The Future of Pharma

to Lindsay, Eleanor, Catherine and Rosalind

The Future of Pharma

Evolutionary Threats and Opportunities

BRIAN D. SMITH
Open University Business School, UK

GOWER

Published by
Gower Publishing Limited
Wey Court East
Union Road
Farnham
Surrey
GU9 7PT
England

Gower Publishing Company
Suite 420
101 Cherry Street
Burlington
VT 05401-4405
USA

www.gowerpublishing.com

Brian D. Smith has asserted his moral right under the Copyright, Designs and Patents Act, 1988, to be identified as the author of this work.

British Library Cataloguing in Publication Data
Smith, Brian D. (Brian David), 1961-
   The future of pharma : evolutionary threats and
   opportunities.
   1. Pharmaceutical industry--Forecasting.
   I. Title
   338.4'76151-dc22

   ISBN: 978-1-4094-3031-5 (hbk)
   ISBN: 978-1-4094-3032-2 (ebk)

Library of Congress Cataloging-in-Publication Data
Smith, Brian D. (Brian David), 1961-
   The future of pharma : evolutionary threats and opportunities / Brian Smith.
     p. cm.
   Includes index.
   ISBN 978-1-4094-3031-5 (hbk) -- ISBN 978-1-4094-3032-2
   (ebook) 1. Pharmaceutical industry. I. Title.
   HD9665.5.S58 2011
   338.4'76151--dc22

                                                                        2011012649

Printed and bound in Great Britain by the
MPG Books Group, UK

Contents

List of Figures and Tables

List of Abbreviations

Biotech	Biotechnology company
CEO	Chief Executive Officer
EU	European Union
FDA	Food and Drug Administration, the United States Regulatory Authority
IPO	Initial public offering; the first sale of stock by a company to the public
NHS	National Health Service, the state healthcare system in the United Kingdom
NICE	National Institute for Healthcare and Clinical Excellence, the United Kingdom's market access authority
OTC	Over-the-counter, referring to medicines that are available to consumers through retail without a medical prescription
Pharma	The pharmaceutical industry, as defined in Chapter 1
R&D	Research and Development
UK	United Kingdom
US, USA	United States, United States of America
VC	Venture capital; funds made available for businesses (usually start-up firms or small businesses) with exceptional growth potential

Acknowledgements

The research for, and writing of, *The Future of Pharma* has been a huge undertaking but something of a labour of love. The future growth and success of the industry is important to me and to every one of us who is mortal and susceptible to injury or illness.

I have however been helped greatly by many people in the preparation of this book. I fear thanking individuals in case I leave anyone out, but there are certain groups of people who I do need to thank.

First, all those senior executives and industry experts, listed in Appendix 2, who gave so freely of their time for the research interviews. I was not surprised by the depth of their knowledge but I was taken aback by their insight, wisdom and generosity. I am also thankful to the innumerable contacts who helped me make contact with these busy and elusive people.

Secondly, the group of critical friends who read early drafts of this work and guided my writing with thought and care. In particular, I wish to thank Andrew Bayode, Andrew MacGarvey, Bhuphendra Patel, Harald Stock, Ian Talmage, Dirk Haasner, Robert Dossin, Diana Stokes, Jim DeMaioriobus, Mitchell Tull, Peter Dumovic and Susan Dorfman.

Thirdly, I want to thank Jonathan Norman at Gower for his wise and gentle guidance.

Fourthly, I want to thank Neil Lewis and the guys at Concept Associates, who did such a great job at taking the ideas out of my head and turning them into interesting figures.

Last, but never, ever least, I want to thank Lindsay Smith who, when editing this book, changed nothing, but changed everything.

Professor Brian D. Smith

About the Author

Professor Brian D. Smith is a world-renowned authority on competitive strategy in pharmaceutical and medical technology markets. Having spent the first two decades of his career in those industries, he has spent the last thirteen years creating, disseminating and transferring knowledge about how firms create and implement strategies in markets where the customer is a healthcare professional and a healthcare system.

He began his career as a research chemist in drug development. He then moved through a series of research and development and marketing roles in the pharmaceutical and medical technology industries before taking up his current tripartite role as academic, author and adviser.

As an academic, Brian is an Adjunct Professor at SDA Bocconi in Milan, Italy and a Visiting Research Fellow at the Open University Business School in Milton Keynes in the UK. His research interests include strategy development and implementation and the socio-economic aspects of medical markets.

As an author, Brian has published over 200 books, papers and articles. His best-selling books include *Making Marketing Happen* and, with Malcolm McDonald and Keith Ward, *Marketing Due Diligence* (both Elsevier, 2005) and, with Paul Raspin *Creating Market Insight* (Wiley, 2008). He is also the Editor of the *Journal of Medical Marketing*, the leading peer-reviewed journal in this field.

As an advisor, Brian leads Pragmedic Limited (www.pragmedic.com) a specialist strategy consultancy that works with many of the leading firms in the pharmaceutical, medical technology and related markets.

Professor Smith welcomes comments, questions and suggestions on his work. He can be contacted at brian.smith@pragmedic.com.

Foreword

ANDREAS FIBIG

Since the rise of the modern pharmaceutical industry over a century ago, pharmaceutical innovation has transformed medicine and the lives of millions of people by eradicating diseases, turning fatal diseases into chronic ones, and vastly reducing the number of deaths from pandemic diseases.

Despite its success and indisputable social and economic impact for many decades, modern pharma is entering the second century of its existence facing a great deal of scepticism over the complex relationship between science and business, the economic sustainability of its business model and its operational capability to act quickly enough to produce the innovative treatment options patients, physicians and global markets expect.

This book provides thoughtful dialogue from diverse viewpoints on how the pharmaceutical industry assesses its situation and how it is likely to evolve over the next couple of decades. It does so by exploring the forces currently reshaping the pharmaceutical marketplace – including the growing power of healthcare payers, providers and patients. It also sheds much light on what the industry needs to change to thrive sustainably, namely, by providing novel treatment options and by being rewarded for innovation in a way that is sustainable to pharmaceutical companies and healthcare systems alike.

Andreas Fibig
Chief Executive Officer
Bayer Schering Pharma
April 2011

Foreword

G. STEVEN BURRILL

There can be no doubt that the pharmaceutical industry, broadly defined to include all those based on life sciences, is at a turning point in its development. Like all evolutionary processes, it is impossible to fix a date when this transformation began, but we can certainly point to specific milestones. In 1953 Watson and Crick discovered the chemical structure of DNA, the double helix, and about 20 years later, in the early 1970s, it begot the beginning of the biotech company revolution with the start of Cetus, Genentech, Biogen and Genex, the early big four. Twenty years later, by the early 90s, we saw the early products and revenues from this industry. Now 20 years later still, and nearly 60 years since the seminal discoveries by Watson and Crick, it is totally transforming the Pharma industry. Not only are firms such as Genentech, Amgen, Gilead and others larger than some of Pharma's historic founders, such as Bristol Myers Squibb and Eli Lilly. but they are the biggest drivers of innovation today.

This evolutionary process continues to accelerate today. The genomics revolution which produced the first sequence of a human being about decade ago, the explosion of knowledge about proteomics and metabalomics and the other -omics and the confluence of other technologies – nanotechnology, high-speed low-cost sequencing, instant communications and enhanced power supplies, visualization technologies and imaging and the beginning of digital medicine – will change everything about the Pharma industry. Not only how we discover and develop new products but how healthcare is delivered globally. The past was the beginning and the future will be unlike anything we know today.

That is why Professor Smith's book is so timely and so relevant. It is the first attempt to not merely speculate on what the future of pharma might be, but to apply evolutionary economics and other ideas from management science to predict what that future might be. As we try to survive and thrive in these interesting times, *The Future of Pharma* is just the sort of guidebook we need.

G. Steven Burrill
Chief Executive Officer
Burrill & Company
April 2011

A Stalling Industry

CHAPTER 1

Whither Pharma? The World's Most Important Industry at a Fork in the Road

'If we could first know where we are, and whither we are tending, we could then better judge what to do, and how to do it.'

Abraham Lincoln

The last time I saw my father, he was wreathed in smiles. Flanked by two of my daughters, he felt fortunate to have lived long enough to see his children grow up and to embed himself in the memories of his grandchildren. Born in 1920, his life expectancy at birth was about 60. That he exceeded that by more than one-third is notable enough in itself, but it is all the more remarkable because he was not unusual in living well into his 80s. That he had survived more than eight decades of injury, illness and infection was, in large part, due to a range of pharmaceutical treatments that didn't exist when he was born. In that context at least, the pharmaceutical industry is the world's most important business. Agriculture and the extractive industries can argue they are 'primary', whilst information technology, aerospace and consumer goods may claim to have changed the world more visibly. But, when you or your family face sickness, disease or hurt then the pharmaceutical industry will usually come top of your list.

This book will discuss how the pharmaceutical industry is likely to evolve over the next couple of decades. In this chapter, I'll describe the enormous societal contribution the industry has made and then suggest that the continuation of that contribution is far from assured. I'll discuss evidence that suggests that we at risk of a world in which, to a large degree, the therapies we have now are the best we will ever have so that the remaining spectres of cancer, degenerative and chronic diseases will remain as terrifying to us in the future as they are today. Then, in later chapters, I'll use the theory of evolution to explain this gloomy scenario and suggest how that explanation might enable us to maintain, or more accurately evolve, a pharmaceutical industry that contributes as much to society in the next century as it has in the last.

But, before we go any further, let us be clear about what we mean by the pharmaceutical industry (also known widely as 'pharma').

Voltaire's Demand – What Do We Mean by Pharma?

Of the many quotes attributed to the French philosopher Voltaire, one in particular is useful to those who, like me, seek to create and disseminate knowledge: 'If you would converse with me, define your terms.'

Were Voltaire editing this book, he would surely have asked what exactly I mean by the pharma industry, because it is not a clear cut entity. When trying to define it, it is hard not to fall into the trap of a circular definition and describe it as the industry that provides us with pharmaceuticals. To an outsider, that industry might include everything from the local pharmacy store to the global pharmaceutical company and, between those two extremes, every size and shape of organization that contributes to the invention, manufacture or distribution of therapeutic compounds. That would be a comprehensive definition but far too broad to speak of as one industry. Instead, I've chosen to define the industry as those companies who develop and/or manufacture therapeutic substances that, initially at least, reach human patients via a doctor or other healthcare professional. So, for the most part, I've ruled out over-the-counter (OTC) consumer products like aspirin or paracetamol and the so-called alternative therapies. I've also put to one side lifesaving equipment such as medical devices and technology. Also out of my remit are drugs intended for animals and biotechnology that is not directed at human therapeutics, such as the rapidly evolving and important technologies for food, fuel or polymer production. To those who know the industry, it is easier to describe pharma in the terms the industry uses. In simple terms, for the purposes of this book, the pharmaceutical industry is the global, research-based firms who invent, make and sell prescription-only pharmaceuticals. These, we tend to call 'big pharma'. Also, their smaller cousins that do similar things and which usually go by the label of 'speciality pharma'. Included, too, are the makers of off-patent pharmaceuticals, usually bracketed under the term 'generics' and, finally, the usually very much smaller biotech companies who, for the most part, invent new pharmaceuticals but tend to sell through the more traditional companies.

I'm aware that this definition leaves room for debate and pedantry, but, as Justice Potter of the United States Supreme Court famously said of obscenity: 'I shall not today attempt further to define it and perhaps I could never succeed in intelligibly doing so. But I know it when I see it.'

So, if I had to reply to Voltaire, I'd say, in short, that the pharma industry is that group of companies, whatever their size, which invent or make prescription drugs. That said, my discussion will necessarily touch on some of the related areas I've chosen to put outside my remit, like over-the-counter drugs and some areas of medical technology. Voltaire would also need to appreciate that the pharma industry has a huge fringe that we also have to consider. There are tens of thousands of companies that supply the pharma industry with various products and services, from specialized materials to qualified labour to industry-specific services, such as market research, clinical trials and contract sales forces. These companies are doing jobs that, until recently, were mostly done inside pharmaceutical companies themselves and, since their activities are vital to the industry, they have to be counted as part of it. That is the pharma industry that this book refers to and, without too much hyperbole, calls the world's most important industry.

A Chance to Skip a Few Pages

This chapter is intended to introduce the problematic situation that the rest of the book examines. That introduction can be summarized in three bullet points:

- Pharma has made and continues to make a huge contribution to our society, both socially and economically.
- That contribution appears to be slowing and there is a threat that the industry will decline into a commodity business that makes much less of a social and economic contribution.
- Within the industry and outside it, we need to understand the problem and ensure that pharma continues to contribute to our well-being and our wealth.

For many people who know the industry, those three statements are completely uncontentious and threaten to be platitudes. If you're one of those, feel free to skip to the end of this chapter, read the closing section (An Unpleasant Prognosis) and move on to Chapter 2, where you will find some new thinking. If you don't know the industry, or if you do know the industry, but don't necessarily accept those three points, you will get more from this book if you read the remainder of this chapter.

Note, however, that this section isn't meant to be an uncritical paean to the pharma industry. As will be discussed at various points later in the book, the industry is far from perfect. Many of its practices and some of its mistakes are open to stern criticism and indeed have been heavily criticized by many authors (see for example 1;2;3). But a central premise of this book is that the industry has made and continues to make a huge contribution both socially and economically and, though we shouldn't ignore its failings, both the industry's critics and its apologists do want that contribution to continue. If that is to be so, we need to understand its future.

Pharma's Social Contribution: Longer, Healthier Lives

Armartya Sen, the Indian-born Harvard professor that *Business Week* called 'the conscience and Mother Theresa of economics', defines something as being of universal value when all people have a reason to believe it has value. From that point of view, the contribution to society made by many industries – the media for example, or financial services – is a matter of subjective opinion that varies between and within cultures. From that same universal values perspective, it seems unarguable that long and healthy lives are one of the few things that are valued equally by all human beings, irrespective of culture. Similarly, few would deny the value of a productive economy that generates wealth and shares it with society. It is worth considering, then, just what the pharmaceutical industry has contributed to those societies, mostly but not entirely in developed economies, which have been touched by it.

At the highest level of analysis, we live much longer. As Figure 1.1 shows, the life expectancy of the average American increased from about age 47 in 1900 to about age 77 in 2000; and similar improvements are seen in the data from other developed economies. An understandable first reaction to this would be to consider the conditions lived in by our Victorian ancestors and attribute this increase in longevity to greater wealth and better living conditions. However, even if we look at more recent times, life expectancy in Western Europe has increased by about ten years since 1960, suggesting there is more to increased life expectancy than increased wealth and living conditions.

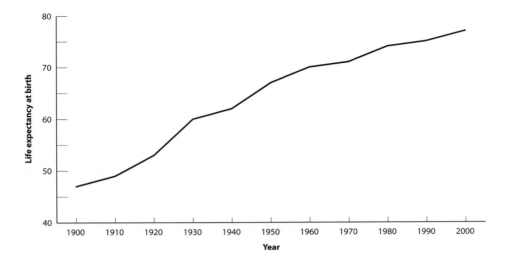

Figure 1.1   United States life expectancy at birth 1900–2000

Source: Elizabeth Arias: United States Life Tables. National Vital Statistic 52 No. 14 Table 1 (2004)

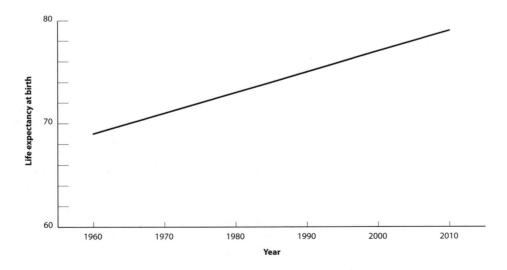

Figure 1.2   European Union life expectancy at birth 1960–2010

Source: OECD

It would, however, be naive in the extreme to attribute all of this increase to the availability of new drugs. Many factors that have nothing to do with the pharmaceutical industry have impacted (both positively and negatively) on life span in the last hundred years. Pharma cannot and does not lay claim to longer lives caused by a reduction in smoking or shorter lives caused by obesity and sedentary lifestyles. Pharma has played a large part, however, in allowing us to live longer, healthier lives and there is a fair amount of research work that demonstrates that. In a 2007 study (4), Frank Lichtenberg of Columbia University and the National Economic Bureau of Research examined why the increase in longevity varied between different states in America. Predictably, he found factors such as obesity, smoking and HIV/AIDS played a part; but the biggest single contributor was medical innovation. Lichtenberg's definition of medical innovation was much broader than the use of new drugs and included new procedures and technologies but, according to his work, the biggest single reason why longevity increased in some places more than others was the use of new drugs. Basing his research on the average vintage (that is, time since approval) of drugs used by Medicare and Medicaid,[1] he attributed about two thirds of the increase in longevity to the use of newer drugs. To be balanced about this, the methodological detail of Lichtenberg's findings have been challenged (5), but not to such an extent as to completely invalidate his work. Even the industry's critics acknowledge that modern pharmaceutical treatments prolong and improve life, even as they debate by how much and criticize the cost and availability of those benefits.

We should not be too simplistic about this. Life expectancy is an extremely complex area and attributing any outcome to any single cause risks painting too simple a picture. Two years after the publication of Lichtenberg's study, Paul Grootendorst, a Canadian academic, published a thorough review of the topic (6) and, in the abstract of his work, captured what seems to be the consensus view of the scientific community:

'Several studies suggest that, on the basis of life expectancy (LE) regressions, new pharmaceutical drugs are responsible for some of the marked gains in LE observed over the last 50 years. We critically appraise these studies. We point out several modelling issues, including disentangling the contribution of new drugs from advances in disease management, changes in the distribution of health care and other confounding factors. We suggest that the studies' estimates of pharmaceutical productivity are implausibly high. Some of the models have very large forecast errors. Finally, the models that we replicated were found to be sensitive to seemingly innocuous changes in specification. We conclude that it is difficult to estimate the bio-medical determinants of LE using aggregate data. Analyses using individual level data or perhaps disease specific data will likely produce more compelling results.'

Paul Grootendorst

And that seems to be the balanced view of researchers at this highest level of analysis: life expectancy is increasing; there are multiple reasons for this; use of newer, better drugs are part of it but it is very difficult to prove the exact contribution of new drugs to increased life expectancy.

---

1   Medicare is the United States government health insurance programme for the aged. Medicaid is the equivalent programme for the needy.

Grootendorst's closing remark suggests that we might find better evidence of pharma's contribution to society if we consider specific disease areas. This could be a huge topic and would fill several books by itself, but a quick tour of the industry's achievements over the last century or so reminds us that most of us live in a different, better world, thanks to pharmaceuticals.

The Pharmaceutical Industry's Greatest Hits

The modern pharma industry usually traces its origins to the point when natural plant extracts gave way to synthetic compounds in the last decade or two of the 19th Century. First among these synthetic compounds were dyestuffs, developed from coal tar, that were found to have antiseptic properties. The stereotypical example is sulphonamides which, in the 1930s, were the first class of compounds found to fight bacterial infection inside the body. Developed initially by Bayer, which remains one of the industry's leading companies, they were the wonder drug of their time. Pharmaceutical chemists of my own generation were raised on World War II stories about sulphonamides, how they changed the course of history by saving Winston Churchill's life in 1943 and how little packets of 'sulpha powder' were issued to American soldiers to sprinkle onto open wounds. Sulphonamides have now been largely superseded as lifesaving drugs, but the numbers of lives saved by them is, literally, countless and they are still benefiting mankind in acne treatments and other applications.

Shortly after sulphonamides, came the antibiotics based on penicillin. Alexander Fleming's famous discovery of penicillin in 1928, combined with Florey and Chain's later work on extracting it, led to a revolution in treating bacterial infections. In the following years, the pharmaceutical industry developed new antibiotic products such as streptomycin (Merck) and the first broad-spectrum antibiotic oxytetracycline (Pfizer). There are now a huge number of antibiotics available, most of them semi-synthetic rather than extracted from moulds as Fleming did. From the comfort of the early 21st century, it is easy to underestimate the impact of antibiotics. A better appreciation is given by medical historian John Parascandola (7) who describes the scale of production of penicillin and its impact in his book *Sickness and Health in America*.

'Production of the drug in the United States jumped from 21 billion units in 1943 to 1663 billion units in 1944 … by 1949, the annual production of penicillin in the United States was 133,229 billion units and the price had dropped from 20 dollars per 100,000 units in 1943 to less than 10 cents … [The Federal Trade Commission] examined mortality statistics for eight important diseases for which antibiotics offered effective therapy: tuberculosis, syphilis, dysentery, diphtheria, whooping cough, meningococcal infections and pneumonia. They found a 56.4 per cent decrease in the total number of deaths for these diseases combined in the period 1945–1955. The decline in all other causes of death over the same period was only 8.1 per cent. The figures were also significant for diseases where antibiotics offered a significant new therapy. For example, the decrease in tuberculosis mortality in this period was 73.5 per cent, as compared with a decrease of 28.6 per cent in the previous ten years.'

John Parascandola, Sickness and Health in America

So the impact of antibiotics, just one example of the pharmaceutical industry picking up an academic discovery and bringing it to the mass market was, and continues to be enormous. No one can accurately estimate the numbers of lives saved by the use of penicillin and its later derivatives, although the figure 200 million is often quoted. Today, it's a routine treatment and most of us living in advanced economies don't fear tuberculosis or many other infectious diseases. Even in a developing country such as India, infectious diseases have given way to cardiovascular disease as the number one cause of mortality in urban settings. Many surgical operations are made possible and much safer by prophylactic antibiotics that prevent post-operative infection and even minor, non-life threatening conditions such as ear infections and dental treatments are made much less onerous by the availability of cheap, effective antibiotics. To the layman and the mass media, it is Fleming, Florey and Chain we must thank for this and, indeed, they richly deserve their fame and honours. But brilliant academic scientists are not responsible for the mass availability of a huge range of antibiotics at a price that makes them accessible to most of us. The reality is that the pharma industry made the drugs available to the mass market and, in doing so, the industry both saved and improved lives.

As important a contribution as it was, the antiquity of the antibiotic revolution has dimmed our memory of it. More recent, but perhaps less broad in its impact has been the pharmaceutical industry's contribution to the fight against HIV/AIDS. Readers who remember the advent of HIV/AIDS will remember how it was seen as an incurable, modern day plague and indeed it is estimated to have killed 25 million people between 1981 and 2006 (8). It remains incurable but the development of antiretrovirals now means that a positive diagnosis of HIV is no longer a short-term life sentence. Studies of the effect of antiretrovirals reveal the real and important impact of these drugs since their introduction in 1989. Walensky (9), for example, estimates that in the United States alone, between three and five million life years were saved by antiretrovirals between 1989 and 2006. His work also finds that a typical patient lives at least 13–14 years longer than if he or she had not had the therapy. More recently, a report by the US Centers for Disease Control and Prevention showed that death rates from HIV/AIDS had fallen by more than 70 per cent between 1995 and 2010 (10). One should not ignore or minimize the threat of HIV/AIDS, especially in sub-Saharan Africa and other developing countries, but antiretrovirals are a potent and recent example of what the pharmaceutical industry, building on academic research and working with healthcare systems, has contributed to society.

Sulphonamides, antibiotics and antiretrovirals are three salient examples of how the pharmaceutical industry has contributed to our society, but sceptics could claim that these contributions are either old, or restricted to the rich world. A fourth example in the infectious disease area points to the contribution made to developing countries in recent times. Haemophilus influenzae type B (Hib) mostly affects babies and young children and leads to brain damage and developmental delays. In the United States and other developed markets, use of Hib vaccines has reduced the incidence of the disease to about one per 100,000 children, but it remains a major problem in some developing countries. Introduced into Uganda in 2002, the Hib vaccine has reduced the incidence to almost zero (11). The same research estimated that the vaccination programme prevented more than 23,000 children from becoming infected and saved 5,000 lives in 2007 alone. The contribution of vaccination to poor countries is measured in more than lives saved; in neighbouring Kenya, a study showed that vaccination for Hib saved 870,000 dollars in healthcare costs for children born in 2004 (12). Hib is just one example of the contribution vaccines have made, and continue to make, to the societies of developing countries.

Pharma's contribution to society is perhaps most obvious in the area of infectious diseases that antibiotics, antiretrovirals and vaccines address. As a curious side effect of modern medicines, these diseases have become less of a concern to most of us. Instead, we worry about diseases, such as cancer and cardiovascular disease, that our ancestors saw as remote threats simply because they usually died from injuries and infections long before cancer and heart disease (typically problems of middle and older age) troubled them. Scientifically, these are harder problems to solve, but in these areas, too, developments in pharmaceutical therapy contribute to our living longer and healthier lives. A 2008 study (cited in (13)) calculated that life expectancy for cancer patients had increased by three years since 1980 and that 83 per cent of that gain was attributable to new treatments, including new drugs. Another study, looking at the increase in cancer survival rates since 1975, attributed 50–60 per cent of the improvement to new drugs (14). In cardiovascular disease, death rates from both strokes and heart disease dropped by about a third in the short period between 1999 and 2005 (15). Not all of this can be claimed by pharmaceuticals, but the use of cholesterol lowering drugs and blood thinners played a big part. The future of this area looks promising, too, with cholesterol-lowering statins being used to prevent health problems by mass administration to people aged over 60. In 2007, for the first time in 50 years, the average cholesterol level for American adults dropped to within the ideal range, largely as a result of statin use (10;13). Statins look to play a bigger role, too, in the prevention of metabolic syndrome, the cluster of diseases, like diabetes and heart disease, associated with obesity.

And the list could go on: diabetes, rheumatoid arthritis, schizophrenia, incontinence, immune system suppression for transplant surgery, clinical depression, erectile dysfunction, contraception, painkillers, fertility treatment and many more. These are all areas where the use of pharmaceuticals has, without exaggeration, changed our lives in the past few decades. Without doubt, this improvement in our lives has been a combined effect of healthcare systems and academic discovery as well as the work of pharmaceutical companies but, without the latter, it wouldn't have happened and our lives would have been much worse for it. Critics are right to point out, as we will later discuss, that the industry is profit driven, that there have been disastrous mistakes like thalidomide and that not enough poor people get access to the medicines they need. But even the biggest detractors of the pharmaceutical industry want to see it reformed whilst still contributing to society as it has in recent generations. And, as we will discuss in the following section, this large, longstanding and ongoing contribution of the industry to our health and wellbeing is not the only value it contributes to our society.

Pharma's Economic Contribution: Good Jobs, Taxes and Cost Savings

The contribution the pharmaceutical industry makes to longer, healthier lives is almost unique amongst manufacturing industries. But it is only half of what the world would miss if the industry went into decline because it is one of the world's largest and most valuable industries, both in size and economic impact.

Beginning again at the highest level of analysis, the global sales of prescription drugs are about 660 billion dollars (16). Approximately speaking, that is about the same as the entire bottom half of the International Monetary Fund's list of national GDPs, all 87 countries from Tanzania to Kiribati via Bolivia and the Congo. To use the well-worn comparison, if the pharmaceutical industry were a country, it would sit about number 16 in the list of world economies, between the Netherlands and Turkey. And those figures are only for the direct sales of the top 500 pharma and biotech companies. They don't count the hundreds of smaller companies or the massive fringe of supporting companies, which has grown rapidly in recent years as pharmaceutical manufacturing companies have outsourced operations that were previously carried out by internal departments.

Like all industries, pharma has an indirect or 'ripple' effect on the rest of the economy as it purchases goods and services from suppliers and as its employees spend their salaries. A 2009 report, using data up to 2006, estimated that the biopharmaceutical sector contributed 88.5 billion dollars directly to the United States economy, a figure that increased to 294 billion dollars when ripple effects were considered (17). Expressed in terms of jobs, the same report identified 668,000 jobs as being directly in the sector and a further 3.2 million jobs supported by the ripple effect of the industry. The salaries paid to direct employees amounted to 61 billion dollars, which contributed 17 billion dollars in federal and state taxes. This is in addition to the taxes paid by the corporations themselves. The contribution to the economy is not, of course, restricted to the United States. The European Union has about 633,000 jobs in the research-based part of the industry (18) (in other words, not including the generics companies) and, although comparable data is not available, a similar ripple effect must work in the European Union as it does in the United States. Japan has a significant pharmaceutical industry too and, in most developed countries, the distribution of pharmaceuticals is a significant sector even if their development and manufacture is not.

The level of jobs and sales generated by the pharmaceutical industry is enough, in itself, to make the industry an important one and this is reflected in the way that most developed and developing economies try to encourage a strong domestic pharmaceutical sector. For example, China, India and Singapore are all supporting the development of national research-based pharmaceutical industries. However, it is the quality of the jobs in the industry and its knowledge-intensive nature that make it more important to national and local economies than even its simple size would suggest. The industry spends about 127 billion dollars a year on Research and Development, about one fifth of its sales (16), an amount that has grown steadily. In short, pharma creates a lot of well paid jobs in knowledge-based work, the kind that governments love. In doing so, it contributes to the 'knowledge economy', supporting educational and technical infrastructures that, without exception, governments see as necessary to a competitive modern economy. By most measures, pharma invests a greater proportion of its sales in research and development than any other industry (18). This is especially true in the three parts of the world – the United States, Europe and Japan – that currently dominate the industry. For example, the industry has a 55 billion euro trade surplus in the European Union (18), one of the few manufacturing sectors in the European Union with a positive trade balance.

As with the industry's contribution to health, it would be possible to cite many more examples of pharma's economic contribution, but this is hardly necessary. Few people, and no one in a position of political power, dispute the value of the industry and the intent of most government strategies, if not always the effect of their policies, is to encourage the industry to keep inventing new drugs and creating more wealth. This clear value of the pharmaceutical industry to society makes pharma genuinely valuable to all of us. It also makes what is happening in the sector genuinely worrying to us all.

The Slowing of Pharma's Contribution

Pharma's value to society depends on two things: firstly, its ability to create new drugs that either cure or manage disease, secondly, its ability to create wealth for its stakeholders and, through taxation, for society at large. Historically, the industry has excelled on both counts. As well as the conspicuous successes discussed in the previous section, in the 18 years from 1992 to 2009, there were 481 new drugs approved by the FDA, roughly equivalent to a new drug every two weeks. In the same period, prescription drug sales increased by 84 per cent from 350 billion dollars to 644 billion dollars. In the years leading up to the financial crisis of 2008/9, growth rates for the industry were between 8 per cent and 15 per cent per annum (16). By most standards, the pharmaceutical industry's history has been a successful one. In addition to its profits and shareholder dividends, pharma has been seen by investors as relatively low risk and, to a large degree, counter-cyclical to stock market trends. To achieve all this whilst also producing products of significant societal value is a great achievement. To achieve it consistently over the decades, as the industry has, is even more remarkable (19). Whether one is an employee of pharma, has a pension fund that invests in the sector or is a consumer of pharmaceutical products, the industry's economic and social contribution is important to us. And therein lies the problem; that important contribution looks like it might be petering out, with significant implications for employees, shareholders and patients. This is not just an artefact of the economic crisis (although that has played a part). Long before this, several distinct but related streams of evidence emerged, that now point to the stalling of the pharmaceutical industry.

Starting again at the highest level of analysis, the strong, steady sales growth that has characterized the industry for most of its history is looking like it will slow dramatically. As shown in Figure 1.3, after growing at 10–15 per cent in the years leading up to around 2007, projections for global sales of prescription drugs expect growth to average out at less than 3 per cent in the ensuing decade projected to 2016. In real, inflation adjusted terms, this is effectively more or less flat.

This top-level trend hides a complex picture. In developed markets, volume growth is anticipated to be low (at around 5 per cent), in many cases completely cancelled out by price reductions. Only in developing markets like Brazil, Russia, India and China are volumes expected to grow quickly and, even in those countries, price reduction is expected to mitigate growth. The result, shown in Figure 1.4, is a mixed picture, but one that is, on the whole, much bleaker than market conditions to which the industry has become accustomed. This slowing of growth has a complex series of causes and effects that together point to the industry's slowing overall contribution to society.

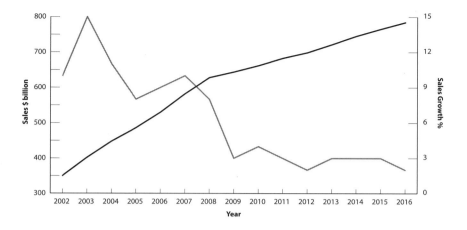

Figure 1.3   The slowing growth of the pharmaceutical industry

Source: Adapted from World Preview 2016 with thanks to EvaluatePharma

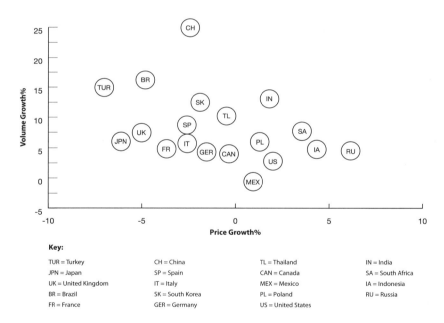

Key:

TUR = Turkey	CH = China	TL = Thailand	IN = India
JPN = Japan	SP = Spain	CAN = Canada	SA = South Africa
UK = United Kingdom	IT = Italy	MEX = Mexico	IA = Indonesia
BR = Brazil	SK = South Korea	PL = Poland	RU = Russia
FR = France	GER = Germany	US = United States	

Figure 1.4   Divergent values and volume trends

Source: IMS Health, Market Prognosis, March 2010

Three interrelated factors explain most of the industry's slowing sales growth. Firstly, there is the replacement of relatively high margin, patent-protected drugs by low-cost copies as patents expire, a process known as genericization. This has been a constant feature of the industry ever since the patent-protected research business model evolved but the years up to 2016 will see patent expiration of a large number of blockbuster drugs with large sales and, almost immediately, the launch of unpatented copies that parsimonious buyers will seize with alacrity. The height of this 'patent cliff', as it is known in the industry, is huge. Industry analysts, EvaluatePharma, estimate that between 2011 and 2016, about 267 billion dollars of sales are at risk and about 141 billion dollars of sales is expected to be lost as blockbusters such as Pfizer's statin Lipitor, and Lilly's Zyprexa and AstraZeneca's Seroquel, both antipsychotics, lose their patent protection and 'go generic'. IMS, an industry market research and consultancy firm, predicts that within the next few years up to 80 per cent of the European market will be generic.

The second cause of slowing sales growth is price erosion, the result mostly of governments and insurance companies forcing pharmaceutical companies to accept lower prices for their products, even while they are still under patent protection. This has, in the last few years, become a standard tactic of many governments. Germany has imposed a price freeze at August 2009 price levels on all drugs reimbursed by the government until the end of 2013. In similar style, the United States Medicaid system demanded an increase in the rebate it obtains on branded drugs from 15 per cent to 23 per cent. Spain, facing a particularly tight fiscal squeeze, expanded its reference pricing system for branded drugs whilst cutting the price it pays for generics. Similar price reductions on both branded and generic drugs were enforced in both developed and developing markets. And the two factors of generic substitution and price reduction work together as in the United Kingdom, where the government used the threat of increased genericization to pressure branded drug manufacturers to reduce their prices. In short, the industry is seeing a huge increase in buyer pressure that is either reducing prices of branded products, increasing substitution by cheaper, unbranded generics or, in many countries, both.

Price pressure and substitution by cheap copies are, however, only the proximate, immediate causes of pharma's discomfort because commoditization, as it is more generally known, is the result of lack of differentiation; and that, in turn, is the consequence of a lack of innovation. In short, the fundamental cause of pharma's slowing growth is its failure to produce enough new drugs that are sufficiently differentiated from their older and increasingly off-patent predecessors. At a quantitative level, this is shown in the relative slowing of new drug approvals in relation to research and development spend, as shown in Figure 1.5.

Compared to the historical trend of a new drug every other week, the industry is currently only about two thirds as productive as it once was, when measured in new drug approvals. And these numbers don't tell the whole story because many of the more recent drug approvals are what are known as me-too drugs, offering only minor improvements over what already exists. As Michael Wokasch, a life-long industry veteran, describes in his critique of the industry (20), this is largely driven by the strategic targeting of large, easy to reach therapy areas that have offered better risk-adjusted rates of return than areas that are smaller and harder to address:

'These days, when promising new drugs are patented, other companies often rush in to create similar but slightly modified "me too" drugs in order to capitalize on lucrative mass markets. While some of these "me too" drugs may have fewer side effects or improved dosing schedules, most provide little therapeutic advantage to drugs that are already available to physicians and patients. Nevertheless, the ability to "pick off" even a small share of the highly lucrative "chronic diseases" market has the potential to generate substantial profits for companies.'

Michael Wokasch, Pharmaplasia

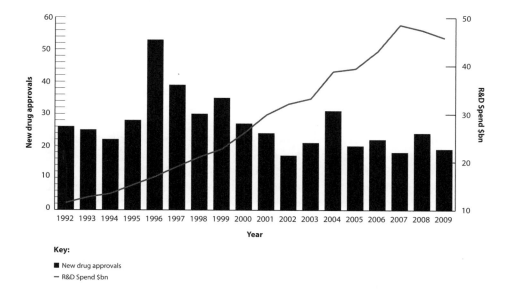

Figure 1.5   The pharma innovation gap

Source: Adapted from World Preview 2016 with thanks to EvaluatePharma

As well as being an indication that the industry is less capable than it was at bringing important new drugs to market, the me-too habit has important financial consequences. Increasingly, to use industry jargon, governments and other bodies will not grant market access to products that are perfectly safe but, which offer no cost-benefit improvement over existing products; in other words, they will not approve such products for sale. Such refusal only directly affects sales to government-funded parts of the market but, since this accounts for most drug spend in the majority of developed economies, such failure to achieve market access means a product is, in practice, a commercial failure even though it has been granted regulatory approval for safety and efficacy.

Interestingly, this lack of innovation is not a result of reduced expenditure on research and development. Rather, the amount that the research-based companies spend on developing new drugs has climbed steadily, from 11.5 billion dollars in 1992 to 45 billion dollars in 2009, but without a commensurate increase in productivity. In practice, the per-dollar productivity of pharma has decreased, at least amongst the big research-based companies. When measured in new drugs per dollar of research and development spend, the research and development machine spends about four times as much for each new drug approval as it did in 1992 which, even allowing for inflation, is a worrying decrease in productivity. The reasons for this are complex and we will touch on them later in the book, but two main reasons are usually cited by the industry. Firstly, the 'low-hanging fruit' of relatively easy to develop products has, to some degree, been taken. What remains are mostly the relatively more technically challenging clinical problems of either very difficult conditions – cancer for example, or the degenerative diseases like Alzheimer's – or making significant improvements on products, like statins or proton pump inhibitors (PPIs), like AstraZeneca's Nexium, that are already very good. Secondly, the regulatory hurdles that new drugs must pass to reach the market are becoming ever more demanding as society becomes less tolerant to the risks that all drugs carry. Since this implies more and larger clinical trials and higher failure rates, this societal aversion to risk embodied in ever more stringent approval processes translates into higher research and development costs.

If lower research and development productivity and consequent lack of differentiation are the causes of slower industry growth, then its consequences are similarly worrying. The most striking of these is the market capitalization of the industry, particularly the top-tier big pharma firms that are its bellwethers. Since this is based on investors' judgement of future cash flows, it has declined as investors have factored in the impact of lower research and development productivity and slower growth, as shown in Figure 1.6. In any industry, let alone one that has traditionally occupied a position perceived as safe in most investment portfolios, a decline of 51 per cent of market capitalization in ten years is dramatic and frightening to investors. And, because the big investors are pension funds, that means most of us.

In response to the threat of further destruction of shareholder value, pharmaceutical companies have embarked on the cost reduction strategies that are a second consequence of lack of differentiation, after slowing sales growth. Even before the financial crisis, most of the major firms began to announce strategic restructuring that was intended both to reduce costs and increase productivity. This restructuring began with the outsourcing of activities that were not considered critical to competitiveness, such as manufacturing and some aspects of clinical development. More recently, however, research-based pharma companies have sought to improve their productivity in the two areas where they enjoyed competitive advantage over generics – research and development, and sales and marketing. In some cases, this has been genuine restructuring, such as the rationalization of research and development centres by AstraZeneca and the restructuring of GSK's research teams

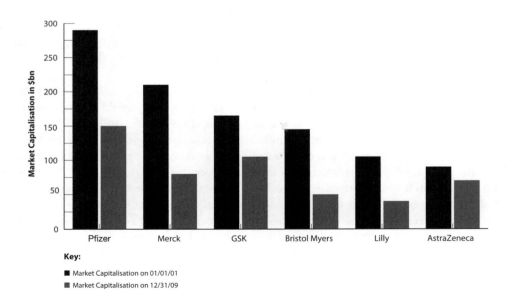

Key:

■ Market Capitalisation on 01/01/01
■ Market Capitalisation on 12/31/09

Figure 1.6   The decline of pharma's market capitalization

Source: Bloomberg

into smaller, self-contained units built around disease areas. Similarly, many firms have shrunk and re-tasked their sales forces to recognize that, in many areas, the prescription decision is no longer made solely by doctors, but by complex decision making units in which clinicians take an advisory role to more financially oriented managers. But although there are many examples of firms reorganising to improve effectiveness, such as Takeda's radical switch from traditional sales representatives to account managers in the UK, the primary driver remains the need to cut costs so as to preserve profit growth in the context of slowing sales growth. Many firms have cut jobs on a scale beyond the career memory of almost all pharma employees. In 2010, Reuters quoted Sam Isaly, the managing partner at OrbiMed Advisors, one of the world's largest healthcare investment firms and responsible for some 5 billion dollars of investments. Isaly predicted that employment in the big pharma companies across the United States, Europe and Japan would fall by 20 per cent between 2009 and 2015, equivalent to 200,000 jobs. Soon after, Roche announced its contribution to fulfilling this prediction by cutting 10 per cent of its workforce. Such shrinkage is, of course, a very significant decline in the industry's economic contribution to society and the ripple effects amplify the job losses in the same way as they amplify the more positive contributions.

Taken together, the causes and effects of pharma's current situation imply that its contribution to society is at best slowing and, perhaps, may be about to decline. Notwithstanding some important new products, it is providing us with fewer new drugs and many of those that it does provide are less innovative and more derivative of existing science. Its financial contribution is slowing, whether looked at from the perspective of a shareholder, an employee or someone who benefits from the ripple effect. Pharma remains a very important industry but its current situation, looked at in the context of its decades-long growth, leads us inevitably to concerns about the future of the industry. The dramatic slowing of growth and innovation suggest that this may be more than a short term stutter and the beginning of a fundamental decline that would see the industry's social and economic contribution shrink, to the detriment of us all. To use a medical analogy, the symptoms we observe cannot help but lead us to ask for a diagnosis and a prognosis.

An Unpleasant Prognosis

The last time I saw my Mother, she couldn't smile. Parkinson's disease, which had started to affect her in middle age, had robbed her of control of her facial muscles and, now in her eighties, Alzheimer's was beginning to steal her memory. I did not take my children to see her because I did not want their memories of her to be clouded with this image of a pathetic figure. As I talked to her, I silently wondered where my genes, lifestyle and environment would lead me and I hoped I will follow my father and not my mother. The contrast between my parents, although personal, is not unusual and is relevant to the future of the pharma industry. My father's good luck was to suffer from conditions like cardiovascular disease, that pharma had understood and provided products for. My mother's bad luck was not simply to be old and ill, but to have conditions for which pharma has not been able to provide cures or palliatives, or at least not to the same extent.

In this chapter, I have taken a brief helicopter flight over the pharma industry. Those who know the industry well will easily notice the things I have omitted, such as the waves of industry consolidation, the blurring of the generic/research-based boundary, the attempts to fill research pipelines by licensing or other arrangements and the rise of newer biotechnologies. These and the other things I have chosen to omit are all important points, and I will address them later in the book, but they risk clouding our view of what is really happening in pharma. In short, the industry is caught between two very strong forces with a predictable outcome. On the one hand, the inability of the industry to produce a stream of highly differentiated products that address unmet needs. On the other, the demands of those who buy the products – mostly governments and insurers, rather than patients themselves – for better results, lower prices and ideally both.

Looked at from that simplified (but not simplistic) perspective, pharma looks like a textbook case of industry life cycle. That model of how industries develop makes a very clear but gloomy prognosis for the industry. In short, it will consolidate and commoditize. The future, if we believe the model, is an industry that looks like steel, packaging or bulk chemicals, an industry dominated by a handful of global firms focussed on reducing costs because they cannot innovate well enough to persuade their customers to pay for innovation. To those who wish to buy a statin or antibiotic at low cost, this is a very attractive scenario. It would certainly reduce price and, for many cases, the drugs we have are more than good enough. But from a wider perspective, a commoditized pharmaceutical industry is truly frightening. Many of us look to our future and fear Alzheimer's or cancer; we wish for cures for spinal cord injury, various genetic disorders and the hundreds of important diseases for which we still lack an effective remedy. Even outside these concerns of an affluent western patient, there remains the need to cure HIV/AIDS in developing countries and to find ways of giving good health to the poor in all countries. And, as HIV/AIDS, SARS and each new influenza strain teach us, there will always be new health threats to shorten and sadden our lives. Despite the advances I have discussed in this chapter, there is still huge unmet need in the pharmaceutical area which, incontestably, a commoditized pharma business cannot meet. Nor will a mostly generic business be able to generate the economic benefits provided by a knowledge intensive, research oriented pharma industry. It will provide fewer and lower paid jobs, contribute less to our knowledge-based society and have a much reduced ripple effect. If the pharma industry is driven towards the commodity conclusion suggested by the industry life cycle model, we will all be poorer and, when new diseases emerge, we will live shorter, unhappier lives. It is indeed an unpleasant prognosis.

But a prognosis does not have to be inevitability. If we can find a way to explain how industries in general develop and then apply that explanation to the specifics of the pharmaceutical industry we might be able to change the path of history. We might be able to engineer a world in which we maintain the trend of longer, happier and richer lives that pharma has brought us in the past. With that explanation, we might even be able to extend the benefits of a successful pharmaceutical industry to those it has so far touched much less, namely the poor and those who suffer from much more difficult illnesses, injuries and infections. It is towards that explanation, its practical application and that goal of a thriving, contributing industry that the rest of this book works.

Reference List

(1)   Bouchard, R.A. 2011. *Patently Innovative: How Pharmaceutical Firms Use Emerging Patent Law to Extend Monopolies on Blockbuster Drugs*. Oxford: Biohealthcare Publishing (Oxford) Limited.

(2)   Moynihan, R. and Cassels, A. 2006. *Selling Sickness: How the World's Biggest Pharmaceutical Companies are Turning Us All into Patients*. New York, NY: Nation Publishing.

(3)   Angell, M. 2005. *The Truth about the Drug Companies: How They Deceive Us and What to Do about It*. London: Random House.

(4)   Lichtenberg, F.R. 2007. Why Has Longevity Increased More in Some States than in Others? The Role of Medical Innovation and Other Factors. Manhattan Institute for Policy Research. Center for Medical Progress.

(5)   Baker, D. and Fugh-Berman, A. 2009. Do New Drugs Increase Life Expectancy? A Critique of a Manhattan Institute Paper. *Journal of General Internal Medicine*; 24(5):678–82.

(6)   Grootendorst, P., Pierard, E. and Shim, M. 2009. Life-Expectancy Gains from Pharmaceutical Drugs: A Critical Appraisal of the Literature. *Expert Review of Pharmaeconomics Outcomes Research*; 9(4): 353–64.

(7)   Parascandola, J. 2006. *The Introduction of Antibiotics in Therapeutics. Sickness and Health in America: Readings in the History of Medicine and Public Health*. 3rd ed. Madison: University of Wisconsin Press; pp. 102–12.

(8)   Overview of the Global Aids Epidemic. Joint United Nations Programme on HIV/AIDS; 2006.

(9)   Walensky, R.P., Paltiel, A.D., Losina, E., Mercincavage, L.M., Schackman, B.R., Sax, P.E., et al. 2006. The Survival Benefits of AIDS Treatment in the United States. *Journal of Infectious Diseases*; 194(1):11–9.

(10)   US Department of Health and Human Services, Centres for Disease Control and Prevention, National Centre for Health Statistics, Health, United States 2009 with Chartbook. Hyattsville, MD; 2010.

(11)   Lewis, R.F., Kisakye, A., Gessner, B.D., Duku, C., Odipio, J.B., Iriso, R., et al. 2008. Action for Child Survival: Elimination of Haemophilus Influenzae Type B Meningitis in Uganda. *Bulletin of the World Health Organization*; 86(4):292–301.

(12)   Akumu, A.O., Mike, E., Scott, J.A. and Griffiths, U.K. 2007. Economic Evaluation of Delivering Haemophilus Influenzae Type B Vaccine in Routine Immunization Services In Kenya. *Bulletin of the World Health Organization*; 85(7):511–8.

(13)   PhRMA. Pharmaceutical Industry Profile. *Pharmaceutical Research and Manufacturers of America*; 2010.

(14)   Sun, E., Lakdawalla, D., Reyes, C., Goldman, D., Philipson, T., and Jena, A. 2008. The Determinants of Recent Gains in Cancer Survival: An Analysis of the Surveillance, Epidemiology and End Results (SEER) Database. *Journal of Clinical Oncology*; 26.

(15)   Lloyd-Jones, D. Heart Disease and Stroke Statistics–2009. Update. ahajournals.org [accessed: 5 January 2011].

(16)   World Preview 2016. EvaluatePharma; 2010.

(17)   Burns, L.R. 2009. The Biopharmaceutical Sectors's Impact on the US Economy: Analysis at National, State and Local Levels. Archstone Consulting PLC.

(18)   The Pharmaceutical Industry in Figures. EFPIA; 2010.

(19)   Demirel, P. and Mazzucato, M. 2010. The Evolution of Firm Growth Dynamics in the US Pharmaceutical Industry. *Regional Studies*; 44(8):1053–66.

(20)   Wokasch, M. 2010. Pharmaplasia. Wokasch Consulting LLC.

2 Universal Acid: A Way to Understand the Complex, Adaptive Pharmaceutical Industry

'There is nothing so practical as a good theory'

Kurt Lewin

We are all theoreticians, every single one of us. Every time we observe something that we don't fully understand – why the train is late, why Apple is so good at innovation, why our toddler is crying – we instinctively try to explain it by relating it to some other phenomenon – leaves on the train line, Steve Job's leadership, the toddler's tiredness. This habit seems to be a fundamental human trait and one that has served us well, especially in the last couple of hundred years when human knowledge has, driven by the scientific method, advanced rapidly. We take things for granted now, but where would we be without atomic theory, germ theory or our theories of electromagnetism? And we don't just apply theory in the physical sciences but also in management science. We set specific objectives according to Locke's goal setting theory (1), devise focussed strategies according to the ideas of Porter (2) and make investment decisions using theories about the time value of money that go back to Martin de Azpilcueta, a 16th Century Spanish theologian. Even executives who eschew theory use theory unconsciously. As John Maynard Keynes famously said:

'Practical men, who believe themselves to be quite exempt from any intellectual influence, are usually the slaves of some defunct economist.'

John Maynard Keynes

So there is no question, in practice, that any attempt to understand the future of pharma will have to use a theory of some sort. The challenge is to be clear about what we mean by theory and then to pick the one that helps us most in practical terms.

Academics like to quibble about what a theory is, especially when we stray away from the physical and natural sciences and into the humanities and social sciences. That debate isn't really relevant to the future of pharma, but readers interested in the topic would do well to look at Hunt's discussion of the morphology of theory (see (3), Chapter 7). In that work, Hunt describes Rudner's view, synthesized from that of many others, as the academic consensus about the purpose of theory:

'The purpose of theory is to increase scientific understanding through a systematized structure capable of both explaining and predicting phenomena.'

Richard Rudner (4)

And that, a systematized structure capable of both explaining and predicting phenomena, is exactly what we need. Faced with the phenomenon of the pharmaceutical industry possibly declining into a commoditized business that contributes much less to our future than it has to our past, we need to understand what has happened in the past and to predict the future of pharma. Armed with that, we may be able to influence or at least cope with the shape of things to come in the pharmaceutical industry.

In researching this book, I considered a number of possible theories as candidates for the practical job in hand. As I describe briefly in the following section, four made the short list and one was selected. Again, readers who want to move quickly can skip this section and pick up the flow at Evolutionary Economics, but readers who wish to know more about why I chose to use evolutionary theory to explain the future of pharma should read the following section.

Why Evolutionary Theory?

With hindsight, evolutionary theory seems an obvious choice to underpin my research for this book. In fact, I carefully considered three other options as well before making my selection. Industry life cycle theory, transaction cost analysis and resource-based theory were early front runners before it became apparent that evolutionary theory would be best placed to predict the future of the industry.

I previously mentioned industry life cycle theory, which purports to explain the growth, maturation and decline of industries. Most examinations of industry life cycle come from the perspective that industry development is driven by technological development (see for example (5)) and describe regularities of firm entry, growth and exit. Other researchers suggest that whilst industry life cycle is a reasonable, approximate generalization, it doesn't predict the patterns that seem to occur as industries mature (6). Still others suggest that the traditional life cycle model doesn't explain or predict very well in situations of radical, discontinuous change (7). Moreover, by focussing on technological change, industry life cycle theory seems to consider only one of the two dimensions that drive an industry. Industry is indeed shaped not only by technological development – as I will come to shortly – but also by changes in the social environment. Industry life cycle theory, which focuses on the aggregate of product life cycles, seems to neglect market changes other than technology. A theoretical purist would probably also class it as a 'Law-like Generalization', a special class of theory that is based on observation but is perhaps weaker in its descriptive mechanism. In any case, industry life cycle theory, when applied to pharma, predicts nothing more than a decline into commodity with perhaps a rump of small, technically advanced companies serving specialist niches. Before we accept such a counsel of despair, we should look harder for a theory that considers both technological and market forces and promises a superior explanation and a more nuanced prediction of the future of pharma.

Resource-based theory attempts to explain the success of firms as the result of its resources, by which is meant its assets, resources, processes and capabilities. In particular, it focuses on resources that are especially valuable, rare and hard to imitate or substitute (see (8)). At a fundamental level, it is not dissimilar to the idea of knowledge accumulation that has been used by Chandler (9) and Mazzucato and Dosi (10) to explain the success of big pharma. But resource-based theory has its critics too (see (11;(12)), who point out that it is tautological and is only really useful if one understands the structure of the industry first. In other words, it explains why one firm will outperform another similar firm, but not why those types of firms exist in the first place. As we will see, resource-based theory and related ideas will help us later in the book when we come to discuss how firms might compete and win in a future pharmaceutical market. In selecting a theory to explain the nature of that future, however, resource-based theory seems to lack both explanatory and predicative power.

Whilst industry life-cycle and resource-based theories come from the strategy departments of business schools, my third candidate came from the economists. Transaction cost economics began with the work of Ronald Coase in the 1930s and came to fruition in the work of his student, Oliver Williamson. In 2009, Williamson and Elinor Ostrom won the Nobel Prize for economics for their work. In essence, this work explains the boundaries of the firm in terms of the cost of exchanges, for instance between the people who invent the product, make it and sell it (see for example (13;14)). Transaction cost economics is an intellectual triumph, as the Nobel committee recognized. It is certainly useful, as I will discuss, in explaining the value of outsourcing and 'virtual' companies we see emerging in pharma. But, like resource-based theory, it seems better suited to explain how firms behave within a structure, rather than for predicting that structure. For that reason, I decided to relegate transaction cost theory, like resource-based theory, to a secondary role. That left me with evolutionary theory, which I will now discuss in more detail, since it is ultimately the one that I have chosen to underpin the research on which this book is based.

Evolutionary Economics

The theory of evolution does, as I will discuss, offer a way to explain the current situation of the pharmaceutical industry and predict how it might look in the future. Before following that line of thought, it is worth going back to Voltaire's demand and being clear what I mean by the word evolution and, just as importantly, what I don't mean. Evolution is one of those words used loosely in common parlance, with its several meanings being confused, conflated and tangled. Typically, evolution is used to describe development over time, usually with overtones of progression and advancement. But that is not the meaning that I use here; I use the term in the Darwinian sense of natural selection. The Darwinian view of evolution has something in common with the everyday, developmental use of the term, but it also implies a mechanism that the ordinary use of the term does not. In addition, the Darwinian use of the word does not imply positive progress because it entails only change, not necessarily in a positive or negative direction. So in the coming section, and the rest of the book, it is worth being clear that I use the word 'evolution' in the Darwinian sense, meaning a process of change with a specific mechanism and without the implication of progress. Now, Voltaire satisfied, let us press on.

Most readers will be familiar with the fundamental mechanism of Darwinian evolution: variation occurs within a population of organisms; some variants are better suited to their environment than others and therefore replicate more; thus, the variation is amplified. By this process, the characteristic traits of a species change over time and new species evolve. I do not propose in this book to enter into the debate about the validity of the theory in the context of biological sciences; I accept it as a well-substantiated explanation and indeed predictor for how biological systems change over time.

And in that word 'systems' lies the clue to how a theory with its origins in biological sciences might be useful in the domain of management science. Whilst ideas about the evolution of companies, business models and industries have been spoken about for many years, this has mostly been in the sense of evolution as a metaphor, not evolution as an actual mechanism of change in the business world. This began to change in 1950 when Alchian (15) introduced the idea of evolution into economics. This, in turn, led eventually to the idea of evolutionary economics, and the seminal text of Nelson and Winter's 1982 work (16), which I will discuss later. Since then, the application of evolutionary theory – the mechanism of variation, selection by environment and amplification – has become a widespread way of looking at economic systems, even having its own, dedicated academic journals. Excellent reviews of how evolutionary thinking has influenced economics and other non-biological areas of study can be found in the work of Beinhocker (17) and Hodgson and Knudson (18). These describe the way that a theory, which emerged from the study of animal and plant species, seems to provide explanations and predictions for many economic, business and social phenomena. To use the phrase coined by philosopher Daniel Dennett (19), evolutionary theory has become a 'universal acid' that can be used to solve a wide range of problems. In essence, this is because evolutionary theory, although developed in a biological context, is a general theory to explain what happens in complex adaptive systems, of which biological systems are just one kind. As Waldrop explains in his excellent non-technical review of the area (20), complex systems are those whose properties are determined by the interaction of its many, diverse parts; complex adaptive systems are a subset of those whose behaviour changes over time. Examples of complex adaptive systems include ecosystems, the immune system, equity markets and industries like pharma. As we will discuss, the economic variants of evolutionary theory have the merit of allowing for both technological and social environments. Because of this, they seem to offer much more hope of understanding the pharmaceutical industry than do other theories. If that is, indeed, the case, the question then is how we might apply evolutionary theory to pharma.

Displacing Evolution to Pharma

The great organizational learning theorist Donald Schön described how we acquire new knowledge: we pick up ideas from one situation and transplant them into another context (21). This neatly describes what we are doing when we use evolutionary theory to understand what is happening in the pharma industry; we are picking up ideas from the biological sciences and transplanting them to the management sciences. In this context, it is an interesting coincidence that, when Schön's book was reissued, its original title, *The Displacement of Concepts*, was changed to *The Invention and the Evolution of Ideas*.

Modern Darwinian thinking – the neo-Darwinism synthesis as it is called – relies on a set of core concepts like replicators, interactors, fitness landscapes, co-evolution and others. If we are to use evolutionary theory as a practical explanation and not just as an extended metaphor, we will need to displace these neo-Darwinian concepts into the realities of the pharmaceutical industry.

The first, perhaps most fundamental, concept to displace is that of a replicator, a term introduced by Richard Dawkins in his first and most famous book, *The Selfish Gene* (22). In biology, genes are the replicators; they dictate the design and behaviour of the organism in which they reside so as to optimize their own replication. That was what Dawkins meant by 'selfish'. But note that the genes themselves don't interact with the environment directly; they do it through the organism, which biologists call the interactor, the second fundamental concept that we have to displace from biology to our examination of pharma. As David Hull neatly defines it in his research (23), an interactor is:

'An entity that directly interacts as a cohesive whole with its environment in such a way that this interaction causes replication to be differential.'

David Hull (23)

In other words, biologists think of organisms as vehicles for genes, which drive their vehicle so that it interacts with the environment in the way that optimizes their (the genes') replication. These are among the basic concepts of evolutionary biology. So, how might we displace them to management science and, in particular, the pharmaceutical industry?

The understanding that all industries, including pharma, have replicators and interactors that are the equivalent of genes and organisms was the big leap forward. Nelson and Winter, who initiated the modern wave of evolutionary economics, were the first to recognize that the equivalent of the genes of a company are its organizational routines, its interwoven pattern of regular and predictable behaviours that enable it to perform certain activities. Just like genes, organizational routines act as a memory, storing both explicit and tacit knowledge about how to do things. And, just as genes express themselves through proteins that do the work, organizational routines express themselves through more observable capabilities. For example, an innovative pharmaceutical company has a set of organizational routines that are visible as the capability to discover new drugs. An effective generic drug company has a set of organizational routines that we observe as the ability to recognize and rapidly respond to opportunities created by patent expiration. From this perspective, any firm can be thought of as a collection of organizational routines that give it the capability to do certain things.

Hodgson and Knudson (24) built on this idea to propose that firms are interactors. Just like organisms, they are driven by their genes (their organizational routines) to interact with their environment more or less well, resulting in better or worse ability to survive and thrive in that environment or, as we would call it in management circles, the market. In their words:

'We argue that the firm is best regarded as an interactor ... upon the outcome of the interactions between the interactor with its environment, the fate of its constituent replicators depends.'

Hodgson and Knudsen, (24), p. 282

So we've made the first, important step in displacing evolutionary theory from biology to our study of the pharma business. Instead of genes expressing proteins that drive organisms in such a way to optimize replication in a particular environment, we have organizational routines expressing capabilities in such a way to optimize replication in a particular market context. If this seems obvious, remember that many useful theories, ones that explain and predict reality, are easy to see with hindsight, just as they were very difficult to see with foresight. Think of atomic theory again. It was not obvious to the ancient Greeks, who thought the elements of earth, air, fire and water were the way to understand matter. Similarly, germ theory was not obvious to those that held that diseases were the result of miasma, or bad air. Today, it is hard to imagine how anything other than atomic theory makes sense of chemistry or germ theory of infectious diseases.

The ideas of organizational routines as replicators and firms as interactors also helps us to understand the industry level equivalent of reproduction by pointing us to situations in which organizational routines (which, remember, are patterns of behaviour) are replicated and spread. The closest to biological sexual behaviour is the joint venture. When Lilly 'mated' with Icos to form the Lilly-Icos joint venture around its Cialis product, the 'offspring' did, indeed, contain some organizational routines (genes) from both 'parents', but was different from each. More usually, the replication of organizational routines is less directly analogous to that of genes. When a successful firm grows, each of its offspring business units is characterized by the organizational routines of its parent. When a new company spins off from an older one, it takes some organizational routines with it. And, when firms imitate the success of other firms, they are replicating the organizational routines of the template company. From this perspective, business schools, consultancies and head-hunters all help the reproduction process along by providing a conduit along which organizational routines are transferred. In a sector with highly incestuous recruitment practices, such as pharma, it is easy to see how organizational routines are replicated from one company to another by job-hopping executives. Indeed, many of us have experienced the effect of a new senior executive who joins from a new company, bringing new ideas about how to do things.

Such new organizational routines do not necessarily have to come from another, successful pharma company. They can be transplanted from other industries, like Six Sigma and other quality management processes. Less commonly perhaps, new organizational routines can be developed from scratch. In reality, firms use a combination of imitation, transplant and other methods to develop new organizational routines. How firms do this is something I will discuss later in the book; for now it is important to grasp that organizational routines do act as replicators like genes. They define the firm, determine its capabilities, drive its behaviour and, by determining its success at interacting with the market, influence their own success in replication.

The next concept we need to displace is that of a species. In biology, species are notoriously difficult to define precisely, but most definitions are based on the idea that species are groups of organisms that interbreed (in other words, swap genes) within, but not outside, the group. That approach has its limitations in the context of an industry, because some organizational routines (genes) tend to be swapped between very different types of companies. For example, Six Sigma originated in Motorola and has been adopted by firms in many sectors, but it does not seem useful to count all companies who use Six Sigma as belonging to the same species of company, even if they do share some characteristics. We can develop a better equivalent of a species if we consider the statistical genetics view of a species. In this view, species are identified by the extent to which they share genes. Within industries, firms cluster according to the organizational routines they use and, whilst no two firms are identical, there are obvious similarities and differences. We would not, for example, class global car companies like General Motors or Toyota, with their capabilities in mass production and global marketing, in the same species as specialist companies like Ferrari, with their own very different set of capabilities. In the same way, we can look at the pharmaceutical industry and recognize 'species' that share similar organizational routines and capabilities, whilst being different and distinctive from other groups of pharma companies. Companies like Pfizer and GSK are more like each other than they are like speciality pharma companies such as Almirall or Norgine and generic companies, like Watson or Mylan, are different again. They differ across a whole host of organizational routines to do with capabilities in how they fund themselves, develop new products, manufacture, commercialize products, and so on.

Within these distinct species of pharmaceutical company, there are individual differences, of course, just as there are differences between your genes and mine, but we can, and usually do pragmatically divide companies according to the organizational routines and capabilities they exhibit. Typically, we refer to groups of companies that exhibit similar routines and capabilities as sharing the same business model. Outwardly, we observe that different business models involve some variations in funding models, structure, strategy, and so on, and that these are underpinned by different capabilities that, in turn, flow from different organizational routines. The parallel with biological species is clear, with different anatomy and behaviours flowing from different genetic makeup. The parallels between species and business models go further. Each business model, which describes a number of firms, is characterized by a set of similar, but not identical, organizational routines and capabilities that add up to what we call the business model. In the same way, each species, which includes many organisms, is characterized by a set of similar, but not identical, genes and traits that add up to what we call a species. And, just as within species there may be sub-species, adapted to a certain environment, there are minor variations within business models adapted, for example, to a particular technology or market.

So the biological concept of a species seems to displace well onto the idea of a business model. If you doubt the usefulness of the comparison, just consider what would happen if you tried to transfer the organizational routines in, say, drug discovery from one of the leading research-based companies to one of the major generics companies. The barriers to such a transfer of organizational routines are hardly less than the barriers to transferring genes from an elephant to a goat.

Another very important concept to displace from the biological sciences to the study of the pharmaceutical industry is the fitness landscape, which is also sometimes called the adaptive landscape. First conceived by Sewall Wright (25), one of the most important figures in evolutionary theory, fitness landscapes are a graphical way of representing the fitness of a certain type of organism. They are usually represented as a three-dimensional graph, in which the vertical axis represents fitness and the horizontal axes represent some variable traits of the interactor and therefore the underlying genes. Note that, in a biological context, 'fitness' means ability to replicate, so that the chart (see Figure 2.1) shows how variation in interactor traits leads to variation in the ability to replicate. In biology, the peaks of the fitness landscape represent species that are well adapted, whilst the troughs represent organisms with weaker traits, which are usually rendered extinct by competitive pressures. Note that there tend to be, in any one environment, several peaks. These equate to different species who occupy different ecological niches within the same environment, just as different ungulates (hoofed animals) share the African savannah and numerous varieties of bacteria occupy your gut.

To displace the fitness landscape concept idea into the pharmaceutical industry, we need to think a bit more about what we mean by both fitness and what the varying traits might be. Fitness is straightforward; it equates to firm performance because it is the best performing firms that become benchmarks, are copied, grow, acquire, have their people head-hunted and otherwise replicate their organizational routines. Firm performance can be expressed in a number of ways, from market capitalization to profitability to market share but, in the end, these come down to the value created, in the eyes of the customer, by the firm.

More problematic is the question of what might equate to variable traits. To have an effect on fitness, it must be variation in some value-creating capabilities, based on differences in organizational routines, but which ones? The answer lies in some of the

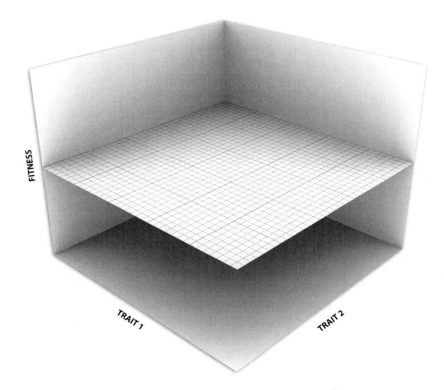

Figure 2.1   The fitness landscape (an example)

later work of Richard Nelson (26), in which he developed the idea of social and physical technologies. In the context of the pharmaceutical industry, physical technologies include all the chemistry and biology we are used to calling technology, but also manufacturing technology, information and communication technology and all the applied science we use to develop, manufacture and distribute a drug. Social technologies, in the context of pharma, include healthcare delivery systems, regulatory systems, health technology assessment and other organizational, legal and social arrangements we have of ensuring the delivery of healthcare. These two dimensions, social and technological, make up the environment against which the fitness of a pharmaceutical business model is defined. In other words, the fitness of any particular pharma business model depends on its ability to create customer value by matching the technology to the market environment. Put more simply, a fitness landscape for the pharmaceutical industry has a vertical axis of firm performance and two horizontal axes corresponding to 'fit with physical technology' and 'fit with social technology', as shown in Figure 2.2. In this example, there are three peaks, corresponding to three business models, each of which creates customer value in different ways, using different capabilities based on different organizational routines. At the simplest level, this fitness landscape might represent big pharma, speciality pharma and generics. In reality, as we will examine later, the picture is more complex than this, but the concept of a fitness landscape is useful in helping us understand the future of pharma.

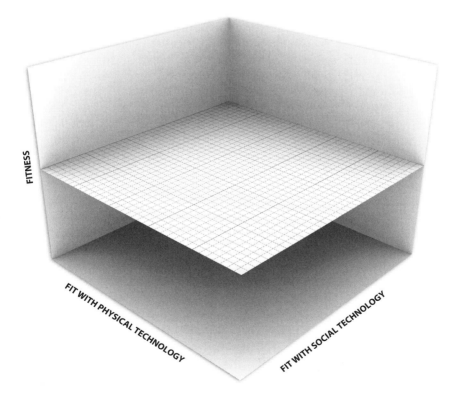

Figure 2.2   The dimensions of the pharma fitness landscape

In biological sciences, the theory of evolution now seems as well proven as any theory can be. Readers seeking a very readable summary of the evidence should read one of Dawkins's later books (27). Beinhocker (17) and Hodgson and Knudsen (24) provide good reviews of the less developed – but still convincing – evidence of evolution's ability to explain and predict business and social phenomena. But what about pharma? Is there any evidence that evolutionary theory, once its concepts of replicator, interactor, species and fitness have been displaced into organizational routines, firms, business models and performance, is a valid explanation, a universal acid, in our attempt to understand the pharmaceutical industry?

In a perfect world, we would construct an experiment; but think for a moment what that would involve and allow me to be slightly facetious. In our facetious experiment, we would start with a hypothesis such as 'a change in the market environment that favours blueness will be followed by a change in the business models of pharmaceutical companies towards increased blueness'. We would execute the experiment by, perhaps, changing the market so that physicians and health providers wrote 'we like blue' into their purchasing and prescribing guidelines. Then we would observe the behaviour of pharmaceutical companies over time. We might expect to see companies who had blue logos start to win over those that had, say, orange logos. We might then see firms adopting more blueness in the colour of their pills or perhaps adopting corporate uniforms for their sales teams. Our hypothesis would be proven by the emergence of several business models all with varying shades of blue and the demise of orange, pink, red and other business models.

What I intend to demonstrate with this flippant example is that it is not possible to set up such an experiment in the real world. Instead, we must observe what is going on in the market and use that as our laboratory, a practice familiar to natural scientists. For example, we observe that the reduced prescribing influence of physicians is associated with the decline of traditional sales teams. The pressure on primary care prices has been followed by a shift in marketing focus to secondary care. The success of biotechs at innovating is being followed by some large pharma companies trying to emulate their research and development routines. The development of biological knowledge is leading to the development of combined diagnostic/therapeutic approaches. All of these are examples of organizational routines being adapted to enable new capabilities that, the firms hope, will create a better fit with the changing technological or market environment. In themselves, they are circumstantial evidence for evolutionary theory in the pharma industry. But these observations of recent trends, informative as they are, are not the strongest evidence we have of evolution in the pharmaceutical industry. For that, we have more than a hundred years of evidence.

Explaining the Past

The long history and massive scale of today's pharmaceutical industry could mislead us into thinking that this has always been the source of our medicines. But, of course, there haven't always been armies of scientists pushing back the frontiers of medicine or huge sales teams patrolling hospitals and doctors' surgeries. Similarly, there has not always been a string of lawyers ready to break patents at the earliest opportunity, nor large, efficient, high quality factories able to produce complex drugs at very low cost. If we go back 150 years, there was the apothecary.

Before the last quarter of the 19th Century, if we were sick and could afford a medicine, we would visit an apothecary, sometimes known as a pharmacist or druggist. Although there were variations on the theme, for example prescribing physicians, this was the dominant 'species' in the market for medicines. At that time, their business model was characterized by small scale use of simple technology and sometimes folklore; furthermore, it was essentially local. Local pharmacies, inventing, making and selling their own medicines, was the successful business model for hundreds of years. It had high fitness in an environment where the technology was simple, healthcare was an individual purchase and the only significant geography was the local one. In scale, scope and strategy, the local apothecary was as unlike a modern pharma company as human beings are unlike the triassic eozostrodon, the shrew like creature that was the first true mammal. The capabilities of the 19th Century pharmacist included sourcing medicinal plant extracts, finding and using novel recipes and winning and maintaining the trust of his local clientele, what we would today call customer relationship management. Each of these capabilities was underpinned by a complex weave of organizational routines that captured and stored the knowledge, explicit and tacit, required of a successful local pharmacist.

Despite surviving for hundreds of years, that business model became extinct within a few decades, evolving into something that was merely a channel for pharmaceutical companies and, in most developed countries, a component of a broader retail business model. In its place, if we are sick today and can afford a medicine, we expect it to come from a pharmaceutical company, either research-based or generic, via a healthcare professional. If evolutionary theory is to explain the future of pharma, it needs to be able to explain the quite revolutionary way that the modern pharmaceutical business model arose to displace the old pharmacy model. More particularly, it needs to explain the way that changes in the social and physical technologies led to different 'fitness criteria' in the medicines environment and how those fitness criteria led to the emergence of different organizational routines, capabilities and business models. To do that, we need to look at what happened in the last quarter of the 19th Century.

The modern pharmaceutical industry began its evolution in a period known as the second industrial revolution, a period characterized by great social and technological change. Technologically, the developments most immediately relevant to pharma were in organic chemistry and biology. In the chemical field, Wohler, in 1828, had synthesized urea for the first time, effectively proving that organic, biologically important chemicals were not fundamentally different from inorganic chemicals. This led to the growth of organic chemistry. In 1856, while attempting to synthesize quinine, William Perkin discovered the first aniline dye, a discovery that led to the rapid development of the synthetic dye industry, particularly in the Rhine Valley. It was from this industry, more than the local pharmacy business model that the pharmaceutical industry was to draw much of its first DNA, its organizational routines for discovering and making drugs. At about the same time, there was an explosion of biological knowledge, especially in bacteriology. To quote one medical historian:

'The decade of the 1870s saw isolation of agents responsible for causing leprosy and anthrax; the 1880s found agents for typhoid, tuberculosis, cholera, diphtheria, and meningococcal meningitis; the 1890s, plague and malaria; and by 1910 pertussis, syphilis, and epidemic typhus.'

Duffy (28)

Soon after this surge of chemical and biological knowledge began, the early drug companies, which included names like Hoffman-La Roche, Sandoz, Schering and Merck, built up research laboratories and relationships with academic scientists in a model that is easily recognizable today. As Alfred Chandler describes so well (9), the birth of what we would call pharmaceutical companies today began in the 1880s and 1890s with first Hoechst and then Bayer using the capabilities they had developed for discovering, making and commercializing dyes to invent, manufacture and market drugs. In that period, Hoechst financed the Robert Koch Institute in Berlin and commercialized serums for diphtheria, early analgesics and Salvarsan, an organoarsenic compound for the treatment of syphilis. At around the same time, Bayer commercialized Aspirin and various sedatives. In terms of evolutionary theory, the second industrial revolution saw significant changes in the chemistry and biological parts of the physical technology environment. Bayer, Hoechst and others adapted to this change faster than pharmacies. They developed new organizational routines that gave them the capability to discover and commercialize new, synthetic drugs that created more value than the apothecary model. In the next few decades, other companies in Europe and the United States would note their success and imitate those capabilities.

However, it would be a mistake to think that the pharmaceutical industry evolved out of the dye industry simply because of changes in the chemical and biological parts of the physical technology environment. At about the same time, there was also a technological revolution in the communications area. Steam trains and steam ships made transport of people and goods easier, faster and more reliable. The development of the telegraph and later the telephone, as well as steam-enabled postal systems, made communication and control over distance possible and affordable. Materials, products and management information could be moved around and between countries better than ever before. From an evolutionary perspective, this meant that the local, small scale business model was no longer the best fit with the environment. Instead, it became possible to build business models first across countries and then internationally. By 1913, over 80 per cent of Bayer's revenues, for example, came from outside Germany.

The same period also saw significant changes in the social technology environment in western countries. The United States was becoming the continent-sized nation and market it is today and both Germany and Italy were consolidating their unification. Developing free-trade arrangements between nation states increasingly opened the western markets. These political changes were accompanied by increasing wealth and levels of education. Primitive social healthcare systems meant that more people had access to more doctors. This period was also characterized by what the sociologist Max Weber called 'disenchantment', a cultural shift away from mysticism and towards rationalization. This is evidenced by advertising of the time, which shifted away from an emphasis on 'secret ingredients' towards the value of 'scientific' remedies. This subtle but fundamental change in social attitudes is beautifully illustrated in a story Sir Michael Rawlins, Chairman of NICE, told at an Oxford lecture in 2009. He described the publication of *Secret Remedies* by the British Medical Association. It was an exposé of the patent drug industry, revealing that they contained nothing but cheap, ineffective materials. Public outrage led to a parliamentary investigation that recommended regulation of the industry. However, as Sir Michael explains, the publication of those recommendations on 4 August 1914, the day World War I broke out, ensured that they were not acted upon for another 50 years.

These social technology changes, taken together, changed the fitness criteria in the pharmaceutical environment as much as did the changes in the physical technology. Small, local business models based on the arcane arts of the pharmacist were a less good fit with this world than the international and scientifically based model that we recognize as characteristic of the pharma industry today. As a result, a relatively small number of companies developed the organizational routines that enabled them to discover, manufacture and commercialize drugs on an international scale. Almost all of the current industry leaders can trace their origins to these companies who, in the Darwinian sense of the term, evolved during the last quarter of the 19th Century and the first quarter of the 20th. Chandler argues that these capabilities provided such a powerful barrier to entry that, unlike most other industries, no new entrants emerged after World War I until the biotech revolution of the late 20th Century. He also argues that the development of research-based companies was only one aspect of the industry's evolution. He describes a bifurcation of the industry into research-based and over-the-counter medicines which, by developing organizational routines and capabilities in branding, distribution and so on, developed a fit with the environment that was different, but equally successful, to that of the research-based industry.

It is not only the emergence of over-the-counter and research-based pharma companies during this period that support the application of evolutionary theory to pharma. There is also strong evidence for the sort of transfer of organizational routines that would be necessary for that evolution to happen. Chandler talks about the German and Swiss companies taking their ideas from British and French scientists. Even more compellingly, Roy Church and Tilli Tansley describe clear processes of imitation in their history of Burroughs-Wellcome (29). This leader of the British pharmaceutical sector was founded by two American pharmacists and adopted a strongly ethical, scientific positioning to differentiate itself from patent medicines. Church and Tansley record how the firm deliberately imported ideas of sales management, down to the level of call rates and detailing aids, from American companies like Parke-Davis. Burroughs-Wellcome also imported routines and capabilities from universities, as they tried to take advantage of the new biological knowledge, based on germ theory. In doing so, they set up the first laboratory in the United Kingdom, licensed for animal experiments outside an academic institution. As Tansley describes in her 2009 lecture to Green-Templeton College, Oxford (30), this laboratory became the source that supplied many of the scientific leaders of the British pharmaceutical industry, a clear example of successful organizational routines being spread across the industry.

So, the birth of the international, science-based pharmaceutical industry that we know today can be explained as an evolutionary response to the developments of the second industrial revolution, both the physical technology of chemistry, biology and transportation, and also the accompanying social technology changes, including the political growth of markets, increased wealth and the shift of social attitudes towards scientific rationalism. But the industry we have known in more modern times is not quite the same as that of the 1920s. Modern companies are larger and were, until very recently, more vertically integrated than those of the inter-war years. By 1939, the larger pharmaceutical companies had many of the capabilities that we recognize as characteristic of the modern 'big pharma' model; nonetheless, their model was different in a number of ways. Capabilities in manufacturing, marketing and sales and, perhaps especially, research and development and regulatory, were all much less developed than today's industry leaders.

This subsequent development of the pharmaceutical industry during the 20th Century can also be explained in evolutionary terms. In the third quarter of the 20th Century, for example, both the social and technical dimensions of the market changed, consequently changing the fitness criteria for the industry and prompting firms to develop new organizational routines and capabilities. On the technical side, there occurred what economist Peter Temin called 'the therapeutic revolution' (31). This included the development of antibiotics described in Chapter 1, but also dramatic developments in other therapeutic areas such as antidepressants and cardiovascular drugs. On the social side, huge changes also served to change the fitness criteria of successful drug companies. At a fundamental level, increased prosperity increased the usage of all medicines, as described dramatically by two 1950s researchers:

'In 1939, total drug (US) sales at manufacturers' prices were 301 million dollars. Eighteen years later in 1957 it had increased to 2,102 million dollars, a seven fold increase. During this period, sales of proprietary drugs advertised direct to the lay public went from 152 million dollars to 425 million dollars, an increase of 2.8 times. But, in contrast, the drugs used solely by physicians, the so called ethical drugs, jumped from 149 million dollars to 1,677 million dollars, an increase of 11.3 times.'

Tainter and Marcelli (32)

Those figures, which reflect a trend in all developed economies following World War II, show that the market environment was changing to place more emphasis on selling to physicians rather than consumers or retailers. This was partly due to legislation; but it was also due to the increasing provision of health services. To quote Temin, speaking of the United States:

'Drug companies in the 1930s were very different from the drug firms of today. They did not advertise to doctors because any nonnarcotic drug could be purchased without a prescription before 1938 and they did not engage in large scale drug research because drug technology was essentially fixed.'

Temin (31)

The 1938 act that began to restrict the availability of drugs in the United States was mirrored in other western countries. In the United Kingdom, for example, the Venereal Diseases Act of 1917 introduced the concept of the prescription only medicine. However, there were few real restrictions on the sale of drugs until much later. The real sea-change in pharmaceutical regulation came in the 1960s as a result of the thalidomide disaster. In 1962, the Kefauver-Harris amendments in the United States gave the Food and Drug Administration (the FDA) the power to demand proof of efficacy, regulate advertising and establish good manufacturing practice. Similar measures followed in other countries. In the United Kingdom, the medicines act of 1968 put into practice many of the recommendations of the 1914 report. This delay in regulating medicines in the United Kingdom meant that, as Sir Michael Rawlins quoted Ronald Mann in his Oxford lecture

(30) 'The thalidomide victims were the last casualties of the first world war.' This early regulation has since, of course, developed into a much more extensive regulatory system that makes much greater demands for safety, efficacy and quality. This is perhaps best illustrated by the development, in 1996, of Good Clinical Practice by the International Harmonisation Conference and its adoption by all the major regulatory agencies. This change in the regulatory element of the social technology environment clearly shifted the fitness criteria for pharmaceutical companies, requiring them to develop organizational routines to enable capabilities in clinical trials and regulatory approval.

The other significant developments in the pharmaceutical social technology environment were those that enabled generic drugs. The turning point here was the 1984 Waxman-Hatch Act in the United States, which provided for market entry of generic versions of all post-1962 drugs in exchange for an extension to the patent period. However, the legal implications of the Act were realized by the development of cost-containment strategies (such as generic substitution) of healthcare providers, Health Maintenance Organizations and Pharmaceutical Benefit Management companies and by government reimbursement policies. Like the other changes in the market, this changed the fitness criteria for the market so that firms would need either low-cost capabilities or the capability to out-sell low cost imitators. That would lead, eventually, to the development of a huge volume, low cost generics market.

Much more recently, in 1997, changes in the legal part of the social environment allowed direct-to-consumer advertising. In the American market, this meant that firms had to import marketing communications and branding capabilities, usually by imitating the organizational routines of consumer goods companies.

Perhaps the biggest change in the social technology environment of the post war years, however, was the rise of social healthcare and, in the United States especially, private health insurance. Germany and Britain had limited health insurance systems before World War II, but great growth followed that conflict. In the United Kingdom, for example, medicines became free at the point of use with the advent of the National Health Service in 1948. In 1965, the Social Security Act established Medicare and Medicaid in the United States, complementing the already booming private healthcare sector. Across the whole of the developed world, demand for drugs was fuelled by the provision of health insurance. This fuelled a huge increase in demand, but it also changed the fitness criteria substantially. It meant that large scale was an advantage in dealing with government payers and new sales capabilities, such as Key Opinion Leader Management, were required to 'pull through' sales against the inertia of these bureaucratic organizations.

Just as the birth of the pharmaceutical industry provides evidence to support evolutionary theory, the post war period also provides compelling substantiation for neo-Darwinian ideas of replicators, interactors and fitness landscapes. As the social technology and physical technology environments have changed, the business models of the industry have also changed. We can show this graphically, using fitness landscape diagrams. In Figure 2.3, representing the period before the second industrial revolution, there was only one group of similar species that included apothecaries, dispensing physicians, patent medicines and perhaps, makers of foods with health claims.

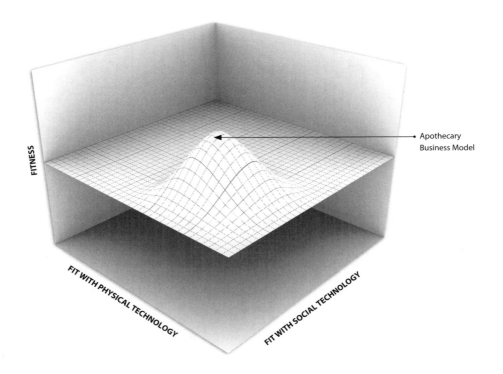

Apothecary
Business Model

FITNESS

FIT WITH PHYSICAL TECHNOLOGY

FIT WITH SOCIAL TECHNOLOGY

Figure 2.3   The pharma fitness landscape circa 1870

In Figure 2.4, representing the first half of the 20th Century, this group has divided into two groups: firstly, the science based companies, both the large, international firms and the smaller, more specialized firms; secondly, the OTC medicine companies. Note that the apothecary model no longer has good fit with the environment. By Figure 2.5, representing the last half of the 20th Century, we see that both the research-based and OTC peaks still exist, although they have moved as they gradually developed organizational routines and capabilities to fit changes in the environment. Further, the research-based peak has split into big pharma and speciality peaks, reflecting adaptation strategies to the cost and difficulty of pharmaceutical innovation. In addition, the OTC and research peaks have been joined by a third, the generic species, which is also a direct adaptation to the social technology changes like Waxman-Hatch. In this interpretation, the biotechs cannot be seen as separate entity. That is because they are either, like Amgen, forms of research-based pharma, or a part of the supply chain of conventional pharma. These illustrations are, of course, an approximation, but they serve to make a point. Evolutionary theory does a good job at explaining how the industry was born and how it developed during the 20th Century. In Part II of the book, I will examine how it can meet the second test of a good theory by predicting the future as well as it explains the past. Before I do that, however, there is one other concept from biological evolution we need to consider and displace into the pharmaceutical industry.

The critical reader will have noticed that, so far, I have not mentioned the important concept of co-evolution. In biology, this refers to mutual adaptation by interacting

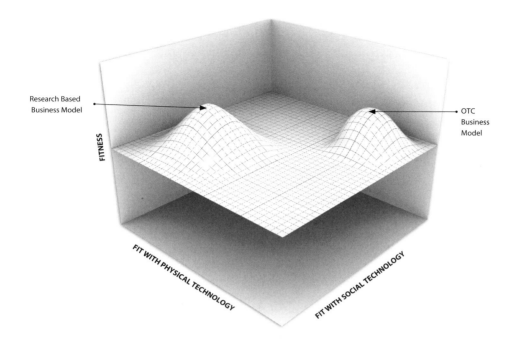

Research Based
Business Model

OTC
Business
Model

FITNESS

FIT WITH PHYSICAL TECHNOLOGY

FIT WITH SOCIAL TECHNOLOGY

Figure 2.4   The pharma fitness landscape circa 1930

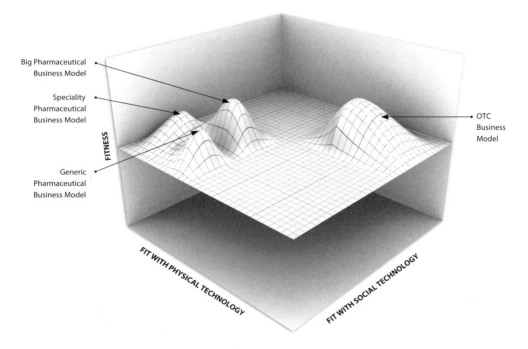

Big Pharmaceutical
Business Model

Speciality
Pharmaceutical
Business Model

Generic
Pharmaceutical
Business Model

OTC
Business
Model

FITNESS

FIT WITH PHYSICAL TECHNOLOGY

FIT WITH SOCIAL TECHNOLOGY

Figure 2.5   The pharma fitness landscape circa 1990

species. Richard Dawkins describes co-evolution in a way that is relevant to the context of pharmaceutical business models, their social environment of healthcare and regulatory systems and their technological environment of fundamental and applied research:

> *'Co-evolution often occurs when organisms that have something to gain from each other, form partnerships in which each side contributes something to the other and both gain from the cooperation.'*

Dawkins (27)

In evolutionary economics, co-evolution refers to mutual adaptation between firms and with social and technological environments. Displacing the concept of co-evolution to pharma suggests that, whilst it is true that pharmaceutical business models have evolved in response to changes in the technological and social environments, those two environments have also been influenced and have adapted to each other and to pharmaceutical business models. Healthcare systems, part of the social environment, have greatly broadened the range of treatments they offer in response to what is technically possible. The fundamental research part of the technical environment has been influenced, at least in part, by the demands of the healthcare system and by commercial imperatives of pharma business models, through mechanisms like joint projects and funding grants. Pharmaceutical business models enabled medication of large populations, leading to incidents, like thalidomide, that shaped the regulatory part of the social environment, and which in turn forced pharmaceutical business models to change. In practice, the evolution of pharma business models, their social environment and their technological environment are intertwined in a massively complex triple helix. Displacing the concept of co-evolution into pharma implies that we need to consider not only how the pharmaceutical industry will adapt to its changing environment but also how the industry might in turn shape its environment. This will add another level of complexity onto how we look at the future of pharma.

Looking to the Future

In this chapter, I've tried to move from the pessimistic prognosis of Chapter 1 – a pharma industry no longer capable of contributing to our society anything like it used to – to the optimistic hope that we have a theory to help us. We are all theorists and, when faced with a problem, our instinct is to begin by theorizing. When faced with the problem of a vital industry in decline, we need a powerful theory that we know works in complex adaptive systems. The evidence that evolutionary theory has explanatory and predictive power in a biological context is as close to complete as we can hope for. Even though it is a newer discipline, it is also compelling in economic and social contexts, which leads us to hope it might help us to understand, predict and, ultimately, manage the pharmaceutical industry. Used retrospectively, evolutionary theory seems to explain the birth of the industry, its post-war adaptation and even, with caution, some of its most recent adaptations. Inevitably, this leads to us ask what the theory predicts for the future of pharma and what those predictions imply for those who work in the industry. Those questions will be addressed in the rest of this book.

Reference List

(1)   Locke, E.A. and Bryan, J.F. 1966. Cognitive Aspects of Psychomotor Performance: The Effects of Performance Goals on Level of Performance. *Journal of Applied Psychology*; 50(4):286–91.

(2)   Porter, M.E. 1980. *Competitive Strategy*. 1st ed. New York, NY: Free Press.

(3)   Hunt, S.D. 2002. *Foundations of Marketing Theory: Towards a General Theory of Marketing*. New York: M.E. Sharpe.

(4)   Rudner, R. 1996. *Philosophy of Social Science*. 1st ed. Englewood Cliffs, NJ: Prentice Hall.

(5)   Simons, K.L. 2003. Industry Life Cycles and their Causes (Synopsis). *Academy of Management*; p. I1–I6.

(6)   Klepper, S. 1997. Industry Life Cycles. *Industrial & Corporate Change*; 6(1):119–43.

(7)   The Industry Life Cycle Revisited. *Harvard Business Review* 2004; 82(10):93.

(8)   Barney, J.B. 1991. Firm Resources and Sustained Competitive Advantage. *Journal of Management*; 17(1):99–120.

(9)   Chandler, A.D. 2005. *Shaping the Industrial Century: The Remarkable Story of the Modern Chemical and Pharmaceutical Industries*. 1st ed. Cambridge, MA: Harvard University Press.

(10)   Mazzucato, M. and Dosi, G. 2006. *Knowledge Accumulation and Industry Evolution: The Case of Pharma Biotech*. Cambridge: Cambridge University Press.

(11)   Priem, R.L. and Butler, J.E. 2001. Is the Resource Based 'View' A Useful Perspective for Strategic Management Research? *Academy of Management Review*; 26(1):22–40.

(12)   Priem, R.L. and Butler, J.E. 2001. Tautology in the Resource-based View and the Implications of Externally Determined Resource Value: Further Comments. *Academy of Management Review*; 26(1):57–66.

(13)   Williamson, O.E. 2008. Transaction Cost Economics: The Precursors. *Economic Affairs*; 28(3):7–14.

(14)   Williamson, O.E. 2010. Transaction Cost Economics: The Origins. *Journal of Retailing*; 86(3):227–31.

(15)   Alchian, A.A. 1950. Uncertainty, Evolution and Economic Theory. *Journal of Political Economy*; 58:211–22.

(16)   Nelson, R.R. and Winter, S.G. 1982. *An Evolutionary Theory of Economic Change*. Cambridge, Mass: Harvard University Press.

(17)   Beinhocker, E.D. 2006. *The Origin of Wealth: Evolution, Complexity and the Radical Remaking of Economics*. London: Random House.

(18)   Hodgson, G.M. and Knudson, T. 2010. *Darwin's Conjecture: The Search for General Principles of Social and Economic Evolution*. Chicago: Chicago University Press.

(19)   Dennett, D.C. 1995. *Darwin's Dangerous Idea*. London: Allen Lane.

(20)   Waldrop, M.M. 1992. *Complexity: The Emerging Science at the Edge of Order and Chaos*. New York: Touchstone.

(21)   Schön, D.A. 1963. *The Displacement of Concepts*. London: Tavistock.

(22)   Dawkins, R. 1976. *The Selfish Gene*. Oxford: OUP.

(23)   Hull, D. 1980. Individuality and Selection. *Annual Review of Ecology and Systematics*; 11:311–32.

(24)   Hodgson, G. and Knudsen, T. 2004. The firm as an interactor: firms as vehicles for habits and routines. *Journal of Evolutionary Economics*. 1;14(3):281–307.

(25)   Wright, S. 1931. Evolution in Mendelian Populations. *Genetics*; 16:97.

(26)   Nelson, R.R. 2008. What enables rapid economic progress: What are the needed institutions? *Research Policy*; 37(1):1–11.

(27)   Dawkins, R. 2009. *The Greatest Show on Earth: The Evidence for Evolution*. London: Bantam Press.

(28)   Duffy, J. 1993. *From Humors to Medical Science: A History of American Medicine*. 2nd ed. Chicago: University of Chicago Press.

(29)   Church, R.A. and Tansley, T. 2010. *Burroughs Wellcome & Co: Knowledge, Trust, Profit, and the Transformation of the British Pharmaceutical Industry, 1880–1940*. London: Carnegie.

(30)   Tansley, T., Rawlins, M., Brinsmead, C., Vallance, P. and Patterson, J. 2009. 'Addicted to Big Pharma? Reconciling business, medical and ethical needs': The Green-Templeton Lectures 2009. Available at: http://www.gtc.ox.ac.uk/academic/lectures-seminars/gtlectures/green-templeton-lectures-2009 html [accessed: 5 January, 2011].

(31)   Temin, P. 1979. Technology, Regulation and Market Structure in the Modern Pharmaceutical Industry. *The Bell Journal of Economics*; 10(2):429–46.

(32)   Tainter, M.L. and Marcelli, G.M.A. 1959. The Rise of Synthetic Drugs in the American Pharmaceutical Industry. *Bulletin of the New York Academy of Medicine*; 35(6):387–405.

A Co-evolving Industry

CHAPTER

3 *An Evolving Social Environment*

'This time, like all times, is a very good one, if we but know what to do with it.'
Ralph Waldo Emerson

In Chapter 2, we introduced the idea of the fitness landscape, which illustrates the strength of a business model, in terms of how well it is adapted to its social and technological environments. We then went on to look at how changes in those two dimensions of the fitness landscape explain the evolution of the pharmaceutical industry from about 1870 to the present day. We saw how the apothecary was replaced as the dominant business model in the Medicines' market by the evolution of two new business models: the research-based and OTC. These two then developed further to become large, international businesses with quite different organizational routines and capabilities. This bifurcation was an adaptation to scientific developments in chemistry, biology and communications but also to social developments such as disenchantment, increased wealth and internationalization. The research-based sector, sometimes described as ethical or prescription-only, was then subject to evolutionary forces from the social and technological environments. In particular, the industry was shaped by publicly funded healthcare, increasing regulation, laws regarding generics and the rapid advance of technology, both pharmaceutical and information. These changes led eventually to a further speciation into generics, biotech, big pharma and speciality pharma.

That we can so clearly correlate these changes in the industry's business models to changes in the environment suggests that evolutionary theory is valid in this context and that it is a reasonable explanation of the industry's past. But hindsight is the easy part; good theories should predict the future as well as explain the past. In this, Part II of this book (Chapters 3, 4, 5 and 6), we'll try to move from the relatively easy task of a posteriori reasoning about what has already happened to the much more difficult task of building a priori postulates about what might happen in the future. In this chapter I will look at the way the social and technological environments are developing now; then, in Chapter 4, I will examine what that seems to imply for the industry's fitness landscape. In Chapter 5, I will attempt to draw these developments together to predict the future of the industry, an altogether more difficult trick. In Part III (Chapter 7 onwards), we will discuss the implications of those changes for individuals and companies involved in the pharma industry. But don't try skipping ahead to Part III just yet; it makes little sense without Part II.

Seven Social Shifts

The research programme for this book (described in Appendix 1: A Pragmatic Research Approach) generated a lot of information that was relevant to the first research question about the way the social environment is changing so as to shape the evolution of the pharmaceutical industry. This information was, as management researchers like to say, 'messy and unstructured'. Respondents each answered the same questions, but from varying perspectives. Even when talking about the same thing, they often used different terms, placed things in different order of priority and drew different conclusions from what they observed. The issues that emerged were also strongly interconnected. For example, important points like the loss of patent exclusivity, genericization and price pressure were often woven together in the respondents' answers. However, by careful analysis seven dominant themes emerged and these seven dominant themes will be used to structure the rest of this chapter. In an approximate order of importance, the seven social environment forces that are shaping the evolution of pharma are:

- A maturing concept of value
- A bigger, more fragmented market
- A more risk averse market
- Stratification of health provision
- A more informed, sceptical and proactive public
- Contemplative investors
- A more preventative approach to healthcare.

A MATURING CONCEPT OF VALUE

Of all the many and varied points made in the research interviews, the theme of the value-seeking customer came out strongest. Typical of this was the observation made by Angus Russell, Chief Executive of Shire:

'The payers, be they governments or managed care, are driving a much harder bargain in terms of the value proposition. Wherever I travel in the world, there's not a government official or payer who doesn't tell me the same story. They say that not only do they have less money but they have greater demands for healthcare provision. They sit there, wring their hands and say "What would you have me do?"'

Angus Russell, Shire

Echoing Russell, Ken Jones, Chief Operating Officer of Astellas Pharma Europe Ltd in Europe, pointed to the economic imperatives facing western governments who are currently the industry's most important customers:

'The reality is an ageing population, a diminishing workforce, a diminishing tax-base to pay for healthcare. So, at the end of the day, government has had to decide what it is worth paying to extend someone's life for a year.'

Ken Jones, Astellas Pharma Europe Ltd

This idea that pharmaceutical companies are under price pressure from the governments and insurers who pay for most healthcare in the developed world was expressed by almost every interviewee but from a number of perspectives. Andreas Fibig, CEO of Bayer Schering Pharma, typified the attitude of many pharma companies, when he expressed the importance of pharmaceutical companies meeting the demands of society:

'Demographics will put a lot of pressure on the industry to make sure that we have relevant therapies and medications available for the people, even if the state and government funds are not as big as they were in the past.'

Andreas Fibig, Bayer Schering Pharma

Closely linked with the frequent mentions of price pressure were descriptions of genericization. These were exemplified by Peter Stein, Chairman of Norgine:

'To me, the biggest force acting on the industry is that the extent to which healthcare problems can be met by commodity – or quasi-commodity – goods and services is changing fundamentally. As a consequence, society's willingness to pay for things where the alternative is a commodity is becoming restricted.'

Peter Stein, Norgine

Almost every respondent saw the growth in generics as inevitable. Harald Stock, CEO of Grünenthal, was representative of the views on this:

'My prediction is that for the next ten years the lion's share of the market, at least half, will be generics, not only in prescriptions volume but also in value.'

Harald Stock, Grünenthal

The genericization trend has also gone far beyond the simple replacement of an off-patent drug with its generic equivalent, as Dr George Chressanthis, a business school professor with an illustrious track record in the industry, points out:

'Generics have gone well beyond replacing the original branded molecule that has lost its patent through bioequivalent generic substitution. More important is the expansion of generic use through therapeutic substitution. This broader degree of generic substitution is driven by economic force. For instance, the increased influence of managed care plans forcing generic use and by public policy that is encouraging generic use on cost grounds.'

George Chressanthis, Fox School of Business, Temple University

Importantly, this phenomenon of payers demanding more value was not seen by the respondents as solely due to economic constraints and the availability of cheap generics. A further, contributory factor was the decline in research and development productivity, mentioned in Chapter 1. George Chressanthis again:

'The first and foremost issue is how the industry will reverse a longstanding decline in research and development pipeline productivity. This long standing, 20-year decline in the outputs of the industry is well documented. While there continue to be increased investments in new chemical entities, outputs have been declining, as seen by new product launches and their degree of innovation. The big question is why this trend is happening and if there is anything the industry can do to reverse this and get productivity increasing again.'

George Chressanthis, Fox School of Business, Temple University

The revenue gap created when products lose patent-protected exclusivity is described by the industry as the 'patent cliff'. In many cases, the precipice created by patent expiry and generic substitution is huge, as observed by Osagie Imasogie, Senior Managing Partner of Phoenix IP Ventures, a venture capital firm:

'The problem is that large pharmaceutical companies look at where their revenue is coming from and see that maybe 50 per cent of it is coming from products that are coming to the end of their patent life. So, there's a huge cliff right in front of you. And how do you manage that? Look at Pfizer and their main product Lipitor generating 13 billion dollars a year, over a billion dollars a month in one product with a 90 per cent plus gross margin. How did you fill a 13 billion dollar hole?'

Osagie Imasogie, Phoenix IP Ventures

Patent loss, genericization and research and development productivity were not the only issues raised in this part of the interviews. The evaluation of new drugs for cost effectiveness, in addition to safety, efficacy and quality, was also perceived as a further aspect of the customers' search for better value. In this respect, the UK's National Institute for Healthcare and Clinical Excellence (NICE) was often cited as a model for what the industry terms 'market access authorities'. Its chairman, Sir Michael Rawlins, expressed the perspective of such agencies very succinctly:

'I think things will have to change. Payers aren't going to be able to pay the money, but nothing can be done about that. The industry is going to have to produce new products more expeditiously if it is going to survive in anything approaching its current form.'

Sir Michael Rawlins

Price controls and market access authorities have been seen as a traditionally European phenomenon but it seems to be accepted that, directly or otherwise, the same strictures will be applied in time to all major markets. Moish Tov of Skila, a pharmaceutical specialized software and services company, noted:

'At the moment, a typical pharmaceutical company gets 60 per cent of its revenue from the US, largely due to the relatively high prices of medicines there, which are among the highest in the world. This model has reached its limits because neither patient, insurer nor government can afford to pay more and payers have now started to push down on price. The Europeans of course have been controlling prices for some time, so cost control will have a large impact on

the industry. We see this already with market access controls, which are evidence of a more educated market realising that the newest drug may not always be the best value.'

Moish Tov, Skila

A similarly global perspective was given by Joe Jimenez, CEO of Novartis, who pointed out that price pressures don't just mean price cuts; they also imply new ways of working with customers:

'Given the increase in healthcare demand, many countries are implementing reforms aimed at controlling rising healthcare costs. They're putting pressure on prices and demanding more evidence for proof of improved efficacy for new drugs. This means that we have to partner in a new way with governments to focus together on better patient outcomes.'

Joe Jimenez, Novartis

Moish Tov's reference to a more 'educated' market and Joe Jimenez's points about 'demanding more evidence' and 'partnering' for better outcomes are indicators of an underlying theme that pervaded the interviews when discussing customer demands for better value. What the respondents described was not simply the predictable attempts of customers to get better prices that we observe in all markets. Instead, what emerged from the interviews was a fundamental shift in the way customers are defining the value of pharmaceuticals. Historically, they defined value as being able to either cure or manage patients and the most valuable drug was the one that cured or managed the patient best. Cost was, if not unimportant, a secondary factor, even when the clinical improvement was small. But this aspect of pharma's social environment has changed, and is continuing to change quite dramatically. Payers are squeezed between increasing demands and increasing costs. The recent surge in me-too or incrementally improved drugs has rendered them sceptical of the value of new products. As a result, they are redefining value in terms of the optimal health outcome per unit of spend. This fundamental shift in what customers want is well recognized by the pharma companies and the research-based companies see demonstrating the value of their innovation as being central to their future success. For example, when he was appointed CEO of Merck in December 2010, Ken Frazier's first press release stressed the importance of demonstrating the value of new products to payers. However, although pharma companies do recognize the shift in customer behaviour from 'best drug first, price second' to 'best outcome for a given budget', they seem less well aware of the evolutionary implications of this shift. It appears to be of the same order of magnitude as earlier great shifts in the social environment, such as the development of socialized healthcare or drug safety legislation. As such, it implies a shift in the fitness landscape that favours companies that have a strong capability to create customer perceived value. Of course, the fitness landscape doesn't care too much about how that value is created. It could be through very low costs, or by much better clinical outcomes, or by some added value service that reduces overall cost or improves clinical outcome. What is clear, however, is that the fitness landscape has shifted against business models that do not create demonstrable value. Along with the other social and technological changes in the medicines market, this will undoubtedly drive the evolution of the pharma industry.

A BIGGER, MORE FRAGMENTED MARKET

In all of the research sources analysed, a theme scarcely less prominent than the maturing concept of value was the way in which the dimensions and granularity of the pharmaceutical market are changing. Respondents described a number of trends, all of which amounted not only to an increase in the number of people needing medicine but also a fragmentation of their needs, whether that was in the sort of diseases they would need treatment for, the way they obtained and used their medicines, or both.

Respondents talked about the volume of the pharmaceutical market growing in all countries, consistent with the discussion in Chapter 1, including mention of well-known phenomena such as the 'baby boomer' demographic bulge in western markets and the access widening effects of the Obama health care reforms in the United States. But by far the most frequently mentioned phenomenon was the rise of emerging markets in Asia, South America and elsewhere and the relative decline in the western markets where pharma has traditionally focussed its efforts. David Norton, Company Group Chairman of Johnson & Johnson, provided a good overview of how the industry sees markets like China and India:

'The emerging markets are where the growth is going to come from, so it will be very important to be there. But they are not going to pay western prices and, whilst companies will make money and sell large volumes, the emerging markets are not going to be the saviour of the industry.'

David Norton, Johnson & Johnson

The same idea, that the emerging markets are important but will not be a new version of western markets, was articulated by Sophia Tickell of PharmFutures, a firm that facilitates the dialogue about long term value between pharmacos and investors:

'A very significant trend is the growth of emerging markets, the potential of which is not yet realized because to do so requires a change in business model that has not yet happened.'

Sophia Tickell, PharmaFutures

In similar vein, Doug McCutcheon of the investment bank UBS, pointed out that the traditional market boundaries of the western pharmaceutical market do not really apply in many of the emerging markets:

'If you look at emerging markets, then generics, consumer and pharma all overlap anyway. When people talk about their emerging market strategy, they really mean they want to grow in the BRIC countries [Brazil, Russia, India, China] and they see branded generics as the way to do that.'

Doug McCutcheon, UBS

The other important reality that emerged from the research is that emerging markets were far from identical, as described by Mike Thomas of A.T. Kearney, a leading consultancy:

'There's no doubt that we're seeing an opening up of the emerging markets – although that word can be misleading, as some of them are no longer emerging – both in the next tier of healthcare markets, like Brazil, Mexico, South Korea, as well as the more emergent large markets like India and China. There are two different tiers of markets. Where the industry growth is happening right now isn't China and India, actually, it's Turkey, South Korea, Mexico and Brazil which are rather more evolved in terms of infrastructure and funding paradigm, and so on. But there's no doubt at all that when you are looking at incremental growth (and this is still an industry that is measured in terms of top line growth) that is where the action and investment is and should be. This is a new tier of markets that is really demonstrating sizeable growth prospects. Many of them are already larger than most European markets.'

Mike Thomas, A.T. Kearney

So the growth of demand for pharmaceuticals in emerging markets is not simply more of the same type of customer as pharma companies are used to in the west. They differ significantly from western markets and, indeed, from each other. This suggests that unlocking the growth potential of these markets will require companies both to adapt their business models and to develop a capability of managing a number of very different markets at once. Compared to the historical base of western markets, which differ in detail but share fundamentals, the emergent markets of Asia, South America, Eastern Europe and elsewhere are not only very large but also much more granular. This granularity or heterogeneity implies a different fitness landscape from that of a largely western market.

The differences between emerging markets were not the only source of market fragmentation mentioned in my research interviews. Many interviews raised the issue of increasing granularity in disease patterns and in healthcare systems. The argument made by Amit Roy of Nomura, a medical doctor turned investment analyst, was especially interesting and worth quoting at some length:

'The industry is very successful in dealing with cardiovascular disease, respiratory disease and even diabetes, so what we will see is the industry trying to deal with cancer. Just push this out a little bit further, another 20 years, and you end up in the neurological period like Parkinson's and Alzheimer's. And the point about this is that, whereas the state of scientific knowledge in the realm of cardiovascular disease is actually very good, the cellular level of scientific understanding of, say, cancer, is a tiny fraction of that of cardiovascular disease. And, if you take that idea a bit further, the level of medical understanding of neurological disease is even less than that of cancer. So what the industry is facing is this massive law of diminishing returns as we get older and we need to find new science and then make drugs to address the next level of conditions.'

Amit Roy, Nomura

Implicit in Amit Roy's cogent line of reasoning is that the social environment faced by pharma in the future will not only involve more people, they will have different diseases that are more difficult to cure. Interestingly, this is a strong example of co-evolution between the industry and the social environment mentioned at the end of Chapter 2. It implies a fragmentation of the fitness landscape corresponding to the different disease classes the industry must deal with.

From a completely different perspective, but with similar outcomes, were a group of comments made about fragmentation of healthcare systems. Characteristic of this were the observations of Chris Wright, Managing Principal at consultancy firm ZS Associates:

> 'The commercial opportunity is becoming more varied across different geographies, both across countries and even within the United States. This is fundamentally driven by variation in market access. Most doctors have to deal with many insurance companies, with many different programmes and they can't keep track of so many companies and products. The market is becoming much more granular, more segmented, than it used to be and the old, mass market sales and marketing model is, in those circumstances, ineffective and wasteful.'

Chris Wright, ZS Associates

So a phenomenon that was expected to emerge from the research – the rise of emerging markets – was, indeed, mentioned by most respondents, but with different ramifications than one might expect. The potential for huge numbers of new customers, as these markets develop state funded insurance, or self-insuring middle classes or other ways of allowing mass access to medicines, is of course important to the industry. So, too, is the less dramatic but important growth as a result of demographic ageing in developed markets. But an increase in the size of the market does not itself change the fitness landscape very much, except perhaps to favour larger companies with global capabilities. From an evolutionary perspective, what is more relevant is that these billions of new customers are not the same as the customers the pharmaceutical industry is used to serving and, indeed, are not the same as each other, either in their clinical needs or how they might access healthcare. As a consequence, the fitness landscape will fragment into more peaks and troughs. This implies that a greater variety of capabilities and business models will be favoured than we have observed in the relatively homogeneous western market in which the modern industry grew up.

A MORE RISK AVERSE MARKET

Another strong theme that emerged from the research data referred to regulatory issues, litigiousness and the implications of these trends for pharmaceutical companies. Many respondents saw this as perhaps the most fundamental of the forces acting on the industry in that it underlies the issue of research and development productivity and, therefore, of cost pressure and genericization. Steve Burrill, CEO of the Life Sciences Merchant Bank Burrill & Company, described it thus:

> 'The big drivers of change in the industry are technology, regulatory and reimbursement.'

Steve Burrill, Burrill & Company

In Chapter 2, we described how the regulatory changes of the 1960s shaped the evolution of the industry, but most respondents commented on how, in recent years, the trend has been strongly towards ever more stringently applied regulation. Sir Richard

Sykes, formerly Chairman of GlaxoSmithKline and now Chair of the prestigious Royal Institution, expressed this in characteristically straightforward style:

'Regulation has had a very significant impact. In the past, you could bring a product to market in less than five years. Today, regulatory authorities are totally risk averse and it is almost impossible to bring some molecules to market.'

Sir Richard Sykes, former Chairman of GlaxoSmithKline

The constraints of regulation on innovation were also well described by Luciano Conde, a Director of Almirall, a Spanish-based speciality pharma company:

'Innovations in healthcare and particularly in the drug industry are very constrained by regulations. We hope to see some genetic treatments being developed, in particular for very severe diseases. However, the complexities and implications from a regulatory and safety point of view are so huge that, as the current regulatory environment stands, it is difficult for me to understand how the full benefits of these treatments are going to be evaluated.'

Luciano Conde, Almirall

Notably, this concern about regulatory constraints was not restricted, as one might expect, to firms producing very new, innovative drugs. Warwick Smith, Director of the British Generic Manufacturers Association (BGMA), pointed to the challenges that face even generic drugs with a long history of usage:

'It shouldn't take two years to get a generic license. We're not dealing with rocket science. The whole system works on the basis that the originator gets their minimum period of monopoly and then the generics launch, which drives the price down. If that launch is delayed, that system starts to fall apart.'

Warwick Smith, BGMA

Nor is the impact of regulation solely restricted to new drug approvals. Every stage of pharmaceutical development, manufacture and promotion is increasingly tightly regulated. This was evidenced, for example, by Brik Eyre of Baxter:

'The increasingly onerous regulatory involvement is another critical factor in the manufacturing of pharmaceuticals. There is increased sensitivity, for example, over particulates. I think this involvement and sensitivity will continue to increase.'

Brik Eyre, Baxter

Of course, it would be easy to see these remarks as simply the self-interested agenda of an industry seeking to reduce its regulatory burden, but the point was made most forcefully by an interviewee who does not work for the industry:

'The demands placed on pharmaceutical companies are just too great ... it's part of the problem. It's not the whole problem, but it's part of the problem of expensive drugs. If we go on like this, they will be unaffordable to anybody and so the industry won't actually be able to make any money.'

Sir Michael Rawlins, NICE

Similar observations to Sir Michael's have been made by others without a pharmaceutical industry bias, such as New York University Law Professor Richard Epstein (2) and former FDA official Henry Miller (3). Overall, the picture that emerges is one of an unbalanced regulatory approach that struggles to balance the task of protecting patients with the challenge of meeting unmet clinical needs.

As with the maturation of value and the growth and fragmentation of markets, the pharmaceutical industry is very well aware of the increasing burden of regulatory approval and its practical implications. From an evolutionary theory perspective, however, this is a shift in the social environment that is likely to shape the fitness landscape just as much in the future as it has since the 1960s. The argument for regulation being a shaper of the industry's future becomes stronger still if we see it as merely a symptom of a broader societal risk aversion. Just as the 'disenchantment' described by Weber and discussed in Chapter 2 was a deep seated, long term societal change, it appears that risk aversion may be the same kind of fundamental shift in the way society thinks. In general terms, the increasing risk aversion of developed societies has been documented by a number of authors (see for example (4)). For individuals, researchers have found that it varies with demographics, including wealth, age and gender (5). And the risk aversion of society seems to be complemented by an increasingly litigious culture that will punish drug companies when drugs that have been approved are subsequently found to cause problems, such as happened with AstraZeneca's Seroquel and Merck's Vioxx. If the regulatory environment is an artefact of a larger cultural trend towards risk aversion, a trend perhaps associated with increased wealth, then it is unlikely to change direction. In a society that mandates a packet of peanuts must bear the legend 'may contain nuts', we are unlikely to see pharmaceutical regulation lessening. Like disenchantment, risk aversion is likely to remain a feature of the fitness landscape and being able to overcome or manage regulatory burden, and indeed litigation action, will be significant fitness criteria.

STRATIFICATION OF HEALTH PROVISION

The fourth major theme that the research revealed concerned the way in which healthcare is provided. In most developed markets, healthcare is provided by some combination of state funding, private or employer funded insurance and a limited amount of self-financing. In a typical western country, most significant healthcare is paid for by the state or health insurance. At the bottom end of treatment significance, only relatively minor ailments are left to the non-prescription, over-the-counter, self-financed sector. Similarly, at the top end, only the most exotic, untried or cosmetic medical treatments are excluded from state and insurance systems. However, two related trends seem set to change this picture. Firstly, I will discuss in Chapter 4, the potential universe of treatments has expanded hugely and will continue to do so. Secondly, as discussed above, the ability and willingness of states and insurers to pay for treatments will decline, at least relative to the number of potential treatments available. Jeff George, Head of Sandoz, expressed this succinctly:

'The growing global population and its changing demographic makeup … are adding additional strains on healthcare systems worldwide. Going forward, there will be fewer active contributors, that is, working population paying into and thus financially supporting the system, challenging the overall sustainability of the public healthcare system.'

Jeff George, Sandoz

Those who study healthcare systems recognize this sustainability problem and, slowly and unevenly, this is leading to a gradual redefinition of healthcare provision. Julia Manning, Director of 2020Health.org, a think tank, put this picture into historical perspective from the perspective of the UK's National Health Service (NHS):

'We've had rationing done on the local level for as long as the NHS has existed. It only provided everything for the first three years of its life, after which some prescriptions, glasses and some dental treatment became a fee-for service. I think we've lived in a state of denial for a long time and sooner or later we're going to have to define core services. I do think the NHS and other health systems, where there isn't a direct payment for services, encourage use and risk displacement. You will take more risk with how you live your life because there is a safety net there; you're not feeling the pain of paying as you use it.'

Julia Manning, 2020Health.org

Manning's comments, although forthright and UK-centric, were borne out by other interviewees. Steve Burrill, for example, stressed the inevitability of having to choose from an effectively limitless supply of healthcare possibilities:

'We have essentially unlimited healthcare. That is to say, we can plug you into enough technology that death becomes controllable. But it's not economically possible to keep everybody alive in the world today and so we are going to have to ration healthcare and decide what we do for whom and why and how much money we're willing to pay to do that. That's why healthcare systems around the world are going through rationing issues to try and figure out what they pay for, and why, and what don't they pay for.'

Steve Burrill, Burrill & Company

The issue of healthcare provision was most commonly mentioned in relation to developed economies caught between demographic ageing and chronic diseases on the one hand, and economic maturity and slow growth on the other. But the issue was not seen purely as a problem of the developed world. David Norton foresaw related issues arising in developing markets:

'The issue around affordability of healthcare is not only affordability in the developed world but also in the developing world; their governments are trying to provide access to their citizens more broadly too. In the developing world, you've got a population that's moving up from low

socioeconomic status that wants health reform and healthcare. Governments are trying to provide healthcare, but they want to do it at an affordable price for their citizens, which may mean [that the industry will] begin to enter a period of, probably, a different pricing mechanism than in the past; there'll be tiered pricing between countries. We have that today, but there might well be tiered pricing within countries.'

David Norton, Johnson & Johnson

This idea of tiering came out in other interviews too. Harald Stack saw it developing differently in markets of differing levels of development:

'In the developed markets, I anticipate more and more of a payer controlled system in the next five to ten years. In the emerging markets, there will still be an end user driven market, both patient and doctor. In the western world, part of the answer will be to allow for more out-of-pocket spending – the patient will have to pay for innovative healthcare. So, in the developed world, part will be reimbursement, part will be patient funded. In some of the emerging markets, as they take on more western characteristics, some of the same thing will be seen in those markets. There will still be a small segment of branded generics, like "aspirins" but I think everything me-too will become the field for the generics, and payers will love that because it will reduce prices. There will be an upper tier segment of innovative products that will either be out-of-pocket or co-payment, but that will need to be innovative and truly differentiated.'

Harald Stock, Grünenthal

A very similar idea of tiering was raised by Steve Burrill:

'There's a kind of three-tiered healthcare system around the world. There is what the government is paying for ... then there's a kind of private system above that, where people can buy insurance and coverage for things that they want; they think it may be better than what the government does. And then there's the third tier above that, a small tier which is really a concierge service where the rich can, and choose to, pay for anything they want anywhere in the world.'

Steve Burrill, Burrill & Company

Taken as a whole, what emerged from this part of the research was an inevitability laced with variability and wrapped in uncertainty. It seems inevitable that there will be a stratification of healthcare provision, in both developed and developing markets, that is much more pronounced than we see today. This is the only way that the almost limitless possibilities of pharmaceutical and healthcare technology can be reconciled with limitations on public spending. There will be something akin to the three tiers of paying customer outlined by Steve Burrill: self-financing patients with minor ailments, state (or health management organization) and then wealthy patients. Almost certainly, these boundaries will be blurred by co-payment in some markets. However, it seems equally certain that the details of how this is implemented in any country or region will vary significantly according to wealth and political choices. Finally, the speed at which this will develop from the existing market will be very hard to predict. Ultimately, the re-trenching or establishment of publicly funded healthcare systems is a highly political issue and will be subject to all the vagaries and illogicality that implies. What is clear is that this tiered, stratified nature of healthcare funding will be a major determinant of the fitness landscape for pharma. This means that the capability to understand and adapt to the multiple market habitats such tiering implies will be important to the survival of pharmaceutical companies.

A MORE INFORMED, SCEPTICAL AND PROACTIVE PUBLIC

Whilst the subjects of value, fragmenting markets, regulation and healthcare systems were the most prominent points to come out of the research, there were three other points that, although slightly less direct in their market influence, were still very significant. The first of these was a set of interrelated themes about public attitudes. Three distinct but interwoven topics arose out of this analysis: informed patients, sceptical attitudes and proactive advocacy.

The concept of the informed patient was described by several respondents as a subtle, gradual but powerful trend. David Redfern, Chief Strategy Officer at GSK, was representative of that view:

> 'I think that there are some subtle changes going on in the role of the patient, and how informed the patient is, facilitated by the internet. This is particularly noticeable outside the Unites States and Europe, where patients have always been pretty informed. I think that is an evolutionary trend that is going at a steady pace.'

> David Redfern, GSK

In addition to being better informed about pharmaceuticals, the public also seems to be more sceptical about the industry's motives, as exemplified in the anecdote told by Andreas Fibig:

> 'Public reputation for us as an industry is probably at an all-time low. When I started in this industry, in the mid-1980s, our industry had, in most countries, a pretty good reputation. That has shifted dramatically. In particular, Big Pharma is seen as extorting price increases from society and faking clinical trial outcomes. And that's even in the United States, [which] was probably the last of the developed markets where we have seen this business trend. When I started with Pfizer around early 2000, my neighbours were very pleased to talk to somebody from Pfizer and said, "It's great. We value what you contribute to society." But this has changed dramatically over the last ten years and we have become the bad guys. This is a huge issue and I believe we have to tackle it in a much better way than we have done in the past.'

> Andreas Fibig, Bayer Schering Pharma

Linked to both better informed and sceptical patients is the rise of patient advocacy groups, as described by Andrew MacGarvey of Quanticate, a firm which carries out clinical trials for pharmaceutical companies:

> 'Patient advocacy groups [PAGs] will become more important and will shape the market much more than at present. They will also begin to interact with charities to become an alternative

source of funding for pharmaceutical research and development. A more long term idea might be that they become channels to market for certain therapy areas. PAGs also link to the idea of informed, motivated patient groups. When that sort of patient, who is well-insured or wealthy, starts demanding a certain drug, perhaps with the help of his PAG, it will shape the market for innovative drugs.'

Andrew MacGarvey, Quanticate

Just as regulatory tightening seems to be a pharma-specific artefact of a more general cultural trend towards risk aversion, the phenomena of a better informed, more assertive patient can be seen as an artefact of what many have called the 'death of deference', a broader shift in social attitudes that is likely to have fundamental, non-trivial effects on the fitness landscape. Supporting evidence for this was provided by a report by the Social Market Foundation (6), a UK think tank, detailing the challenges to healthcare systems created by better educated, less deferential patients. Notably, this work was supported by data from the World Values Survey, which as the name suggests, measures shifting cultural values on a world-wide basis. If it is indeed true that patients and their families are becoming more assertively involved in demanding healthcare and influencing the choice of treatment, then this will undoubtedly shape the fitness landscape for pharmaceuticals. To succeed in this environment, firms will need to develop the capability to manage their public image, communicate to patients as much as to doctors and healthcare organizations and to shift negative public perceptions. Of course, not all parts of the fitness landscape for pharma will be equally demanding of public and patient management, but significant parts might be expected to require such skills.

CONTEMPLATIVE INVESTORS

Ownership structures seem to have played a role in the past evolution of the industry. Roche, one of the big pharma giants, has an unusual dual share structure that has contributed to its development. The survival of many of the speciality pharma companies can be attributed, in part at least, to the fact that they remain privately, often family, owned. And the growth of the biotech sector has been heavily dependent on the rise of venture capitalism and its associated risk management processes. It was no surprise, therefore, that a minor but still significant theme that arose from the research concerned the funding of the industry, be it by owners, shareholders or other investors. As mentioned in Chapter 2, the financial performance of pharma has slipped in recent years and, unsurprisingly, this has led to a shift in investors' perspective on the sector. Brian McNamee, CEO of CSL Ltd, an Australian-based speciality pharmaceutical company, provided an interesting view on this:

'I would say that investors are also seeing the pharmaceutical industry, or at least a large part of it, as moving from being a high growth, high margin, high returning sector to something very different. Clearly, the most obvious example is the tremendous compression of price/earnings ratios. I would say that investors have lost faith in the growth of the larger companies and see them merely as value plays. In fact they are probably encouraging those companies to significantly reduce their research and development investment because there's little evidence that many of them have earned an economic return on their research and development

investment for the last decade. So I'd say the investor perception is significantly changing the view of the industry, the way in which the industry operates and the way they can access funding.'

Dr Brian McNamee, CSL Ltd.

Sophia Tickell, as the leader of a company that facilitates discussions between pharma and investors, is especially well placed to observe this situation and reinforces Brian McNamee's comments:

'Investors have already concluded that pharma companies will no longer hold the same place in their investment portfolio as they have in the past. If you look at the discount rates, they are assuming that pharma companies are going to make smaller margins anyway. From an investor perspective, that has already happened.'

Sophia Tickell, PharmaFutures

The implications of this shift in investor perceptions were spelt out by Doug McCutcheon:

'Essentially, what's happened in the last several years is that the investors' perception of the industry has changed. It's gone from being an industry that had double digit top line growth and was perceived as relatively safe and predictable, to being one with single digit top line growth and with risks greater than previously perceived. So investors still have a place in their portfolio for pharmaceuticals, but what investors are saying is, "If that's what you are, a 5 per cent growth company with a massive dividend, that's a nice thing for my portfolio but we want you to do two things. Firstly, search out incremental growth wherever you can find it – new places basically – and the relatively new dynamic is that we want you to de-risk your business. Because, if you're not going to deliver the growth, we're certainly not going to take the same risk profile."'

Doug McCutcheon, UBS

The public company model is not the only one seen in the pharmaceutical industry, however. In the smaller pharma companies, there was a strong feeling that the privately owned nature of many of those businesses provided them with an advantage, in that they were shielded from short term investor pressures. A good example of this view was that of Bert Tjeenk Willink, a main board director of Boehringer Ingelheim, which remains a family-owned company:

'I think that one of the main backgrounds is the short-term focus that is enforced on most of the big pharma companies as a consequence of being publicly traded … You see our shareholder family has been with this company for 125 years and plan to be there for the next 125 years … The majority of the shareholders of a big pharma buy shares today and would be quite happy to sell tomorrow if they can make a profit. The privately-owned companies have some advantages in terms of being able to drive transformational and radical change compared to

the large publicly-owned companies … Our single biggest competitive advantage is the fact that we're privately held.'

Bert Tjeenk Willink, Boehringer Ingelheim

The other main funding model seen in the industry, especially in the smaller, highly innovative and risky biotechs, is venture capital (VC). This model has been particularly affected by the financial crisis of 2007 and, at the time the research was done in 2010, the viability of the model was in doubt both financially and scientifically, as two complementary views show, firstly from Doug McCutcheon:

'I think the biotech model will have to change and a lot of it comes down to money. I don't think they can depend on the VC followed by IPO model anymore; the returns just aren't there. The big pharmas prefer targeted acquisitions and licensing. This suggests the biotech model will shift from backing a CEO to backing a particular product. This has huge implications as it demands less infrastructure … There may be exceptions – platform companies and spin-outs – but there has been a huge retrenchment in biotech funding.'

Doug McCutcheon, UBS

Secondly, from Merv Turner, Chief Strategy Officer for Merck:

'I think today there's an open question about how the private biotech companies will fare, but they're certainly going through a very difficult period at the moment. They're having much more difficulty raising capital than previously and, with no evidence that the public markets are going to open again, which would allow them to exit through IPO. So, for venture capitalists, the model is now very much "build to sell". And the ability of that as a model to really generate innovative molecules still has to be indisputably proven. I mean, historically biotech has been a losing proposition until the last couple of years. There have, of course, been some spectacular hits.'

Merv Turner, Merck

Funding models are part of the social environment that shapes the fitness landscape and the general tenor of the research findings was that the investor environment was reflecting the changes in other parts of the industry's social setting. Not only were price controls and slow growth in traditional markets reducing expectations, but innovation and market risks were also eroding the once unassailable position of pharma in investors' portfolios. And, because the underlying causes of this shift in investor views are long term, the investor environment has also shifted fundamentally. As ever, short term factors will play a part in investor sentiment towards pharma but, overriding this, there seems to be a longer term change going on. In evolutionary terms, this is likely to affect the fitness landscape in two ways. Firstly, it increases the importance of capabilities in investor relations management, of demonstrating the value of the business model to investors in parallel with demonstrating the value of the products to the customers. Secondly, and with rather less certainty, this shift may impact on the relative fitness of public, private and venture capital models.

A MORE PREVENTATIVE APPROACH TO HEALTHCARE

The six themes discussed in the preceding paragraphs all emerged from the research interviews but were prefigured by previously published work, either academic research, industry publications or both. For these six themes, rather than throw up surprising new phenomena affecting the fitness landscape, the interviews added colour and depth to things already suggested by the existing work. Examples of this, as discussed above, were when they revealed the fragmenting effect of globalization or the stratification of healthcare systems that followed from financial constraints and technological development.

There was, however, one theme that registered only fleetingly in the content analysis of the interviews, even though it came out strongly in the preparatory literature searches. This was the topic of preventative medicine, a shift in healthcare practice towards preventing, rather than curing, disease. It came up in the discussion with Julia Manning, who has the task of looking at healthcare trends 'over the horizon':

'I would hope that there could be an improvement in the willingness to take more responsibility for the way that we live our lives and the medical repercussions of our behaviour with the knowledge that, if we want either our relatives or ourselves to have life-saving interventions still freely available, then we can help facilitate that by taking more care about ourselves.'

Julia Manning, 2020Health.org

But preventative medicine was only mentioned indirectly in the interviews with pharmaceutical company executives when they referred to the burden of lifestyle diseases, such as smoking related cancers and the array of conditions associated with sedentary lifestyles and obesity. Joe Jimenez's remarks were typical of many on this subject:

'We are seeing a dramatic increase in demand for healthcare around the world as rapidly aging populations, along with lifestyle changes, are leading to more and more chronic illnesses. For instance, because of the growing overweight and obese population, chronic diseases like hypertension and diabetes are on the rise. This is creating a major shift in healthcare needs around the world.'

Joe Jimenez, Novartis

Logically, there are three possible reasons for this atypical mismatch between the social market shifts predicted by the literature and those suggested by the interviewees. Firstly, the interviewees could have been ignorant of the trend. Secondly, they could have been aware of the trend but regarded it as too trivial to discuss. Neither of these two explanations seems plausible. The interviewees were chosen for their depth of knowledge and many less important market changes were mentioned in the course of the interview which translated to around 300,000 words of transcript. A simpler and more compelling explanation is that this discrepancy was simply an artefact of the methodology I used. In qualitative interviews, the interviewer inevitably 'leads' the interviewee a little, through the choice of questions and even by body language. Despite attempts to avoid this, it seems likely that I inadvertently led the interviewees away from mentioning preventative medicine. The interviewees were asked to discuss the pharmaceutical industry and, for the industry, with the notable exceptions of vaccines and a few other smaller therapy areas, preventative medicine usually takes second place to cures or palliatives. Instead, preventative medicine is typically perceived to be in the remit of governments and healthcare systems.

Despite this methodological glitch, it seems likely that preventative medicine will be a significant shift in the social environment that will shape the fitness landscape. Preventable causes of death, such as smoking, diet and sedentary lifestyles are estimated to account for 40 per cent of deaths in the United States (7) and promoting smoking cessation, screening for cancer and lifestyle changes are widely seen as a way to improve health and reduce overall healthcare costs (see for example (8)). In addition to the obvious benefits of smoking cessation and cancer screening, lifestyle changes such as diet and exercise have been suggested to reduce the incidence of coronary heart disease, diabetes, various cancers and degenerative diseases such as Alzheimer's and dementia. Almost all governments in the developed world, along with many in the developing world, have some kind of policy towards preventative medicine. These range from encouraging lifestyle changes to active medication, such as vaccines or the use of statins to manage lipid levels. Consistent with this is growth of an already significant market in foods that make clinical claims, known as 'nutraceuticals', as well as functional foods and dietary supplements (9). Interestingly, this market is shifting towards the sort of specific claim usually associated with drugs, as indicated by Anna Ibbotson, a consultant with Kline and Company:

> 'About ten years ago, the nutraceuticals message was very much about general wellness – take this supplement and it'll enhance your wellbeing. But over the past five years, the trend is more towards promoting an ingredient to address a specific health issue.'

> Anna Ibbotson, Kline and Company

These various factors: clinical evidence about the value of preventative medicine, the convergence of food and pharma, government policies and extant mass medication programmes, all suggest that the future fitness landscape for pharma will include a greater, perhaps much greater, element of preventative medicine than at present. This may not imply a necessary capability for all companies, but it does imply that certain 'peaks' of the landscape may require some of the capabilities normally associated with food companies or perhaps other industries associated with health maintenance.

The Times They Are A-Changing

Today's pharmaceutical industry, with its handful of business models each characterized by a specific set of capabilities, looks very different from that of the past. Those differences emerged as the industry co-evolved with its social and technological environment. In the social environment in particular, changes in societal attitudes, healthcare systems, regulation and other factors all helped to shape what we see today. In the same way, the pharmaceutical industry of the future will look different from that of today, and those differences will be shaped by changes in the social environment. In this chapter, I have looked at the social changes that are emerging and which, along with the technological changes I will discuss in Chapter 4, are driving the evolution of the pharmaceutical industry. From a large, messy and unstructured data set, seven key themes have come to light. Each of these social shifts, from how value is defined, to who pays for drugs, to how much we respect authority, will shape the peaks and troughs of the fitness landscape. However, before we can think about the shape of that landscape and what it implies for the future of pharma, we need to look for the corresponding shift in the technological environment. That is the subject of Chapter 4.

Reference List

(1)   Mazzucato, M. and Dosi, G. 2006. *Knowledge Accumulation and Industry Evolution: The Case of Pharma Biotech*. Cambridge: Cambridge University Press.

(2)   Epstein, R.A. 2006. *Overdose: How Excessive Government Regulation Stifles Pharmaceutical Innovation*. 1st ed. New Haven, CT: Yale University Press.

(3)   Miller, H.I. 2010. The FDA's Imprudent Caution. *Policy Review*; (161):73–85.

(4)   Gill. T. 2007. *No Fear: Growing Up in a Risk Averse Society*. Calouste Gulbenkian Foundation.

(5)   Halek, M. and Eisenhauer, J.G. 2001. Demography of Risk Aversion. *Journal of Risk & Insurance*; 68(1):1–24.

(6)   Griffiths, S. 2008. The Death of Deference and its Impact on Social Care. *Social Market Foundation*.

(7)   Mokdad, A.H., Marks, J.S., Stroup, D.F. and Gerberding, J.L. 2004. Actual Causes of Death in the United States. *Journal of the American Medical Association*; 291(10):1238–45.

(8)   Maciosek, M.V., Coffield, A.B., Edwards, N.M., Flottenmesch, T.J., Goodman, M.J. and Solberg, L.I. 2006. Priorities Among Effective Clinical Preventative Services: Results of a Systematic Review and Analysis. *American Journal of Preventative Medicine*; 31:52–61.

(9)   Hayden, T. 2007. Getting to Know Nutraceuticals. *Scientific American*; 17(4):38–44.

CHAPTER

4 *An Evolving Technological Environment*

'We've arranged a civilization in which most crucial elements depend profoundly on science and technology.'

Carl Sagan

In Chapter 3, I attempted to make sense of the large number of social environment factors that are shaping the pharmaceutical industry. From the flood of issues that gushed from the research, I structured the data into seven coherent streams, each of which has implications for the future of pharma. In this chapter, I will attempt a similar exercise with the technological factors, weaving the outputs of the research into a pattern of technological change that, acting together with social change, will shape the future of pharma. In the next chapter, I will draw together these social and technological trends to predict how they will create a new fitness landscape for the industry and how its business models will evolve to fit with that landscape.

Just as in Chapter 3, the sources for this chapter are a combination of peer reviewed research, trade publications, including industry news, consultants' reports and the rich, varied results of the research interviews. As you will read, the technological environment revealed by these sources and to which pharma business models will have to adapt is changing across a very wide range of technologies. These can broadly be divided into two categories: external and internal. External technological changes are those that have their origins mostly outside pharmaceutical companies and include new scientific knowledge and new ways in which healthcare can be delivered. Internal technological changes are those that have their origins mostly within the pharmaceutical industry value chain and include technologies applied in research and development, supply chain management and sales and marketing. Both internal and external technological trends are determining the direction of the pharma industry to a greater or lesser extent. Importantly, however, these forces don't act on the industry in a simple, bilateral manner. Rather, they interact with each other and the industry in the nature of a complex, adaptive system. Hence my approach in this part of the book (Part II, comprising Chapters 3, 4, 5 and 6), will not be simply to list and prioritize the various factors but to synthesize them so that we can understand how they are shaping the fitness landscape for the pharmaceutical industry.

Just as the various social trends could be structured into seven social shifts, the multifarious technical factors can be integrated into five technical transformations discussed overleaf.

Five Technological Transformations

As with the analysis of the social shifts affecting the industry, the data about the technological environment was messy and unstructured. Moreover, in the data there was a greater degree of uncertainty about the technological environment, if not about the existence of technological developments, then about the way they would play out. For example, in the social environment, there was little doubt that the trend of more and older people suffering diseases associated with lifestyle would manifest itself as increased demand and tighter cost management. By contrast, in the technological environment, it was much less clear how personalized medicine, for example, would develop and change the market. Notwithstanding that uncertainty, it was possible to discern five forces that are shaping the technological environment for the pharma industry. The first two, new therapeutic possibilities and telemedicine, are external technologies, originating mostly outside of pharmaceutical companies, whilst the next three are internal technologies, applied within the three main stages of a pharmaceutical company's value chain.

A SECOND THERAPEUTIC REVOLUTION

The most dominant theme to emerge from this part of the research was the development of new biological knowledge and its translation into exciting new therapeutic possibilities. This topic is often clouded by speculation and hyperbole but, underlying that, there is no doubt that a major leap forward, neatly labelled by the Economist as 'Biology 2.0', is taking place in the biological sciences (1). Importantly, this advance is not based on a single, momentous discovery but rather on a complex set of recent discoveries in biological and related sciences. Although discussion of this biological revolution is frequently conflated with our understanding of the human genome, such a genomic focussed view of the biological revolution is an unbalanced one. The consensus view of those working in the area is that our increased understanding of systems biology is the key factor, with genomics, proteomics and epigenetics playing an important but supporting part. This new level of biological understanding, and the place of genomics in it, is well summarized in a recent report by the International Pharmaceutical Federation, a global federation representing about two million pharmaceutical scientists. In the words of this well informed group:

> 'The trend to moving away from reductionist towards a more holistic approach … is likely to continue with the belated realisation that "omics" as such are not the solution to everything but should be incorporated into a fuller mechanistic and quantitative appreciation of biological systems. The latter is expected to develop not just at a cellular level but also in a broader framework of pharmacokinetics and pharmacodynamics (including biomarker development) at the organ and whole body levels.' (2)

The holistic trend in also reflected in the increasingly important shift towards translational research in medicine, which seeks to solve health issues by integrating knowledge from biological, physical and social sciences.

Steve Burrill described the implications of this surge of new biological knowledge more graphically:

'We have massive technology today, like coming out of the end of a fire hose, providing data about how you and I work and why you and I work a little differently and how those differences between us – our systems biology if you will – cause us to be tall or short or skinny or fat or get diabetes or have cancer or die early or die late and so forth.'

Steve Burrill, Burrill & Company

This same point about the vast, untapped potential of the new biology cropped up persistently in the research, but many of those close to the topic qualified it carefully. Merv Turner's comments were a good example of this:

'We are in the century of biology and, eventually, all this information must ultimately pay off – genomics information, our understanding of how cellular pathways act together, our understanding of the working of the cell and the relationship of all this to disease. But I think that, being realistic, we have to say that it's going to be five or ten years before you really start to see the fruits of that knowledge impact on our industry.'

Merv Turner, Merck

Complementing that view, Julia Manning elucidated the reason why pharmacogenomics alone is not a short term answer to pharma's challenges, whilst pointing to where we might expect to see advances:

'The greatest hope for the pharmaceutical industry in this area is identification of appropriate prescribing of medicines and appropriate dosage of medicines. But the progress is much slower than people anticipated, even though there have been notable examples of applications that have been extremely important. It is one of the great hopes of the biotech industry, but I'm just not seeing the results. There is a huge gap between the science and our ability to apply it. Although we are able to identify specific genes, we know so little of how and why they are expressed, the role of epigenetics and the role the environment. It seems to me that we have uncovered one area but found one hundred others leading off it that we have very little information about. So I think actual progress is going to remain slow, even though there's a huge amount of money being put into this. The greatest advances are happening in the whole area of application to regenerative medicine, adult stem cells and so on, and application of those technologies seems to be going in leaps and bounds.'

Julia Manning, 2020health.org

In the same vein, the loosely-used term 'personalized medicine' occurred frequently in the research but the reality seems to be that, for the foreseeable future, genomics will help us identify patient populations better rather than truly personalize treatment. Even with this qualification, it still promises much, as expressed by David Norton:

'That promise of your genes telling you exactly what to take – it is unlikely we will be able to do that because we're not going to get to individualize drugs and individualize diagnostics. Personalized medicine means more than one, it means a population or sub-population. It's a broader scale. But I think we will get there. I'm optimistic about scientific capabilities. I'm

optimistic about a promise of ingenuity of people to find those solutions, and I think we'll get there, both for biologics and also for small molecules.'

David Norton, Johnson & Johnson

In that last comment lies the true picture of how new biological knowledge are likely to shape the pharmaceutical market. Systems biology will give us gradually better understanding of how our bodies work, how to keep them working and how to fix them when we become diseased. Further, genomics, proteomics and epigenetics will help us differentiate between different patient populations so that we can target treatments and get better results. Other, related technical advances, such as gene therapy and regenerative medicine, will also play a part. But the advance towards this new world will be gradual and will be marked by the convergence of pharmaceuticals with more advanced diagnostics, particularly biomarkers that indicate a specific disease state. We see the first signs of the future now with biologics, often called 'large molecules' in industry parlance to distinguish them from traditional, small molecule, products. Biologic products are derived from biological processes and include Abbott's Humira for rheumatoid arthritis and Roche's Herceptin for breast cancer. But the science fiction world of truly personalized medicine is some way off, perhaps decades away, and then even its technical feasibility will not guarantee its economic viability. This was pointed out in a 2010 McKinsey report (3), which suggested that whilst personalized medicine faced significant technical and operational issues, the biggest challenge remains economic, as these new treatments have huge development costs that can be spread over a relatively small target market.

In addition to the impact of systems biology and pharmacogenomics, one contiguous and important area that emerged from the research was the combination of pharmaceuticals and medical devices. This idea was expressed by Osagie Imasogie, who saw only industry history and inertia as slowing the convergence of the two industries:

'I think that there is a false divide that exists in the industry between pharma, device companies and diagnostics. Diagnostic companies are really not a treatment or cure for disease but will help you identify the condition. Now, in my view, there is a false divide because the patient doesn't care. The patient wants their problem solved. So what you are going to be seeing in the near future is companies that are actually going to be integrated across therapeutics, diagnostics and devices.'

Osagie Imasogie, Phoenix Ventures

This convergence of pharmaceuticals and devices into so called combination products is in its early days. It is, at present, a small business compared to traditional pharmaceuticals and is currently restricted to only a few therapeutic areas. That said, the global market for combinations of drugs and devices, such as drug eluting stents and transdermal patches, is estimated to be 40–50 billion US dollars and growing at 14 per cent, according to Chris Cramer, Principal of PRTM Management Consultants. Further, a 2007 white paper by Microtest Inc. suggested that 30 per cent of the medical devices that were under development at that time were combination products (4). In the related area of materials science, the convergence of pharmacology and nanotechnology seems likely to offer great potential for improving the therapeutic effects of both existing and new drugs (see for example 5). According to consultancy PricewaterhouseCoopers, over 100 nanotech-based medicines and delivery systems are under development (6). Taken together, the multiple strands of pharmaceuticals convergence with devices and materials science will improve the delivery of medicines and enhance the developments arising from Biology 2.0.

So, what emerges from this complex picture of systems biology, genomics and convergence of drug, device and diagnostics is something that looks like a second therapeutic revolution, as important as that which followed World War II. In the future, we will be able to prevent and treat more diseases more effectively than ever before, by the application of biological sciences, material sciences and diagnostics. But, importantly, the speed at which this part of the technological environment changes will be inversely proportional to its scientific and regulatory complexity. We should, therefore, expect the new technological environment to take longer to develop than the new social environment and to arrive in many, uneven steps rather than a big, single leap. And not only will this revolution be more gradual than we might hope, it will mostly result in more complex, costlier treatments aimed at smaller and more distinct populations of patients. As a result, the impact of Biology 2.0 on society is likely to be less widespread than that of, for example, antibiotics in the 1940s and 1950s. Those who expect the second therapeutic revolution to mimic the first and provide a cornucopia of new drugs that can be mass marketed are undoubtedly drawing too close an analogy between the two revolutions.

As it develops, we should expect the Biology 2.0 to shape the fitness landscape for the pharmaceutical industry, creating one or more peaks that demand the capability to master the advanced new technologies such as biologics, biomarkers and device/drug combinations. It will also, inevitably, demand new capabilities in demonstrating the economic value of some very expensive treatments. However, this selection pressure for these more advanced technological and health economic capabilities might not have the simple effect of driving the evolution of more technically advanced companies. Rather, the history of the industry suggests that we should anticipate a fragmentation. The 'new science' of the second industrial revolution in the late-19th Century led some companies to give up the technological chase, choosing instead to follow the OTC route. The technological shifts of the mid-20th Century equally gave opportunities to companies, like Pfizer, to grow faster than they otherwise would and overtake their rivals. It seems likely that the second therapeutic revolution will facilitate a quite significant change in pharma's fitness landscape but also that we should not expect simplistically that the current technological leaders will evolve into new, super-technology leaders. Some may choose other evolutionary routes and it may be that the species most able to adapt to that new world are not the current research-based leaders but business models and firms that are currently undreamt of.

A BLACKBERRY WORLD

The idea that advances in non-pharmaceutical technology would accompany and complement advances in pharmaceutical technology emerged frequently during the research. Some of these ideas, the convergence of pharmaceuticals with devices, material sciences and diagnostics, have already been mentioned in the previous section, pointing to much more effective, but potentially more expensive, therapeutic possibilities. But another non-pharmaceutical technical advance, which is distinct from that convergence and which has big implications for the fitness landscape of the industry, is worth considering separately. This is the advent of telemedicine, a broad and varied area that, simply put, concerns the transfer of medical information, either to or from the patient, to enable healthcare without the direct presence of a healthcare professional. Current discussion of telemedicine focuses mainly on its use in geographically remote or economically undeveloped areas (see for example (7) and (8)), but it seems clear that it has huge potential to augment or replace current healthcare systems in developed and well served markets. Telemedicine's value has been demonstrated in clinical applications as varied as cognitive impairment (9), diabetes (10) and dermatology (9) and there seem few situations in which it does not have the potential to improve the effectiveness of or access to healthcare, whilst also reducing its relative cost.

The current applications of telehealth have all the characteristics of an embryonic technology, with many varied, niche approaches that are developing quickly; and pharmaceutical companies are very aware of their likely future impact on the industry, as Joe Jimenez pointed out:

'New technologies are also transforming the healthcare landscape. Telehealth technology is allowing healthcare providers to connect with their patients for remote monitoring of key health indicators and compliance, which can correctly diagnose and identify problems earlier. This is promising for both improving patient outcomes and reducing costs. iPhone apps are providing patients with new ways to track and control their families' health. One example is the Novartis VaxTrak application, which helps families track routine immunizations and recommends nearby locations for vaccinations. We need to continue to take advantage of these tools to connect with our customers and patients, as well as improve outcomes.'

Joe Jimenez, Novartis

Jeff Kiesling of Pfizer made a similar point:

'Information and communications technology has a phenomenal capability to deliver value, to streamline the overhead and the administrative cost of healthcare systems and I think [healthcare systems] have underperformed in terms of what the technology can do in terms of streamlining when compared to, say, financial services. This would bring a value to patients around the world, so we can't afford not to follow up this problem. We are working with a number of healthcare systems directly, using health information technology to improve the delivery of the right therapy to the right patients at the right time. We just want to make sure that people are using the medicines faithfully and effectively. We have a number of very successful programs and in the near and long term there needs to be much greater investment in that space, both from the public and private sectors. I think there are 30 per cent cost-savings opportunities out there just by taking inefficiencies out of the systems.'

Jeff Kielsling, Pfizer

It is not only pharmaceutical companies who see telemedicine as a shaper of the market. Vodafone is working with partners to create patient monitoring systems that allow patients' vital signs to be communicated in real time to monitoring centres;

and Cisco Systems are trialling advanced interactive video systems for remote medical consultations. Datamonitor, the market research company, claim that the global market for telemedicine is 3.9 billion US dollars and is growing at 10 per cent per annum. This looks likely to be an underestimate, as the category shifts from enabling conventional medical services to creating new ways of accessing medical knowledge, via handheld computers and smart phones. At the time of writing, for example, Apple's iPhone had almost 5,000 health and fitness apps and, whilst only a minority of these relate to pharmaceuticals, those that do, like Medscape, point to a future in which much medical knowledge and therapeutic guidance comes from a device rather than a doctor. Steve Burrill graphically articulated this vision of the telemedicine future:

> 'We're heading to a Blackberry/smartphone centric world, in which we have enormous amount of both real time information and communication technology, microfluidics chips buried in handheld palm devices that enable us [in some way] to deliver healthcare and healthcare information at a consumer level that will dramatically change the world of doctors and hospitals and the patient experience.'

Steve Burrill, Burrill & Company

The rise of telemedicine, an artefact of the wider information technology revolution, seems assured. However, at first sight it seems merely an important but parallel trend to the biotechnology revolution with only tangential relevance to the future of the pharmaceutical industry. However, there is a perspective that suggests that telemedicine will have a more significant impact on the industry. This is the idea of disruptive technology, a term coined and popularized by Clayton Christensen (11). Disruptive technologies are those that disrupt an existing market, typically by creating value in new ways. iTunes, for example, disrupted the music market and now seems set to do the same in other media markets too. From a pharma perspective, there are least two ways that telemedicine is likely to be disruptive. The first is to decouple healthcare more from healthcare professionals. Telemedicine will, of course, enable doctors to treat their patients in a way that is complementary to (or, to use Christensen's term, sustaining of) the traditional doctor-led healthcare market. However, it will also enable patients to get at least some of their healthcare information without using an expensive doctor. Coupled with the ability to buy drugs over the internet, this suggests that at least some of the pharmaceutical market will become decoupled from its traditional route to market of healthcare professionals. Already, some patients choose to bypass doctors for financial or other reasons. Access to good quality clinical information and cheap drugs will increase the part of the market that 'goes direct' in the same way that some consumers do with PCs and financial services. This won't happen for all customers or for all conditions; serious or poorly understood conditions will continue to require a physician. But for well-educated patients with minor or well understood conditions, the value of direct medical advice may not seem worth its cost. For pharmaceutical companies, this implies a whole new set of capabilities that will be needed to reach this market. The second way that telemedicine may disrupt the pharma market is by providing new ways for pharmaceutical companies to create value. One way of looking at the pharmaceutical market is that the active ingredients and pills that pharmaceutical companies currently sell are simply vehicles for their knowledge about disease management. When we buy a drug, we are simply buying a package of knowledge that the pharmaceutical company has created about, for example, hypertension, diabetes or asthma. To use it well, we also buy some knowledge, usually from a doctor, about diagnosis, side effects and the way it interacts with any other treatments. But in a Blackberry or iPhone world, to borrow Steve Burrill's phrase, we might get that knowledge more cheaply, more conveniently and perhaps better from a portable device connected to the internet. This sort of diagnosing/consulting app, combined with a link to an online drugstore, may come to replace the doctor and pharmacy for some 'prescribing' contexts, in the same way that many other markets, from music to pensions, have been 'disintermediated'. And of course, telemedicine has just as much potential to reshape the 'wellness' market as it does the 'illness' market. There are already applications that help us manage our diet and weight. From there it is short step to preventing lifestyle diseases such as cardiovascular disease and diabetes.

This raises the obvious question of who is best placed to package and distribute medical knowledge in this way? In certain circumstances, it is hard to see who is better placed than pharmaceutical companies to do this. Their drug development capabilities have given them a store of valuable knowledge about disease mechanisms, epidemiology and therapy. Many of the larger firms are also relatively cash rich and capable of developing or acquiring telemedicine capabilities. The telemedicine trend therefore implies a new peak, or set of peaks, in the pharma fitness landscape that demands capabilities in packaging and delivering knowledge about disease management for individuals, rather than doctors and healthcare professionals. As with new therapeutic opportunities, these new peaks will not necessarily be most accessible to the most successful traditional pharma business models. The disruption of telemedicine may lead to smaller, innovative companies overtaking larger incumbents. Similarly, the disintermediation of the healthcare professional, which complements the stratification of healthcare concept that emerged in Chapter 3, may initiate a fragmentation of business models between those that choose to package their knowledge in pills and those that package theirs in apps. In short, the 'death of distance', a phrase coined by Frances Caincross (12) to describe the effects of the information and telecommunications revolution, will have a disruptive effect on the pharma fitness landscape that will, inevitably, lead to the evolution of new business models.

A second therapeutic revolution and the death of distance were clear trends in the research. They can be seen as external technological changes that are creating directly observable trends in the market. The link between these observable phenomena and the industry's fitness landscape is quite obvious, even as the details of how the technologies will manifest themselves are not. However, there were visible in the research many other technological developments that appeared to be in a different category from the first two. These are the internal technological changes that are occurring inside the value chain of the pharmaceutical industry. They can, therefore, be categorized according to where they exert most influence on the value chain – research and development, operations or commercialization.

NEW RESEARCH AND DEVELOPMENT TECHNOLOGIES

In Chapter 2, I described how the problem of research and development productivity is central to the future of pharma. Only about one in ten drugs that enter preclinical development reach the market (13) and as long ago as 2003 an academic study put the cost of developing a new drug at 868 million US dollars. Partly in response to this, the technological environment in which drugs are discovered and developed is changing rapidly and these changes will, along with other factors, shape the industry's fitness landscape. These changes in research and development technology are complex and hard to untangle from one another, but they can be broadly divided into two groups: changes in how information is managed and changes in how people and processes are managed.

The need to manage information in research and development is pressing. The pharma industry is similar to many other knowledge-based sectors inasmuch as the information it creates and uses is expanding at a prodigious rate. Many of the factors we have already mentioned – new disease patterns, the need to demonstrate value and Biology 2.0 – all produce and demand vast amounts of data. Some estimates suggest that a single pharmaceutical laboratory can generate 100 gigabytes of data per day (14). It seems inevitable therefore that the ability to manage and extract value from data will be essential for firms wishing to be part of the future of pharma. Historically, the industry is seen by some to have lagged behind in this area, as was eloquently captured by Brian McNamee:

'In the last decade or two, what I've witnessed is that our industry has been marvellous at building larger haystacks and very poor at developing the needle-finding skills.'

Brian McNamee, CSL

The technological developments in information management form an intricate web of new technologies to do with generating and making use of clinical information. The dominant theme in this area is bioinformatics. Perhaps more usefully described by an older term of computational biology, this is the use of data analytical techniques to better understand biological processes at a molecular level. This domain is very fragmented and ranges from understanding gene expression to structural biology (see for example (15)). Bioinformatics is complemented by semantics, the process of systematically searching the large amounts of existing research through web-enabled databases (16). The practical application of bioinformatics is the increasing development of in silico (computer-based) research to complement or replace drug development processes that were previously carried out *in vivo* or *in vitro* (in animals or in laboratory experiments). At the leading edge of this area are attempts to build virtual biological systems, such as the virtual lab rat created by Entelos. As PricewaterhouseCoopers point out (17), bioinformatics approaches improve the efficiency of pharma research and development by enabling drug candidates to 'fail fast and fail cheaply'. As David Norton pointed out, this is seen by the industry as a critical competency for the future of innovative pharma companies:

'First of all, we need to fail fast. If a product cannot deliver the appropriate value, we need to fail fast rather than invest big dollars. By failing fast, I don't mean only in the safety quality and efficacy stakes, it's in the value stakes as well.'

David Norton, Johnson & Johnson

Changes in information management are not, however, the only significant internal change in the technology environment of pharma. The second way concerns changes in how research and development is organized. Within this theme, there seem to be four important strands. The first is the way research and development is structured within the company where, increasingly, the trend is towards breaking down research and development into smaller units in order to improve flexibility and effectiveness. The archetype of this approach is GSK (18), although some other companies have now adopted similar approaches. Linked to this search for more responsive research and development is the strong trend towards outsourcing (see for example (19), (20)). Although the efficacy of this approach is not fully proven and it carries some risks, the trend is now firmly established in the industry. The third trend in the organisation of pharma research and development is that towards 'open source' innovation, the idea of pooling knowledge as opposed to protecting it by intellectual property rights (21). Recent examples of this include both GSK and Novartis depositing data on hundreds of thousands of compounds active against the malaria parasite with the European Bioinformatics Institute. Although issues remain around how open innovation fits into the traditional, protected intellectual property business model, this approach does seem to be a significant and long term trend in pharma, as in some other industries. The final strand of developments in how pharma research and development is organized is that of collaborative research and development. Of itself, this is not a new development (22) and licensing of products from other companies is, of course, common in the industry. However, there are signs that this activity is moving away from opportunistically filling pipeline gaps and towards a more systematic approach with the aim of managing risk ((23), (24)).

We know that technological developments shape the fitness landscape of an industry. In pharma, developments in the research and development technologies used by some companies were part of what shaped both the emergence of the industry in the late-19th and early-20th Centuries. Later, in the mid-20th century, new technological approaches shaped the industry further. In the themes examined in this section – concerning the management of both information and people – we see trends that are also likely to shape the sector. However, they will inevitably do so in conjunction with technological developments in the rest of pharma's value chain.

THE EFFICIENCY IMPERATIVE

In Porter's classic description of how firms create value along a chain of activity (25), new product development is followed by supply chain management, an umbrella term that includes all those activities involved in making and supplying the product or service. Historically, this has not been as strong a focus for pharmaceutical companies as research and development or commercialization. The margins available, especially on innovative products, have meant that investment in supply chain efficiency has not offered high returns on investment. In addition, the need to ensure high quality and pass regulatory authority inspection has always been more important than driving down manufacturing costs. That is not to say that pharmaceutical operations are unimportant or inefficient but it does seem that pharmaceutical companies generally do not view supply chain management as source of competitive advantage. In one cross-sector study, for example, not one of the strongest supply chain companies came from the sector (26). Of course, this is not unexpected, given the past cost structure of the industry, especially that of the research-based companies. In very high margin businesses, the return on investment from increasing operational efficiency is less than in low margin businesses. However, one might reasonably expect this situation to change as innovation becomes harder and margins come under pressure; and, in this context, the supply chain aspects of the industry's technological environment will become more important. Significantly, however, technology in the supply chain has a broad meaning. It refers not only to specific technologies, but also to the structuring and management of the different parts of the supply chain. In our research, we tried to identify the important developments of both these aspect of supply chain technology.

Three overriding factors came out of the research concerning pharmaceutical supply chains. The first was that the industry has a substantial overcapacity. According to McKinsey (27), the industry could shut down three out of four manufacturing plants and still meet demand. Clearly, this is unsustainable in the long run and suggests change is imminent. The second was the application of information technology to improve both the efficiency of supply chains and their effectiveness, especially as regards security and quality. Foremost amongst this was the application of radio frequency identification (RFID) which, although at an early stage of market penetration, seems set to transform the industry's supply chains. The third was the strong trend towards outsourcing of manufacturing. Two representative quotes illustrate this point:

'In the supply chain, third party manufacturing and in-licensing will become dominant.'

Mike Thomas, A.T. Kearney

'A whole host of suppliers have developed over the past ten years that are now able to provide quality in scale.'

Blane Walter, Inventive Health

Whilst many interviewees spoke of outsourcing manufacturing to reduce costs, McKinsey sees the dominant model of supply chain as a little more mixed between in-house and outsourced operations. This suggests that the challenge for pharma is to manage a network on internal and external operations, as identified by Andreas Fibig:

'Manufacturing will go into a transitional period and we'll have to figure out a way to manage that in a global network. We have to figure out what we have to do on our own and what can be done by third parties and how to squeeze out some more margin points out of every function we have within our companies. And manufacturing is certainly a big one.'

Andreas Fibig, Bayer Schering Pharma

Nestling within the big issues of overcapacity, information technology and outsourcing, a whole series of important secondary issues emerged. Importantly, these formed a sort of dichotomy for the industry. On the one hand were issues related to efficiency: driving down costs, managing outsourced networks, moving manufacturing to emerging markets and other efficiency issues. On the other hand were issues related to effectiveness: improving flexibility and security, meeting increased regulatory demands, manufacturing more complex products and other effectiveness issues. Just as the capacity, information technology and outsourcing trends point to significant change in the industry supply chain, so too does this tension between efficiency and effectiveness.

From an evolutionary perspective, changes in the technological environment for making and supplying pharmaceuticals seem to portend significant change. Capabilities in supply chain management will be more important in the future than they have in the past. The difficulty of becoming both efficient and effective will challenge all companies and, like the challenges of the second therapeutic revolution, might drive bifurcation of business models. We might, for example, see a clear division between those companies for which supply chain management is critical to competitive advantage and those for which it is a necessary-but-not-sufficient hygiene factor, important to get right but not deserving of large investment. However, it seems unlikely that pharmaceutical companies manufacturing strategies will be as 'binary' as in the past, stark choices between efficiency and effectiveness. Instead, a more nuanced set of options will lead to greater variation in business models in which efficiency is as imperative as effectiveness.

DEATH OF A TRADITIONAL SALESMAN

After new product development and supply chain management, the final stage of the internal value chain is customer relationship management. Whilst this term has been hijacked in recent years by software vendors, I use it here in its original sense, meaning the set of activities related to creating and keeping customers. In most industries, this is synonymous with sales and marketing, but in pharma it also (and increasingly) includes the activities of medical affairs, scientific liaison, market access and other customer contact functions.

As with research and development, the customer relationship management part of the pharma value chain is being shaped by a number of developments in its technological environment that can broadly be divided into two categories: how information is managed and how the process is organized.

Historically, information technology has had less impact on the customer relationship part of the pharma business model than it has on the preceding research and development and supply chain stages. The long-standing pre-eminence of the sales force, established communications channels such as congresses and advertising, and the importance of physician relationships have meant that, until quite recently, the commercial models of pharma have been relatively undifferentiated from each other, and mostly unchanged from previous decades. However, three strong trends are discernible in the research concerning the customer relationship management.

The first can broadly be classed as customer analytics. The ubiquity of information technology is increasingly allowing pharmaceutical companies to replace or augment relatively ad hoc targeting of prescribers and opinion leaders by systematic use of data. Companies like IMS offer pharmaceutical marketers the ability to target more precisely, based on current prescribing patterns. Other companies, such as Cegedim, are able to use social network analysis to identify how influence diffuses through clinical 'communities of practice'. Increasingly, this IT-based targeting activity is complemented by extensive use of sales force automation, a slightly misleading term that refers to the recording and control of sales force activity through the use of laptops and handheld devices.

The second technological change in pharmaceutical sales and marketing is the shift towards IT-enabled channels and away from the traditional detailing and advertising approaches. The use of websites, email and laptop or tablet detailing is now ubiquitous, since it offers lower costs and better compliance with regulatory codes (see for example (28)). Similarly, social media are beginning to impact on how pharmaceutical companies communicate with both prescribers and patients (see for example (29)).

The final strong trend observed in my research, concerns the management of the commercial function. This is closely linked to the shifting definition of customer value described in Chapter 3. As part of this, the traditional role of the prescriber as decision maker has been eroded and access to them reduced, as described graphically by Angus Russell:

'When I go to see my physician, there's a big poster on her door saying, "Absolutely no medical reps will be seen other than for one hour on a Wednesday morning between the hours of eight and nine o'clock."'

Angus Russell, Shire

In response, pharma companies are changing the way they organize marketing and sales teams; focussing them on where the decision is now made, and structuring them to deal with different sorts of decision makers. An example of this was described by Sean McCrae:

'We're seeing a dramatic drop in access [to physicians], so companies are both downsizing and changing focus, using people like medical liaisons to focus on key opinion leaders more. So it's more of a push approach in terms of these high level people because we can't see each individual doctor. We see companies creating very, very specialized teams here in the United States – just five or ten people nationally, focussed only on the highest level accounts, the most important hospitals to drive products usage in major medical centres.'

Sean McCrea, Pharmaforce

In addition to the changes in how existing sales and marketing tasks are performed, a new layer of tasks is being grafted on to the commercial function. These include market access processes that apply health economics outcomes research with the goal of being granted reimbursement or other market access rights. They also include added value services that were not traditionally part of the sales and marketing role, such as logistics, medical education and support.

From the perspective of the pharma industry's evolution, these changes in the technology of customer relationship management imply significant changes in the fitness landscape because they change the capabilities that confer fitness on a business model. Certain capabilities that conferred high fitness in the past are now less important. For example, the management of large, detailing sales teams, the ability to implement large scale advertising campaigns, the management of opinion leading physicians are all possible candidates for capabilities that will have less importance in the future. Other capabilities are becoming essential characteristics of high fitness business models. These may include the management of specialized key account teams, the manipulation of social media or the understanding of communities of practice. Whilst the details may vary, it is clear that the customer relationship management capabilities of successful business models will not be exactly the same as in even the recent past.

From Analysis to Synthesis

In this chapter and in Chapter 3, I've attempted to make sense of a large amount of messy and unstructured data. I have followed the advice of Professor McDonald by trying to understand what is going on in the industry rather than prove a particular point. What have emerged in these two chapters are changes that are undoubtedly important in the industry's social and technological environments. The structuring and simplification of myriad different phenomena into seven social shifts and five technological transformations allows us to understand the climate in which the industry is evolving. From a cacophony of information, a number of messages become clear. These don't yet tell us the future of pharma, but they tell us what forces are acting to shape the industry's fitness landscape.

In Chapter 5, I will move from analysis of data to synthesis of the main findings. In particular, I will try to extrapolate from the historical changes in fitness landscape described in Chapter 2 to predict a fitness landscape of the future. The peaks and valleys of that future landscape will be sculpted by the social and technological changes described in Chapters 3 and 4, just as a geographical landscape is shaped by plate tectonics, glaciations or weathering. Then, having made an informed prediction of the future landscape, the rest of Chapter 5 is dedicated to describing how pharmaceutical business models will evolve – or more accurately co-evolve – to fit that landscape, just as our ancestors adapted to the savannah of the east African rift valley. Once that is done, we will be able to discuss the implications, choices and challenges for pharmaceutical companies of today who wish to be part of the future of pharma. That will be the subject of Part III of this book, Chapter 7 onwards.

Reference List

(1)   Carr, G. 2010. Biology 2.0. *The Economist* 395(8687): special edition pp.3–5.
(2)   Shah, V., Besancon, L., Stolk, P., Tucker, G. and Crommelin, D. 2010. The Pharmaceutical Sciences in 2020: Report of a Conference Organized by the Board of Pharmaceutical Sciences of the International Pharmaceutical Federation. *Pharmaceutical Research*; 27(3):396–9.
(3)   *Invention Reinvented: McKinsey Perspectives on Pharmaceutical R&D*. New York and London: McKinsey; 2010.
(4)   Richeter, S. 2007. *Combination Products: Navigating Two FDA Systems*. Agawam, MA: Microtest Laboratories Inc.
(5)   Park, K. 2007. Nanotechnology: What Can It Do For Drug Delivery. *Journal of Controlled Release*; 20(1–2):1–3.
(6)   *Pharma 2020: Virtual R&D. Which Path Will You Take?* London: PricewaterhouseCoopers; 2007.
(7)   Mbarika, V.W.A. 2004. Is Telemedicine the Panacea for Sub-Saharan Africa's Medical Nightmare? *Communications of the ACM*; 47(7):21–4.
(8)   Sudhamony, S., Nandakumar, K., Binu, P.J.and Niwas, S.I. 2008. Telemedicine and Tele-Health Services for Cancer-care Delivery in India. *IET Communications*; 2(2):231–6.

(9)   Martin-Khan, M., Wooton, R. and Gray, L. A 2010. Systematic Review of the Reliability of Screening for Cognitive Impairment in Older Adults by Use of Standardized Assessment Tools Administered via the Telephone. *Journal of Telemedicine and Telecare*; 16:422–8.

(10)   Larsen, M.E., Turner, J., Farmer, A., Neil, A. and Tarassenko, L. 2010. Telemedicine-Supported Insulin Optimization in Primary Care. *Journal of Telemedicine and Telecare*; 16:433–40.

(11)   Christensen, C.M. 1997. *The Innovators' Dilemma: When New Technologies Cause Great Firms to Fail*. Cambridge, MA: Harvard Business School Press.

(12)   Caincross, F. 2001. *The Death of Distance*. Cambridge MA: Harvard Business School Press.

(13)   *Pharmaceutical R&D Statistical Sourcebook*. Parexel; 2001.

(14)   Gassmann, O., Gerrit, R. and Von Zedtwitz, M. 2008. *Leading Pharmaceutical Innovation*. 2nd ed. Berlin: Springer.

(15)   Larson, R.S. 2006. *Bioinformatics in Drug Discovery*. Totowa, NJ: Humana.

(16)   Stephens, S., LaVigna, D., DiLascio, M. and Luciano, J. 2006. Aggregation of Bioinforatics Data Using Semantic Web Technology. *Web Semantics*; 4(3):216–21.

(17)   *Pharma2020: Virtual R&D: Which Path Will You Take?* London: PricewaterhouseCoopers; 2008.

(18)   Garnier, J-P. 2008. Rebuilding the R&D Engine in Big Pharma. *Harvard Business Review*; 86(5):68–76.

(19)   Sen, A.K. 2009. Outsourcing of Research and Development Activities: Evidence from US Biopharmaceutical Firms. *Global Journal of Business Research (GJBR)*; 3(1):73–82.

(20)   Howells, J., Gagliardi, D. and Malik, K. 2008. The Growth and Management of R&D Outsourcing: Evidence from UK Pharmaceuticals. *R&D Management*; 38(2):205–19.

(21)   Hodgson, J. 2010. Pharma Embraces Open Source Models. *Nature Biotechnology*; 28(7):631–4.

(22)   Hagedoorn, J. 2002. Inter-firm R&D partnerships: An Overview of Major Trends and Patterns Since 1960. *Research Policy*; 31(4):477.

(23)   McGrath, R.G. and Nerkar, A. 2004. Real Options Reasoning and a New Look at the R&D Investment Strategies of Pharmaceutical Firms. *Strategic Management Journal*; 25(1):1–21.

(24)   Gassmann, O. and Reepmeyer, G. 2005. Organizing Pharmaceutical Innovation: From Science-based Knowledge Creators to Drug-oriented Knowledge Brokers. *Creativity & Innovation Management*; 14(3):233–45.

(25)   Porter, M.E. 1980. *Competitive Strategy*. 1st ed. Free Press.

(26)   Harrison, A. and New, C. 2002. The Role of Coherent Supply Chain Strategy and Performance Management in Achieving Competitive Advantage: An International Survey. *Journal of the Operational Research Society*; 53(3):263.

(27)   *Outpacing Change In Pharma Operations*. McKinsey; 2010.

(28)   Alkhateeb, F.M., Khanfar, N.M., Doucette, W.R. and Loudon, D.A.V.I. Characteristics of Physicians Targeted by the Pharmaceutical Industry to Participate in E-detailing. *Health Marketing Quarterly*; 26(2):98–116.

(29)   Pfizer, A.W. 2008. Soon to Launch Pfacebook. *Strategic Communication Management*; 12(4):9.

5 The Evolution of the Pharmaceutical Industry

'Prediction is very difficult, especially if it is about the future.'

Neils Bohr

In this chapter, despite Bohr's admonition, I am going to predict the future of pharma. Because the pharmaceutical industry is a complex, adaptive system I will use the theory of evolution, discussed in Chapter 2 as my guiding principal. I will use the social and technological changes that the research uncovered, as discussed in Chapters 3 and 4 respectively, and combine facts and theory to make a prediction that has both practical relevance and academic rigour.

I will do this in three steps. First, I will explore the different ways that the seven social and five technological forces will act on the industry to shape its fitness landscape. Then, I will predict the future fitness landscape for pharma that will result from that shaping action. Finally, I will predict how the industry's business models will evolve to fit that landscape. That prediction will then allow me, from Chapter 6 onwards, to discuss the implications for firms in the industry.

This is, in many ways, the most important chapter of the book. In it, I use the research findings as a platform to make conceptual leaps from the present to the future. Since many readers will approach this chapter with much experience of the pharmaceutical industry and their own ideas about how it will happen, it may challenge your existing views and you might be tempted to look for the weaknesses in the arguments rather than the strengths. As with any learning experience, you will get the most out of this chapter if you remember the old maxim that your mind is like a parachute: it works best when it is open; although it will get you to your conclusion faster, if you keep it closed.

How Social and Technological Forces Act on the Pharmaceutical Industry

In the preceding chapters, I discussed at length a large number of factors that are shaping the future of pharma. In order to better understand how they are influencing the industry, I then wove them into seven social shifts and five technological transformations. For convenience, these are reiterated succinctly in Table 5.1. They contain little that will surprise industry experts but their synthesis and interpretation helps us see how they change the fitness criteria for pharmaceutical business models, which is what ultimately interests us. The challenge now is to calculate how this complex set of forces will shape and sculpt the peaks and troughs of the pharma fitness landscape. The starting point for this calculation is to understand how each of the forces acts on the industry differently.

Table 5.1   Forces shaping the pharmaceutical industry landscape

Social Environment Forces	Technological Environment Forces
A maturing concept of value: Most customers will now define value in terms of health benefit per unit cost.	A second therapeutic revolution: The number and effectiveness of pharmaceutical treatments will increase significantly, but new treatments will be more specific and relatively more expensive than in the past.
A bigger, more fragmented market: There will be more customers and they will vary more in what they want and how they purchase.	A Blackberry world: Information and communications technology will provide new ways to deliver and use healthcare, including pharmaceuticals.
A more risk averse market: Customers will continue to become less tolerant of the risks associated with healthcare treatment.	New research and development technologies: New methods of organizing and new information management will improve the effectiveness of research and development.
A stratification of health provision: Retrenchment of state provision will lead to a stratification of health service provision.	The efficiency imperative: New ways of organizing manufacturing and the supply chain will make it possible to improve efficiency and address demands for quality and risk management.
A more informed, sceptical and proactive public: Laypeople will continue to become more informed about medical matters, less likely to defer to medical authority and doubt the motives of profit oriented organizations.	Death of a traditional salesman: New organizational structures will replace the traditional methods of marketing and selling pharmaceuticals and will be enabled by information technology.
Contemplative investors: Investors will reappraise the place of pharmaceuticals in their portfolio, become more sensitive to risks and less willing to grant executives freedom of action.	
A more preventative approach to healthcare: Both patients and providers will become more willing to invest directly and indirectly in prophylaxis.	

At first sight, this combination of forces looks like what one research respondent called 'a perfect storm'. In other words, we can see it heading our way but it is hard to predict what things will look like after it has wreaked its havoc. On the other hand, if we look carefully at these twelve forces, we can see that, whilst they all have significant influence on the industry, they affect the fitness landscape in different ways and to different degrees. In particular, they differ in whether their effect on the fitness landscape is continuous or discontinuous and whether the changes they imply are operational or strategic. This is an important observation because it helps us understand how the forces shape the fitness landscape and it is worth spending a couple of paragraphs appreciating these different effects.

One way in which the effects of these forces differ is their continuity. Some of these forces are continuous, that is, their effect on the fitness criteria is to develop existing criteria rather than to create new ones. Contemplative investors, a sceptical public, and risk-averse regulators all fit into this category. They demand capabilities, such as those in investor relations, corporate social responsibility and regulatory approval, that most pharmaceutical firms currently possess to some degree. Continuous market changes may imply a significant upgrading of these extant capabilities, but they don't imply development of a wholly new set of capabilities. On their own, they may modify the existing fitness landscape but they will not create a radically new one. In contrast to the continuous forces, some of the forces are discontinuous in that they create new fitness criteria. The stratification of healthcare provision and new therapeutic opportunities seem to fit into this category. The capabilities necessary to adapt to these trends, such as selling to patients and combining diagnostics, devices and drugs, are new ones when compared to existing business models. Forces with discontinuous effects imply the creation of new peaks and troughs in the fitness landscape and not just a modification of the existing one.

The forces also differ in whether they demand adaptation at a strategic or operational level. Some of the forces demand changes in capabilities that are very important but operational, such as restructuring of sales organizations or outsourcing of manufacturing. These are essentially decisions about how to deliver a value proposition to the market, not about which market to serve or what to offer it. Whilst they are not less important than other decisions, they typically follow, rather than precede, strategic decisions about which parts of the market in which to compete and with what offer. Some of the social and technical forces identified in Table 5.1 do demand decisions at an earlier, more strategic level. For example, the rise of a preventative healthcare market and the emergence of more stratified healthcare provision both imply strategic decisions about which parts of the market to serve and what kind of value propositions are required. By contrast, the availability of new customer analytic technology or the option of outsourcing manufacturing demand decisions are essentially operational in nature and follow on from strategic decisions.

Understanding this variation in the action and impact of the five technological transformations and seven social shifts enables us to better interpret how they shape the fitness landscape. Although all of the changes in the environment imply some changes in the fitness criteria against which business models are selected, not all of the changes shape the fitness landscape to the same degree. Some of the forces merely tweak its evolutionary path and lead to gradual, incremental changes in the fitness landscape, which retains a similar pattern of peaks and troughs to the past. By contrast, other changes imply more discrete, distinct changes in the fitness landscape, which will, as a result, have a significantly different pattern of troughs and peaks. And, of these discontinuous forces, some are strategic in that they create broad new peaks in the landscape, whilst others are more operational, leading to a fine detail of ridges and valleys on the broad, strategic uplands. So, armed with this more detailed appreciation of how the environmental changes act on the fitness landscape, what does that imply for how it will be shaped? As I will now go on to describe, these forces will expand and fragment the fitness landscape for pharma, creating a series of new market habitats and causing new business models to develop and old business models to fail.

A Fragmented Fitness Landscape of Habitats

As discussed in Chapter 3, the most fundamental finding of the research was that customers have changed the way they define value. For the traditional customer of the pharmaceutical industry, the state or private insurer, value now means healthcare outcomes per unit spend. This is a major shift from the past, in which value was largely a function of how well disease was cured or managed. As a result, customer-perceived value creation is the dominant, overriding fitness criteria for the future of pharma. Business models that create customer-perceived value will survive and be copied by other firms. Those that don't create customer-perceived value will fail and become extinct.

This maturing of the value concept is very important to the shaping of the future pharma fitness landscape, since we know that customer-perceived value has two components or factors. Value creation is dependent on how it is created by the firm and how it is defined and perceived by the customer. It follows that the two basic dimensions of the fitness landscape will reflect who defines value and how that value is created. This is illustrated in Figure 5.1.

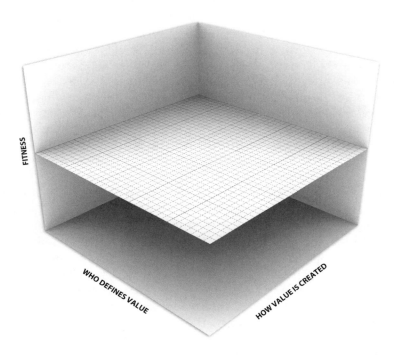

Figure 5.1   The basic framework of the future pharma fitness landscape

Until recently, both of these dimensions have been relatively narrow. The axis: 'who defines value', was mostly restricted to healthcare providers such as governments, insurance companies and health management organizations. Indeed, until very recently, it was still more restricted than that in many markets and value was defined by the prescribing physician in most cases. For the sake of brevity, I'll call this type of value definer the 'institutional buyer'. Similarly, the axis: 'how value is created', has been restricted to only one approach, that of research-based innovation that resulted in small molecules administered mostly by pill or injection. True, this value creation approach is manifested in slightly different forms – big pharma and speciality pharma – and it is augmented by a complementary and somewhat dependent generics sector. But, in essence, value in pharma has mostly been the result of what I'll call for brevity 'research-based innovation'. And, by and large, value in the pharmaceutical industry has been defined by institutional customers and created by research-based innovation.

But now, both dimension (that is, who defines value and how value is created) are evolving from their present state under the pressure of social and technological forces. As healthcare systems retreat to core provision in developed markets and emerging markets develop carefully restricted healthcare systems, the 'who defines value' dimension of the fitness landscape is expanding and subdividing. Both developed and developing markets will stratify into mass-market consumers, institutional buyers and wealthy self-payers. It is very clear how the environment forces are causing this. It is an inevitable corollary of the expansion of what is technically possible outstripping what states and other institutional buyers are able to fund, whilst individuals with varying degrees of disposable income choose to spend it on healthcare. The very wealthy will want therapies that the state cannot afford to provide and the majority will be forced to pay for more minor treatments that the state judges beneath its remit to provide. Of course, at a detailed level there will be many shades of grey, for example co-payment for drugs by state and individual and top-up insurance to augment state provision. But the basic stratification of healthcare provision, identified by Steve Burrill, Julia Manning and many others, will be a fundamental determinant of the pharma fitness landscape. We see the harbingers of each of the three customer strata today. Some Americans buy their own medications over the internet; state and insurer systems already limit what they will pay for, and health tourists travel to obtain what they won't. From the perspective of the future, these nascent trends are simply early signs of what will become fundamental features of the pharma fitness landscape.

At the same time as the 'who defines value' dimension is stratifying, the means by which value is created are also evolving and subdividing. There is, at present, relatively little value (with the emphasis here on the word relatively) created in the supply chain and customer management parts of pharma's value chain, which have historically played only a supporting role to research and development. The external and internal technological forces described in Chapter 4 (see Table 5.1) will change this dramatically. The second therapeutic revolution, telemedicine and the new technologies in research and development, supply chain and customer management will open up new ways to create and deliver customer-perceived value, ways that are very different from the research intensive, small molecule pill that is the dominant value proposition today. Supply chain rationalization, information technology and outsourcing will enable new business models in which value is created by the supply chain, almost certainly by reducing costs drastically, as we have seen in low cost airlines and retailing. At the same time, reorganizing of commercial models and, especially, information technology and telemedicine will enable new business models in which value is created by customer management, usually by some form of customization or tailoring of the value proposition, as we have seen in financial services and business logistics services. Very importantly, these technological factors will do much more than enable more ways to create value. They will also polarize the core strategies of pharmaceutical companies, so that firms focus on excellence in either innovation, supply chain or customer management but will not attempt excellence in all three parts of their value chain. The root cause of this polarization is the reality that, because of cultural constraints and resource limitations, firms can very rarely excel, in the true sense of the word, relative to their competition in more than one part of their value chain. To attempt to do so risks a straddling or stuck-in-the-middle strategy in which innovation, supply chain and customer management are all more than adequate but are none of them superior to the competition. Some readers will recognize the industrial economics ideas of Michael Porter (1) and his apologists Treacy and Wiersema (2), and I commend those who are not familiar with their work to read it. But, for our present purposes, it is sufficient to recognize that 'cost leading innovators' and 'premium priced commodities' will be as unlikely in pharma as they are in other markets. Value creation will be led by innovative research and development, or by efficient operations or by insightful customer management, but not by all three at the same time. The net result of this subdivision of value creation approaches will be that the present situation in pharma, where research-based and generics are pretty much the only two games in town, will polarize so that the price/performance gap between these two approaches will become much greater than at present. In addition, telemedicine, customer analytics and personalized medicine will allow the emergence of a third value creation mechanism by tailoring the solution more specifically to customers' clinical and other needs. As with adaptations to customer stratification, we can see some harbingers of the future of value creation today. Customer management and tailoring is the core strategy behind what Fresenius does when it manages dialysis patients. Diagnostic enabled biologics and drug/device combinations are examples of innovative core strategies. Generics are examples of core strategies based on efficient supply chains. But all of these are early examples, embryonic and primitive in comparison to what will evolve in the future. The pharma fitness landscape of the future will be able to trace its origins to these existing business models just as we human can trace our origins to the triassic eozostrodon, but it will look as different from present business models as we look compared to that shrew-like creature.

This expansion and fragmentation of the fitness landscape is a fundamental factor in the understanding of the future of pharma. The pharmaceutical market was, until quite recently, limited for the most part to pills containing small molecules, sold to institutions such as the healthcare systems of developed countries. The forces I have described are stretching that market into one that sells everything from small molecules to diagnostic-enabled gene therapy, to everyone from poor consumers with an ear infection to the fabulously wealthy who want to live forever. This expansion of the pharma market environment will lead to its subdivision into a number of distinct and differing habitats, formed at the intersection of different ways of defining and creating value, as illustrated in Figure 5.2. Each of these different habitats will have different fitness criteria and demand different capabilities of successful business models. For example, the habitat in which value is defined by mass market consumers and created by customer management will have different fitness criteria from the habitat where value is defined by state provided healthcare systems and created by an efficient supply chain. The former may demand, for example, routines and capabilities in segmentation and branding. By contrast, the latter may demand lean operations and key account management as essential components of its business model. Where there was one basic habitat that the pharma industry needed to adapt to – that created by state healthcare systems asking for small molecule pills – there will now be many habitats, each defined by a different combination of value definer and value creation approach.

Simplistically, Figure 5.2 and the reasoning behind it suggests nine different pharma market habitats, each with one corresponding business model that meets that habitat's particular fitness criteria. But reality will be more complicated. As the research identified, the maturing concept of value, who defines value and how it might be created are not the only forces acting on the market. The action and interaction of the full range of forces has to be factored in to understand how the fitness landscape will be shaped. So, before taking the next step in predicting the future pharma fitness landscape, it is worth considering three important details about how the theory is likely to play out in practice.

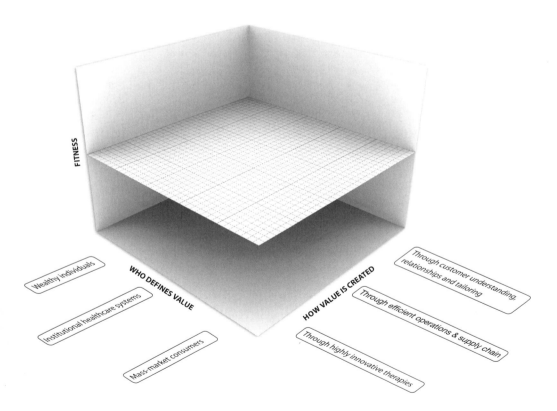

Figure 5.2   The structure of the pharma fitness landscape

Firstly, the three-by-three structure of the landscape does not necessarily imply the arithmetical outcome of nine fitness peaks. Some of the fitness criteria may contradict each other, for instance the clinical performance demanded by wealthy individuals and the very low cost offered implied by efficient supply chains are unlikely to be simultaneously possible. Contradictory fitness criteria like this are more likely to lead to troughs in the fitness landscape, indicating that any business model attempting this would not survive. For a biological analogy, try to imagine a cheetah born with a turtle's shell.

The second important detail to consider is that each habitat may lead to more than one peak. In essence, several sub-habitats may arise within a broader habitat, each of which meets similar but not identical fitness criteria. The intersection of institutional buyers who demand low overall costs and insightful customer management processes and who deliver this by understanding the customer and tailoring the value proposition may represent a broad habitat . But there may be more than one way of surviving in this habitat. For example, providing tailored management of chronically ill diabetes patients and providing prophylactic health maintenance to prevent diabetes might be two different, although similar, fitness peaks in the same part of the landscape. For a biological analogy, think of antelope and giraffes occupying similar but not identical parts of the same African savannah habitat.

The third consideration is that the fitness landscape will not be restricted to a particular national or regional geography. The global nature of the business and the fundamental nature of human health needs mean that each of these habitats will exist to a greater or lesser extent in all parts of the world. Clearly, we might expect more wealthy individuals in California than in Zimbabwe, but even the latter will have some people who wish to use their wealth to buy extended and enhanced life. Similarly, institutional systems will exist in both developed and developing markets, even though what they provide and to whom may vary significantly. Mass consumers will exist not only in the west but also in emerging economies. And, wherever those customer types exist, globalization will enable the transplantation of different value creation approaches from one country to another, so that the same intersections of value definer and value creation process will exist, to some extent, in almost every geography.

Furthermore, the direction transplantation of value creation approaches will not always be from the developed to the developing world. We are familiar with products developed by innovative research and development being exported from developed to developing economies and low cost products of efficient operations going in the other direction. This is will inevitably increase and become more complex and bilateral, even as the distinction between developed and developing economies becomes less clear.

These detailed considerations make an important difference to how the social and technological changes shape the future of pharma. Combining them with the basic structure of pharma's fitness landscape shown in Figure 5.2 allows us to predict the future fitness landscape of the industry, as shown in Figure 5.3. This is a significant step in our exploration of the future of pharma and it is worth spending some time explaining the reasoning behind it. In particular, whilst I have already discussed the ideas behind the basic structure shown in Figure 5.2, it is important to understand the detailed structure of Figure 5.3 and how it results from the forces summarized previously in Table 5.1.

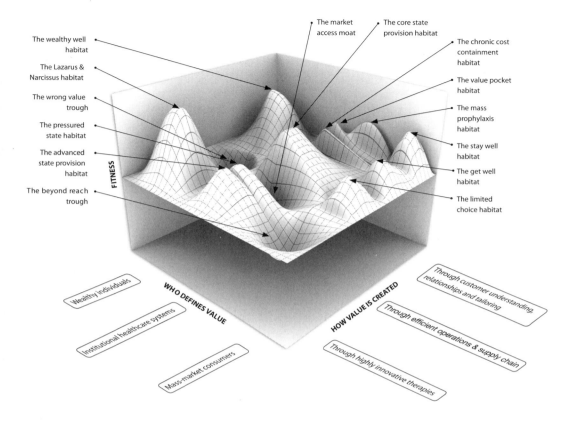

Figure 5.3   The future pharma fitness landscape

Those habitats in which value is defined by wealthy individuals are a good place for me to start an explanation of pharma's future fitness landscape. They have most in common with the traditional, late-20th Century pharma market since, as in that period, the overriding fitness criterion is optimal clinical efficacy with cost as a secondary consideration. In all three of the wealthy individual habitats, survival of the business model will depend on clinical efficacy; but exactly how efficacy is defined will, of course, be specific to the context of the clinical condition. In oncology, it might be remission rate or survival. In dementia, it might be preservation of cognitive abilities. It might equally, in the case of elective or cosmetic treatments, be some measure of appearance, emotional wellbeing or physical performance. The critical point is that, to survive in these habitats, firms must be able to deliver clearly superior performance by whatever criterion is used by the wealthy individual who is paying for the treatment.

In the habitat I have labelled Lazarus and Narcissus, the value proposition will be based on innovative research and product development. This is the territory of very innovative treatments involving personalized medicine, biologics, stem cells, gene therapy other technically advanced therapies. Equally, the therapy may be combined with diagnostics and delivery devices. The Lazarus and Narcissus decision makers' comparators will be the core, typically small molecule, therapies available through institutional health systems and Lazarus and Narcissus' customers will expect their therapies to be both much more expensive and much more effective than those comparators. The Lazarus and Narcissus habitat is complemented by the Wealthy Well habitat which shares the overriding fitness criterion of optimal clinical efficacy, with cost as a secondary consideration. The difference between them is that surviving in the Wealthy Well habitat demands maintaining health or managing minor ailments and value is created not by pharmacological innovation but by an insightful customer management process that achieves what Treacy and Wiersema called 'customer intimacy'. In other words, optimal clinical outcome is achieved by understanding and acting on the specific health needs of the individual patient. This is the realm of health monitoring, personal genetic screening and tailored prophylactic treatments. In this habitat, very innovative therapies may be superfluous, but the value of telemedicine, health data analytics and customized service is very high. The wealthy individual will compare the benefits of his or her concierge service with those of the more limited public health programmes provided by the state or other institutions. He or she will expect the Wealthy Well value proposition to be both much more effective and significantly more costly than the institutionally provided options.

Between the Lazarus and Narcissus and the Wealthy Well habitats, at the intersection of the wealthy patient and efficient supply chains, lies the area I have labelled the Wrong Kind of Value trough. Survival in this habitat would require a business model that met the overriding fitness criterion of optimal clinical efficacy through operational efficiency. Given the costs associated with achieving optimal clinical efficacy, this is very unlikely. In addition, the low costs that could be created by efficient operations would not be valued by the wealthy individuals if, as is inevitable, efficiency compromised clinical outcome. Such a business model would, therefore, be unfit in the evolutionary sense and would not survive. So although the landscape has room for three potential habitats involving wealthy, self-financing individuals, reality dictates that only two – those I have labelled Lazarus and Narcissus and Wealthy Well – will in fact emerge.

Let me now move from that part of the landscape where value is defined by wealthy individuals to that where value is defined by institutional buyers, such as state healthcare systems or perhaps health management organizations. This part of the landscape has some superficial similarities to existing pharma markets, in that the value definer is the same as for most of today's pharmaceutical market. But the institutional customer of tomorrow will differ greatly from that of yesterday in terms of how they define value, as we have already discussed.

In this part of the fitness landscape, the overriding fitness criterion will be comparative cost effectiveness, although politics and scale will mean the pattern of peaks and troughs will be more complex than in the wealthy individual area. Value will be determined by market access authorities, perhaps enabled by more advanced analytics or more sophisticated in-market assessments, risk sharing arrangements or value-based pricing. In the central part of the landscape will be the Core State Provision habitat. Here, the fitness criterion of comparative value will demand a value proposition based on operational efficiency. To survive, a business model will have to be capable of delivering very low cost therapies, mostly generic small molecules but gradually extending to biosimilars and eventually other more advanced treatments as their product life cycles age and they become genericized.

This Core State Provision will also leave room for other habitats that involve institutions. Adjacent to Core State Provision will be two sub-habitats in which institutional providers will seek value created by innovative product development. In the first, the Advanced State Provision sub-habitat, the fitness criterion of comparative value will demand a value proposition based on innovative product development with demonstrable comparative value. To survive, a business model will have to be capable of delivering advanced therapies that can be proven to deliver value compared to the very cheap, small molecule therapy available through Core State Provision. Next to the Advanced State Provision sub-habitat will lie the Pressured State habitat in which the fitness criterion is the resolution of certain high profile diseases that the state healthcare system is obliged to fund by the political pressure of patient advocacy groups and others. Treating such diseases will probably not meet the comparative value tests applied to other diseases, but this habitat will be the direct consequence of more informed, less deferent and more proactive patients, as previously discussed. This Pressured State habitat may include emotive diseases like rare cancers or politically sensitive conditions such as *in vitro* fertilization.

The value proposition in both Advanced State Provision and Pressured State habitats will be based on innovative research and product development and will share some features with the Lazarus and Narcissus habitat, of which it will be a pale, state funded reflection. Of course, the extent and boundaries of the Core, Advanced and Pressured State provision will vary greatly between countries, dictated by national wealth, political policy and local needs, but it will of necessity exclude many treatments at the most expensive and least clinically important ends of the therapy spectrum. This exclusion of very sophisticated and very simple therapies will create the preconditions for the wealthy individual and mass consumer habitats.

Complementing Core State Provision will be the habitat in which governments or other institutions define value but in which that value is created by insightful customer management rather than supply chain efficiency or innovative research and product development. There are at least three sub-habitats imaginable in this area. The first involves the management of chronic diseases which, as already discussed, are expected to consume much of states healthcare resources. I have labelled this the Chronic Cost Containment habitat. Here, the overriding fitness criterion is creating comparative value by reducing the overall cost of managing a huge and expensive patient population. In this case, the costs and efficacy of the drug will be secondary considerations in value creation, since the drug is likely to form only a tiny part of the overall management cost. More important will be the reduction of care costs by personalized management of each patient's condition and therefore avoidance of expensive deterioration or complications.

The second sub-habitat involving customer management and institutional value-definers is the Mass Prophylaxis habitat. This differs from the Chronic Cost Containment habitat, in that the fitness criterion is creating comparative value by preventing, rather than managing, the development of expensive, 'avoidable' conditions. Again, drug costs and efficacy will be secondary issues in this habitat because even if the 'treatment' does involve prophylactic drugs such as statins, they will be a small component of overall management costs. In the Mass Prophylaxis habitat, value will be created by, and survival will demand, understanding disease aetiology and patient behaviour, and using that understanding to reduce disease incidence, probably by a combination of patient monitoring, lifestyle management and prophylactic treatments.

The third likely sub habitat in this institutional buyer/customer management area will be the Value Pockets habitat. Here, the fitness criterion will be to find pockets of comparative value that have been neglected by large scale, undifferentiated therapeutic regimes typically used in Core State Provision. Value will be created by formulating and combining drugs in novel ways, extending their use into under-served therapeutic areas or other product 'line extensions' based on some insight into the weaknesses of prevalent mass treatment regimes. Notably, in the institutional area there will be a trough where innovative products, despite their clinical superiority to cheap generics, either fail to demonstrate cost effectiveness in comparison to very cheap generics or fail to garner political support. This trough, which I have labelled the Market Access Moat, will be the graveyard of business models that fail to be appropriately innovative, politically astute or both.

Having explored the parts of the landscape that most resemble the current prescription medicine market, we can now look at the part that is most like the current OTC medicine market and indeed, at its edges, blurs into that market. However, the consumer driven part of the pharmaceutical market can still be distinguished from the purely OTC market by the severity of the conditions, the need for health care professional involvement and local regulation of access. The habitats I will discuss here are those in which the consumer perceives the treatment as something of greater consequence than popping an aspirin, although I acknowledge that it varies greatly from person to person where that line lies and it is hard to define, especially in many emerging markets.

In these habitats, value is defined by ordinary individuals who do not fall into the wealthy category and whose conditions are not provided for by institutional healthcare systems. At present, it is mostly very expensive treatments that are excluded but one might reasonably expect an increasing number of conditions that are not life threatening – erectile dysfunction, perhaps, mild forms of depression or minor infections – to become excluded from Core State Provision as cost containment becomes ever more important. For institutional healthcare systems, abdicating this part of the market to self-funding consumers offers large cost saving opportunities in both drugs and labour costs. For mass consumers, even relatively affluent middle class ones, there will of course be a trough in the fitness landscape, where highly innovative but expensive therapies are simply out of the financial reach of the consumer. I have labelled this the Beyond Reach trough. Self-evidently, business models that depend on selling very expensive treatments to ordinary consumers are not likely to succeed. That said, a few anomalous consumers will, through great sacrifice, family or charitable support, manage to afford such expensive treatments and these will have, de facto, become émigrés to the Lazarus and Narcissus habitat.

Close to this Beyond Reach trough is the Limited Choice habitat, comprised of consumers who can barely afford pharmaceuticals at all. In this habitat, the overriding fitness criterion is low cost and the comparator is not other treatments, but non-treatment or non-pharmaceutical folk remedies. In this habitat, only extremely low cost business models will survive and, as a corollary of this, this habitat will be especially prone to counterfeits and other illegal or low quality products. This threat of cheap, useless or potentially dangerous products will shape the fitness criterion on the last part of the landscape I will discuss. This is where value is defined by a consumer who is sufficiently affluent not to have to choose on price alone but is not so wealthy that price is irrelevant. In this habitat, cost and trust will be dual fitness criteria as consumers seek to obtain medicines at the lowest trustworthy price, avoiding the risks of useless or harmful products.

This part of the landscape will, in a parallel of the corresponding institutional habitat, contain at least two sub habitats: firstly, the Get Well habitat, based around treatment;

secondly, the Stay Well habitat, based around prevention of illness. Since a primary fitness criterion will be trust, the value created by the clinical innovation and supply chain efficiency will be secondary to that created by strong brands built upon consumer insight and socially responsible behaviour. Business models that do not create trust, even if they produce effective and inexpensive products, will fail in this habitat.

And so we have a prediction of the future fitness landscape of pharma. The odd looking set of contours shown in Figure 5.3 is not simply the creation of my fevered imagination. It is what we should expect to see, if the five technological transformations and seven social shifts act on the pharmaceutical market in the way I have described. Indeed, if we accept that those forces are acting on the market, it would be surprising if the fitness landscape did not evolve into something close to this predicted shape. For example, it would be remarkable if, in a world where exotic, effective but expensive treatments were available but not provided by the state, rich individuals did not spend their money to buy extra years of good life for themselves or their loved ones. It would be equally extraordinary if, faced with the clear economic argument for preventing chronic disease rather than managing it, governments were not willing to pay for mass prophylaxis programmes and companies did not combine drugs and information technology to meet that need. And in a world where brands command a premium in food, automobile and other consumer goods markets, it would be very odd indeed if consumers did not use brands as a way to reassure themselves that their medicine was safe and effective.

The peaks predicted by evolutionary theory and shown in Figure 5.3 are, in effect, parts of the market that make a specific set of demands on any business model that attempts to operate in that area. The troughs and spaces between the peaks are, by extension, parts of the market where business models are not likely to be viable. Mostly, these are simple valleys that represent suboptimal straddling, stuck in the middle strategies that do not create enough customer perceived value.

In some cases, the troughs represent particular situations where the certain attributes of a business model would make it extinct. It is no surprise, for example, the model predicts that selling very expensive therapies to ordinary consumers will not work, and such therapies will only be accepted by institutional providers if supported with extraordinary political or market access capabilities. And, as I have already noted, we can see embryonic examples of all these things happening already today, from private healthcare to nutraceuticals, from smoking prevention programmes to OTC brands, from online pharmacies to market access departments. In other words, the evolution of the pharmaceutical market into something resembling Figure 5.3 is not merely an unsupported theory. It is already happening in a thousand small variations of business models that are gradually being selected for and amplified.

Given Bohr's admonition, it would be surprising if the predicted fitness landscape was absolutely accurate. Orgel's 2nd law (3) states that 'Evolution is cleverer than you are' and it is certainly clever than I am. I would not be surprised if the reality is the emergence of a landscape even more complicated than the one I have predicted, with more detail superimposed on the basic ideas I have proposed. But if, as I argue, the fitness landscape shown in Figure 5.3 is broadly correct and captures the most important features of the landscape, it serves my purpose as a basis for predicting the future of pharma.

What remains for this chapter is to take the step from what the landscape will look like to what business models might evolve to fit that environment. To take that step, I follow the example of Charles Darwin and the story of an orchid pollinating moth.

Xanthopan Morganii Praedicta: Predicting Pharma's Business Models

As Gene Kritsky recounts (4), one day in January 1862 Charles Darwin received a parcel from Robert Bateman. The parcel contained specimens of *Angraecum sesquipedale*, a very unusual orchid from Madagascar that surprised Darwin because of its nectary, which was almost 12 inches (30 centimetres) long. Since no known creature could reach its nectar, this orchid seemed designed to thwart pollination and so challenged evolutionary theory. Such a challenge pushes knowledge forward because it demands explanation or revision of the theory and that is exactly what happened in this case. Because the orchid belonged to a family that was usually pollinated by moths, Darwin predicted that:

> *'In Madagascar, there must be moths with proboscises capable of extension to a length of between 10 and 11 inches.'*

Charles Darwin (5)

Although not until 1903, just such a moth was found on Madagascar and it was named, appropriately, Xanthopan morganii praedicta, in honour of the prediction that Darwin had made. This example of the predictive power of the theory of evolution is now one of the most famous in scientific history and is often used as a demonstration of co-evolution in practice.

I use the famous praedicta story as an analogy to help take the next step in understanding the future of pharma. The premise of the preceding section is that the pharma market environment has comprised, until recently, of only one type of orchid, the 'state provider wanting to buy small molecules based on research' variety. And three species of moth have evolved to feed from this orchid – big pharma, speciality pharma and generic pharma – although, given their interdependency and the similarities of their DNA-like capabilities, one might consider them symbiotic sub-species rather than distinct creatures. Taking the analogy a step further, I then predicted, based on the effects of the seven social shifts and five technological transformations, that eleven new varieties of orchids would evolve and replace the existing one. Each of these, from the Lazarus and Narcissus to the Stay Well variety and all those in between, would demand different characteristics of any moth who wishes to feed from it. The implication of the analogy is that we might expect to see eleven new species and sub-species of moth evolve.

Stepping back from the analogy, we should expect to see new pharma industry business models evolve whose characteristics, like the ten inch proboscis of praedicta, are dictated and prophesied by the demands of the market habitat they choose to occupy. To express the same idea in terms of the variation, selection, amplification algorithm that underpins evolution, we should expect pharmaceutical and other companies to experiment with various business models, which will be selected for or against by the market environment described by the future pharma fitness landscape. Many will fail, but the successful ones will grow and be imitated until the industry is characterized by a set of business models that climb the peaks of the fitness landscape. Thus, the industry will transform from a relatively simple one of three closely related business models to a menagerie of many different models serving different customers and creating value in different ways. In the remainder of this chapter, we'll outline some of the basic characteristics of the multiple business models predicted by evolutionary theory. That will complete most of the three part promise to predict the future of the industry, which I made at the beginning of this important chapter. Then, from Chapter 6 onwards, I will examine the implications of that future for those firms that wish to be part of it.

As I described earlier in our reference to Voltaire, there is little point in using a term if I have not defined what I mean. This is especially true when I discuss business models, since the term is very loosely used by both academics and executives. In 1960, the first academic paper to use the term in its title (6) does not even describe what a business model is. After that, the term is barely used until its use explodes in the 1990s and early 2000s, when Joan Magretta's definition is often quoted:

'Business models are, at heart, stories that explain how enterprises work. Like a good story, robust business models contain precisely delineated characters, plausible motivations and a plot that turns on an insight about value. It answers certain questions: Who is the customer? How do we make money? What underlying logic explains how we can deliver value to the customer at an appropriate cost?'

Joan Magretta (7)

PricewaterhouseCoopers, in their series of reports about the pharma industry, used the term business model in a sense that had much in common with Magretta's definition:

'A company's business model is the means by which it makes a profit – how it addresses its marketplace, the offerings it develops and the business relationships it deploys to do so.'

PricewaterhouseCoopers (8)

The problem with these and many other uses of the term is that they tend to conflate business models with strategy when, in fact, a business model is an umbrella term, covering many things. For our purposes, I am going to define business model thus: a business model is a description of the way a firm or group of firms operate and includes three principal components:

- The firm's strategy, meaning that set of resource allocation decisions about which customers to serve and what to offer them.
- The firm's capabilities, meaning the set of assets, resources and routines and processes that enable it to operate and to create value.
- The firm's structure, meaning the set of organizational relationships between functions within the firm and between the firm and its suppliers and other partners.

As knowledgeable readers will notice, this definition synthesizes the ideas of several leading management thinkers, but especially Drucker (9;10), Mintzberg (11), Barney (12) and Teece and Pisano (13;14) and Dosi, Nelson and Winter (15).

Using this definition implies that predicting how pharma's business models will evolve means predicting how their strategies, capabilities and structures will evolve. Importantly, this does not just mean predicting the evolution of strategy, capabilities and structure of those firms that are currently operating in the industry. It must also include those firms that are not yet part of the industry, and may not yet even exist, but who will eventually be part of the future of pharma. Clearly, this is not a straightforward, simple task. But we do have the future pharma fitness landscape as a platform on which to build and, as we shall see, that takes us quite a long way.

To extrapolate directly from Figure 5.3 to the future strategies, capabilities and structures of those firms that are already in the industry and also those that may be, we have to proceed with caution. Firstly, we have to treat the strategic choice about which habitats to serve as the independent variable, a starting point, and assume that it is a decision made by the firm's executive team. I will return, in Chapter 6, to the hows and whys of this decision but, for now, let us assume that the decision is a given. Secondly, we can assume the choice of which habitat to serve defines the basic outline of the sort of offer that has to be made.

Clearly, since each habitat demands a particular value proposition that meets the fitness criteria for that habitat, the executive choice of which habitat to serve also defines, at least to a first approximation, the nature of the value proposition. The choice of which habitats to serve and broadly what value propositions to offer is, by definition, the firm's strategy. The nature of the strategy then delineates, again to a first approximation, the distinctive or core competency needed by the firm. This idea, coined by Philip Selznick (16) and developed by Kenneth Andrews (17) and Gary Hamel and C.K. Prahalad (18) simply means the thing that the organization is especially or particularly good at. The core competency of a firm is the result of a number of capabilities, each of which is the result of a combination of assets, resources and organizational routines.

In Table 5.2, I have identified the distinctive or core competencies required of a firm seeking to meet the fitness criteria of each of the eleven sub-habitats described above and in Figure 5.3. Note that the capabilities that lead to the distinctive or core competencies are not the only capabilities implied by each habitat. All of the strategies, for example, still demand the ability to do certain essential things like get basic regulatory approval and meet basic quality standards. But these essential capabilities are merely what is required to operate at a basic level in the chosen habitat. At most, these essential capabilities are necessary for competitive parity, not sufficient for competitive superiority. Distinctive capabilities are what implies and enables competitive superiority.

Table 5.2   Distinctive capabilities for each chosen habitat

Habitat chosen	Distinctive capabilities
Lazarus & Narcissus	Invent and develop treatments that cure or manage difficult-to-treat ailments with significantly greater efficacy than any other treatment.
Wealthy Well	Develop and implement patient management processes that maintain wellness and cure or manage minor ailments with significantly greater efficacy than any other process.
Core State Provision	Manufacture and distribute treatments for ailments funded by institutional buyers at the lowest possible cost, consistent with quality standards.
Advanced State Provision	Invent and develop treatments that cure or manage difficult-to-treat ailments and demonstrate comparative value to institutional buyers.

Table 5.2   *Concluded*

Habitat chosen	Distinctive capabilities
Pressured State	Invent and develop treatments that cure or manage difficult-to-treat ailments, and enable political pressure to allow access to those treatments in institutional health systems.
Chronic Cost Containment	Develop and implement processes for institutional buyers that manage populations of chronically ill patients at the lowest possible cost consistent with quality standards.
Mass Prophylaxis	Develop and implement processes for institutional buyers that minimize the development of ailments in at-risk populations at the lowest possible cost consistent with quality standards.
Value Pockets	Identify and fill areas in current mass-treatment regimes where product modification can deliver better comparative value for institutional buyers.
Limited Choice	Manufacture and distribute treatments for ailments not funded by institutional buyers at the lowest possible cost consistent with quality standards.
Get Well	Manufacture and distribute treatments for ailments not funded by institutional buyers and establish trusted brands.
Stay Well	Develop and implement processes that maintain the health of self-funded consumers and establish trusted brands.

With Figure 5.3 and its list of distinctive capabilities, Table 5.2 makes a good start to predicting the future business models of the pharmaceutical industry. But there's still work to be done.

From Habitat to Biosphere

In this chapter, I have done most of the three things I promised at its beginning. I have looked at how the social and technological forces shape the fitness landscape. Then I predicted the resultant landscape. The combination of theory and facts predicts that no fewer than eleven fitness peaks, or habitats, will evolve in the pharmaceutical market, each with its own particular set of fitness criteria. Then I began to predict how the industry's business models will have to evolve to fit that landscape. We can say that any given choice of habitat implies a particular business model and for each particular business model, and it is now possible to make a first, broad approximation of the value proposition and distinctive competency that is required. Having done that, we have made significant progress towards understanding the future of pharma.

We can predict that the industry will evolve new business models with new strategies, new capabilities and new organizational forms. We can predict that new strategies will involve targeting one or more of the habitats in the fitness landscape. We can predict that the value propositions of those strategies will attempt to meet the fitness criteria of the targeted habitats. And we can predict that successful business models will have the distinctive competencies required to develop and deliver those value propositions.

But this is only an outline of the future of pharma and still leaves several questions unanswered. We don't yet know whether the eleven habitats will lead to eleven, distinct business models or a smaller number of aggregated business models, each of which attempts to address more than one habitat. And, for each business model that does evolve, we only know the fundamentals of what it will need to be capable of – its distinctive competency. We still need to understand the separate capabilities and organizational routines that will underpin each distinctive competency. Crucially, we don't know how firms will develop any new capabilities that are critical to survival. To understand the future of pharma, we also need to understand how firms will organize themselves to deliver the value required by their chosen habitat. Finally, we still need to understand how firms will manage the change that is implied by this evolution.

In short, we need to make the leap from understanding the habitat of hills and valleys to seeing the biosphere, populated with a number of distinct species of business model, all trying to survive by creating value in different ways for different customers. The research underpinning this book, after exploring the forces shaping the industry and its fitness landscape, went on to investigate precisely that question and its findings will be the subject of Part III of this book, Chapters 7, 8 and 9.

Reference List

(1)   Porter, M.E. 1980. *Competitive Strategy*. 1st ed. Free Press.

(2)   Treacy, M. and Wiersema, M. 1995. *The Discipline of the Market Leaders*. London: Harper Collins.

(3)   Dennett, D.C. 1995. *Darwin's Dangerous Idea*. London: Allen Lane.

(4)   Kritsky, G. 2001. Darwin's Madagascan Hawk Moth Prediction. *American Entomologist*; 37:206–10.

(5)   Darwin, C. 1862. *On the Various Contrivances by which British and Foreign Orchids are Fertilized by Insects*. London: John Murray.

(6)   Jones, G.M. 1960. Educators, Electrons and Business Models, A Problem In Synthesis. *Accounting Review*; 35(4):619.

(7)   Magretta, J. 2002. Why Business Models Matter. *Harvard Business Review*; (May):86–92.

(8)   *Pharma 2020. Challenging Business Models. Which Path Will You Take*. PricewaterhouseCoopers; 2010.

(9)   Drucker, P.F. 1954. *The Practice of Management*. New York: Harper & Row.

(10)   Drucker, P.F. 1974. *Management: Tasks, Responsibilities, Practices*. First ed. Oxford: Butterworth-Heinemann; 1974.

(11)   Mintzberg, H. 2000. View from the Top: Henry Mintzberg on Strategy and Management. *Academy of Management Review*; 14(3):31–42.

(12)   Barney, J.B. 1991. Firm Resources and Sustained Competitive Advantage. *Journal of Management*; 17(1):99–120.

(13)   Teece, D. and Pisano, G. 1994. The Dynamic Capabilities of Firms: an Introduction. *Industrial & Corporate Change*; 3(3):537–56.

(14)   Teece, D.J., Pisano, G.P. and Shuen, A. 1997. Dynamic Capabilities and Strategic Management. *Strategic Management Journal*; 18(7):509–33.

(15)   Dosi, G., Nelson, R.R. and Winter, S.G. 2010. *The Nature and Dynamics of Organisational Capabilities*. Oxford: OUP.

(16) Selznick, P. 1957. *Leadership in Administration: A Sociological Interpretation.* 1st ed. New York: Harper and Row.

(17) Andrews, K.R. 1971. *The Concept of Corporate Strategy.* Homewood: Dow-Jones Irwin.

(18) Prahalad, C.K. and Hamel, G. 1990. The Core Competence of the Corporation. *Harvard Business Review;* 68(3):79–91.

6 *The Speciation of Pharma: The New Business Models that Will Transform the Industry*

'It may be said that natural selection is daily and hourly scrutinising, throughout the world, every variation, even the slightest; rejecting that which is bad, preserving and adding up all that is good; silently and insensibly working, whenever and wherever opportunity offers, at the improvement of each organic being in relation to its organic and inorganic conditions of life.'

Charles Darwin, The Origin of Species

In Part II of this book (Chapters 3, 4, 5 and 6), we combined facts with theory; facts about the forces shaping the pharmaceutical industry and the economic variants of the theory of evolution, which explains how industries develop and predicts their future. The result was a complex, new fitness landscape that is very different from the present, filled with steep, demanding peaks and deep, swampy troughs. In this chapter, I will populate that landscape with a range of new business models that will roam that landscape in the future. To do that, I will again combine facts and theory: facts observed in the early signs of evolution by pharmaceutical companies and theory from strategic management research, which explains why some business models work and others don't.

Punctuated Equilibrium and Extinction

Before I start combining fact and theory again, it is worth making a small detour into two other bodies of knowledge, one from evolutionary biology and the other from management research, both of which will help us understand, and place in context, what is going on in the pharmaceutical industry. The first, from evolutionary biology, is the concept of punctuated equilibrium, first posited by Niles Eldredge and Stephen Jay Gould in the 1970s (1). They suggested that evolution, far from being a constant, gradual process, may occur in leaps of rapid change that punctuate long periods of stability. The most commonly cited example of one of these periods of rapid evolution is the Cambrian explosion or, to use biologists' preferred but less dramatic term, radiation. This describes a period about 530 million years ago when the number of different species increased rapidly in a relatively short space of time and the diversity of life increased to something approaching what it is today. Evolutionary scientists argue about punctuated equilibrium and debate the exact causes of the Cambrian radiation, but the general tenor of the debate is that rapid environmental change and competition between species can drive a sudden surge of speciation.

Because both biological systems and industries like pharma are complex, adaptive systems, punctuated equilibrium is a useful way of looking at what is happening in the pharmaceutical industry in the first quarter of the 21st Century. As we've seen, the industry is in a period of rapid environmental change and intense competition, following a relatively long period of industry stability in which the same business models have dominated for many decades. It takes little stretch of the imagination to see that, just as the Cambrian period provided the right conditions for a radiation of biological species, the present conditions in the pharmaceutical industry provide appropriate conditions for a radiation of pharma business models.

The second useful aside, this time from management research, concerns extinction rates, the corollary of the emergence of new species. Extinction rates are useful data because they are, in effect, the opposite of replication; they tell us when a business model was not well adapted to the market environment.

This is particularly true for large firms that, to some extent, are insulated from the chance and circumstance that makes the survival of small firms so unpredictable. In a landmark piece of research, Hannah Marshall, tracked the survival of the 100 largest, most powerful firms from 1912 to 1995 and found that only 52 survived and only 19 were still in the top 100 list (2). In a complementary piece of work, Neil Fligstein (3) tracked the 100 largest United States firms from 1919 to 1979, a total of 234 firms altogether. Of the top 100 firms in 1919, only 34 were still on the list in 1979. Both these pieces show that even giant companies are susceptible to high extinction rates and, although they didn't examine pharmaceutical companies specifically, it would be naive to take the continued existence of our industry giants for granted.

In an interesting extension of this extinction rate work, Paul Ormerod (4;5) compared extinction rates of large companies (whose evolution is driven by the careful thought of executives), with that of biological species (whose evolution is driven only by the blind process of DNA mutation and evolutionary variation, selection and amplification). Contrary to what executives might hope, random DNA mutations and thoughtful executive decisions seem to lead to pretty much the same extinction rates. This surprising result led Ormerod to conclude:

> 'The implication is that it is as is … firms acted at random … Firms try all the time to achieve favourable outcomes but they often fail. And they often become extinct.'

Paul Ormerod (5)

This detour via punctuated equilibrium and extinction rates tells us two things that are important to our prediction of the future of pharma. Firstly, that evolution need not be gradual; it can happen in 'spurts' if the environmental conditions and competitive environment drive it that way. Secondly, despite the careful plans of bright executives, companies are just as likely to become extinct as blindly mutating biological species. If we displace these ideas back to the pharma industry and its current conditions, we should anticipate an explosion or radiation of pharma business models that will be accompanied by the extinction of many existing firms. It is, in short, going to be an interesting time.

This brief diversion helps set the scene for exploring how the evolution and extinction of business models will populate the industry landscape. We are looking for how firms will adapt to the fitness landscape and how that will lead to the evolution of new species of business model and the extinction of others. We will begin this exploration by discussing what companies are doing now, which tells us a lot but also has its limitations as a data source. Then we'll add in ideas from strategic management research to move beyond those limitations and paint a picture of the beasts that will roam the future pharma landscape.

Evidence of Variation, Variation of Evidence

As we have discussed, the evolutionary process is an algorithm – a three step process of variation, selection and amplification that leads eventually to species that meet the fitness criteria of the habitat they occupy. To gain insight into where the evolution of pharma might be taking us, therefore, we need to look first for evidence of variation and then, if possible, selection and amplification.

This was the direction the research took after examining the forces shaping the pharmaceutical environment, and I began to look for evidence of variation in firms' business models. The first step was to look for variation in the foundations of the business models, namely that set of strategic decisions about which customers to serve and what to offer them. In particular, I sought to identify variations that indicated firms were adapting to new habitats, either the ones suggested in Chapter 5 (Figure 5.3) or some other habitats that I had not anticipated.

As with the 'forces shaping the industry' research, the raw data were messy and unstructured and, in this case, often disguised by investor relations hyperbole. But analysing the data reveals six overarching trends in how companies are varying their business models. In the following sections, I will discuss these patterns briefly and separately before synthesizing them and drawing implications for the future of pharma.

THE QUEST FOR INNOVATION LEADERSHIP

Looking for signs where companies are trying to be innovation leaders is especially hindered by the way firms manage their public pronouncements. Even technological laggards declare that what they do is innovative and pioneering whilst few firms will admit to weaknesses in their innovation, even when it is patently clear. In this context, identifying instance of where firms are really focussing on innovation is difficult, but careful parsing does reveal a number of illuminating examples. Roche, for example, seem clearly set on occupying the innovative habitats of the pharma landscape. Its CEO, Severin Schwann, told the *Financial Times* in November 2010:

> *'It's true we invest over proportionately on research and development. But that's a reflection of our business strategy and we will continue to do so. Science is at the core of driving innovation and our future growth.'*

Severin Schwann, Roche (6)

This proclaimed strategy is little different from many other companies that are clearly less innovative than Roche, but the Swiss giant's actions substantiate their claims. As long ago as 1998, they acquired Boehringer Mannheim not for its pharma business, but in order to combine diagnostic and therapeutic capabilities. Their longstanding focus on oncology, their acquisition of Genetech, a substantial biotech firm, and their relatively strong pipeline of innovative products, such as Taspoglutide, a new drug for type 2 diabetes, are indicators that they trying to climb those peaks in the landscape for which innovative capabilities are the most important selection criteria. Equally telling is their strategic choice not to become involved in generics, which differs from their neighbours at Novartis, for example.

We see similar attempts to climb the innovation fitness peak at many of the other major pharma companies. David Brennan, CEO of AstraZeneca, has poached research and development leaders from Pfizer and Wyeth, narrowed the scope of its research and development, and reorganized AstraZeneca's development process quite radically. Speaking to *Business Week*, Jane E. Henney, representing AstraZeneca's Board, said of their commitment to innovative development:

> *'I don't sense there's any feeling among the board that we should move in another direction. It's the path that we've chosen. Only history is going to be able to judge if we were correct.'*

> Jane E. Henney, AstraZeneca (7)

The same sentiment was enunciated by many other pharmaceutical companies, large and small:

> *'We will continue to be innovation driven.'*

> Bert Tjeenk Willink, Boehringer Ingelheim

> *'The answer for those who still want to innovate is going to be true innovation.'*

> Harald Stock, Grünenthal

On this evidence, many of the existing players are exhibiting variations in their business model by trying to out-compete their rivals in an innovation sense. This is unsurprising, given that many of the existing players got where they are today by innovating better than other companies. Innovation is a continuous, rather than discontinuous, change. It is a case of doing more of the same, only more so. But, like a giraffe's neck, it is a variation nevertheless and such firms will either achieve innovation leadership or they won't; and those that don't will either become extinct or adapt to a habitat in which innovation is not a key fitness criteria.

It's worth noting, too, that variation in innovation capabilities is not restricted to the large, established pharmaceutical companies we've already mentioned. Below the level of the major pharmaceutical companies lies a very large number of life sciences companies that are examples of variations from 'value as a small molecule pill' strategies, whether that is in biotechnology or information technology.

Two examples from the many hundreds possible illustrate the point. Sangamo Biosciences is working on gene regulation technology that, in early trials, seems to prevent HIV infection. Proteus Biomedical is trialling a pill containing a chip that can measure patient compliance and so improve therapy effectiveness. And, of course, this list of examples could go on endlessly. What these and other examples demonstrate, in evolutionary terms, is variation in business models; strategies that are not 'small molecules pushed by heavy detailing' but are much closer to the 'distinctly better outcomes from combined technology' aimed at the Lazarus and Narcissus, Advanced State Provision and Pressured State habitats. There is also evidence that some of this variation has been successful or, in evolutionary terms, selected and replicated. For example, the success of Roche's Herceptin and other monoclonal antibodies is a clear example of how innovative variations in strategy, such as these, have been selected by the market. Similarly, Roche's early focus on oncology has been mimicked by other companies that have shifted focus from primary to secondary care, an example of replication of that particular 'gene' for focussing on more technically demanding markets.

THE EXPANSION OUT OF THE DEVELOPED MARKETS

The quest for innovation leadership is an example of variation in the 'what to offer' part of the business model. In the same way, expansion out of developed markets is an example of variation in the 'to whom to offer it' component of the business model. It is in contrast with the 'focus on the United States and western markets' that has been typical of the industry. As we already discussed in Chapter 2, the most important point about emerging markets is not simply that these markets are large, but that they are and will be different from the western markets that the pharmaceutical companies have traditionally targeted: pricing, the scope of institutional provision and the importance of consumers are all very different in, say, India than in the United States or Western Europe. The understanding of this and the shift from the United States and European Union to emerging marketing were among the clearer, less ambiguous, findings of the research. Jeffrey Keilsing's comment captured Pfizer's view of the complexity of emerging markets and their response:

> 'They say emerging markets only emerge once; they will become broader and more mature markets. So we have a specific set of entities, business units that focus on making sure we understand those sets of customers.'

> Jeffery Keisling, Pfizer

Two aspects of emerging markets – their consumer nature and their price sensitivity – are clearly important environmental differences to which pharma business models will have to adapt. David Norton described the consumer nature of the emerging markets well and hinted at the way his company will use its strengths there:

> 'If you look at the developing world, like India for example, the majority of people who are getting medication are paying for themselves. And that's a very different environment. So, yes, people are moving in to sell non patent-protected products; but the concept is, "I want to build

a brand in the emerging market and maintain that brand for 20, 30, 40 years." Then it's about the consumer brand. Johnson & Johnson knows that well; Tylenol is nearly 60 years old.'

David Norton, Johnson & Johnson

The second issue of pricing will obviously be another part of emerging markets that firms will try to address. Teva's Aharon Schwartz pointed to how this will be an important part of their strategy:

'We are putting more emphasis on the emerging markets simply because this is a growth area and we believe that we have a very unique advantage because we do know how to be cost effective because of our sheer size.'

Aharon Schwartz, Teva

Variation of strategy to address emerging markets is also demonstrated by merger, acquisition and partnership activity of pharmaceuticals. For example, Nycomed has acquired China's Guangdong Techpool Bio-Pharma; Daiichi Sankyo acquired India's Ranbaxy and Pfizer has acquired Brazil's Tueto. These are just a few of the steady stream of acquisitions of emerging market pharmaceutical companies. Another variation on the same theme is AstraZeneca's agreement with Torrent to market the latter's branded generics, again designed to address the needs for low cost products in emerging and, increasingly, developed markets. Nor are these strategy variations restricted to commercial operations. Speaking to Reuters, Pfizer's head of clinical development in Asia drew a clear picture of how research and development strategy is varying to address emerging markets:

'The old model for pharmaceutical research and development does not work. Going into risk sharing, collaboration and partnerships would be one way of lowering costs. The old model, where you build laboratories and you have a whole lot of bricks and mortar, is not the way to go in China … we can basically do full research using partners instead of our own laboratories. In the research space, we have a very small footprint in our office. But we have hundreds of scientists who work on Pfizer projects. They are sitting in laboratories in Chinese companies.'

Bradley Marchant, Pfizer (8)

As with the quest for innovation leadership, these incidents of expansion out of developed markets and into various parts of the emerging markets are examples of attempts to climb parts of the fitness landscape. In particular, they point to variations that might be selected for in the context of the Core State Provision, Limited Choice and Get Well habitats, which will exist to varying degrees in all geographies but which will be key to penetrating emerging markets.

THE GROWTH OF GENERIC APPROACHES

In addition to innovation leadership and expansion from traditional markets, a third clear variation in pharmaceutical business models observed in the research is the expansion and consolidation of generics. Whilst a strong generics sector has existed for almost 30 years, it has been relatively small in value terms, fragmented relative to research-based pharma and, for most of its history, quite distinct from research-based pharma. However, this sub-species of business model is changing, becoming larger, consolidated and less distinct from big pharma. Three specific sub-trends have contributed to this: the tendency of research-based pharma to develop generic arms; the growth of generics companies to become substantial and more technically competent; and the development of economic nationalism in some developing markets, leading to the growth of national champions. The archetype of the first approach is, of course, Sandoz, the Novartis generic business unit; but other leading research-based companies have developed – and are developing – stronger generic arms, such as Pfizer's Greenstone and Sanofi-aventis's Winthrop. Notably, these companies are not following a pure-play, lowest cost strategy but something more akin to a 'premium generic' strategy, similar to the differentiated brands used by retailers in consumer markets. Jeff George of Sandoz describes several strands of differentiation in their strategy:

'Sandoz derives competitive advantage from its expertise in the development, production and commercialization of differentiated products. Our portfolio ranges from advanced application forms such as oral solids to complex technologies, such as injectables, biosimilars, inhalers, transdermal patches, and implants.'

Jeff George, Sandoz

If the blurring of the generics/innovative distinction is one aspect of strategy variation, the consolidation and growth of generics firms is the other side of this picture. Leading companies that used to be classed as simple generics firms are both growing and expanding away from simple copies of off-patent molecules. Mylan's acquisition of Merck KGaA, Teva's acquisition of Barr and Ratiopharm and Watson's acquisition of Arrow are all examples of this. Warwick Smith of the British Generic Manufacturers' Association (BGMA) predicts the trend in this area:

'I think the top six could easily be 50 per cent of the market and I expect to see some continuing consolidation. My guess would be that we will see what's happening in other similar commodity type markets. You will get a polarization and you will lose the middle players. You'll end up with the niche players and the global players. And you will lose what 15 years ago was the bulk of the industry, which were the big national players.'

Warwick Smith, BGMA

Warwick Smith's well informed prediction did not preclude a third noticeable variation in this area, the rise of national champions supported by economic nationalism. As large, typically western, companies have acquired interests in emerging markets, a counter trend is developing towards a kind of economic nationalism in pharmaceuticals, including legislation to protect local manufacturers. Brazil, India and China all support local pharmaceutical industries that are currently basic generic manufacturers, although one would expect that they would try to progress up the ladder of technical complexity in due course.

These variations in strategy – convergence of generics and innovative products, growth and consolidation of generics firms and national champions – are particularly interesting, in that they seem to be aimed towards adapting to the habitats ignored by the research and development innovators and, to a lesser extent, by those firms depending on brands to help them penetrate emerging markets. Instead, the variations in generic strategies that involve moving upmarket seem to be adaptations to the core state provision habitat, with its demands for cheap but effective and good quality drugs. At the same time, building of scale and the national champions of the generics area suggest adaptation to a very low cost market, such as the Limited Choice habitat. Both Core state Provision and Limited Choice habitats are not, of course, restricted to emerging markets and will exist in developed markets too so, what appear at first to be emerging market strategies are in fact related to developed markets too and will influence fitness in a given habitat, irrespective of geography.

THE DRIVE TO DEMONSTRATE VALUE

A fourth significant variation in the strategies of pharmaceutical companies has been the focus of considerable resources on demonstrating the value of their products. It used to be traditional, when a new Chief Executive took office, to hear boast of the wonderful new products that were emerging from the pipeline. It is noticeable that, in recent times, emphasis has shifted to demonstrating the value of those products. Ken Frazier's first public statement on his appointment to Pfizer's top job in 2010 (mentioned earlier) was an example of just that. In my research, numerous other examples came up. For example, it is part of the future scenario planning of Merck, as described by Merv Turner:

'You could think about a future, which we call rationality where, yes, innovation is rewarded, but you absolutely have to have outcomes data in hand to demonstrate a value for the payer. And without that, you're just not going to get reimbursed.'

Merv Turner – Merck

The same idea of value demonstration was also mentioned by several research respondents with respect to the product development process. Angus Russell of Shire was typical of many who raised this point:

'I think there is a growing realization, in the whole industry, that value and reimbursement is something you need to contemplate almost at the point that you take a drug from research and nominate it for clinical development. You need to be thinking very carefully about what the value proposition is.'

Angus Russell, Shire

The drive to demonstrate value is shown in more than just the awareness of senior executives in the industry. Various firms are beginning to work with payers to introduce some form of pricing that is related to outcomes. For example, GSK entered into a deal with the United Kingdom's National Health Service that allows for a partial rebate if the performance of its kidney cancer drug, Votrient, does not match its rival, Pfizer's

Stutent. This arrangement, although novel, is an example of a broad class of variations in pharmaceutical pricing strategies. These include Bayer's Nexavar cancer drug, and two osteoporosis drugs, Novartis's Aclasta and Sanofi-aventis's Actonel. In various parts of Europe and the United States, pharmaceutical companies have agreed plans such as to provide a drug free if no improvement is seen after initial treatment, or, in the case of osteoporosis, to reimburse the payer if bone fractures occur despite the therapy.

Like variations in innovation, emerging markets and generics, these variations in the value demonstration part of pharma business models represent attempts to climb demanding fitness peaks. In particular, selection for some of these variations will allow firms to meet the fitness criteria of habitats that demand comparative value. Whilst to some extent comparative value is a fitness criteria in all of the habitats we've described, it will be especially true in the Advanced State Provision habitat. Given that this habitat may combine the volume of state provision with the higher margins associated with differentiated products, it's not hard to see why this is a desirable trait in some pharma business models.

THE POLARIZATION OF RISK MANAGEMENT

A fifth stream of variation in business model that emerged from the research concerns the management of strategic risk. The traditional pharma model has always contained a significant element of risk, but changes in the environment have amplified that risk, as described by David Redfern:

> 'In the 80s and 90s [Big Pharma] had broadly the same strategy. We spent about 15 per cent of our sales on research and development, often in the same areas and producing me-toos, and we commercialized what we produced, particularly in the Western markets and in the United States. And broadly that was successful but it's very clear that isn't going to be sustainable going forward.'

David Redfern, GSK

One response to this amplified risk has been diversification, as described by George Chressanthis:

> 'We've also seen many companies diversifying. They've acquired consumer healthcare, medical devices and diagnostic companies ... This moving of assets into related areas has two reasons behind it. It may become important when payers require a more integrated solution – for instance a diagnostic tool to accompany a pharmaceutical therapy – that can allow better targeting of patients or demonstrate that the therapy has achieved its goals. And it may allow better margins and lower risks than are available to the company by investing the same money into a pharmaceutical product alone.'

George Chressanthis, Fox School of Business

David Norton emphasized the risk management rationale behind diversification, from the position of a firm that has always been unusually diversified:

'The industry will still be a place for large multinationals [which] may not be necessarily pure play pharma companies. Some will be, but I think you see the diversification coming back into the industry. Johnson & Johnson has always been very diversified with consumer, diagnostics and devices. But if you look now, GSK is trying to expand its consumer business. Sanofi-aventis is trying to get back into the consumer business. Pfizer, who sold their consumer business to us, is trying to get back into the consumer business. And one of the rationales behind that is to smooth out the cycle of seeing huge ups and downs from patent expirations.'

David Norton, Johnson & Johnson

Boehringer Ingelheim, although different in scale and focus from Johnson & Johnson, expressed a similar sentiment:

'Something we see happening at the moment, that is going to continue, is diversification. We're in a cyclical behaviour pattern as an industry where, in the past, everybody wanted to be diversified and companies were actually quite radical … But in the 80s, everybody was focussing and now people like to be diversified again … I think that's a trend which will continue during the next years … Pfizer has bought Wyeth and they intend to keep the consumer healthcare business which they sold in 2006 to GSK. Merck may consider keeping its shares in the consumer healthcare business. For big firms with products the size of [something like] Zyprexa or Lipitor, it is very difficult to manage volatility over time. Diversification helps manage risk and volatility. I see that industry trend continuing in the industry. Boehringer Ingelheim has always been diversified with a strategic intent. Beyond classical pharma, we've always been in consumer health care. And we have biopharmaceutical and animal health production. We have a generics leg in the United States. I am not aware of any trend within our company or its shareholders to change that at this point in time.'

Bert Tjeenk Willink, Boehringer Ingelheim

The early 21st Century diversification of some pharma strategies does indeed echo a strategy of the 1960s and 1970s which was then reversed, but the more modern version seems to be more focussed and more related to core business; it typically involves other kinds of therapy rather than, as in the earlier wave, unrelated products. That said, the current wave of diversification is certainly a variation in business model, but what makes it especially interesting is that the major players in the industry seem to be polarising between those who are choosing to diversify, albeit in a related way, and those who are instead focussing heavily on research-based innovation to develop advanced therapies. David Redfern describes this well:

'So you've got the diversifiers, of which GSK is one, [along with] others like Novartis and Sanofi-aventis to some degree … Whilst developing innovative medicines remains the core of the business, [these companies] have chosen to allocate capital more broadly and invest in our more stable income flows, whether it's a consumer business, animal health, vaccines and also increasing our emerging market capability to try and develop a more stable income flow that is less susceptible to the sort of US blockbusters and then patent erosion. So that's one response. Clearly, BMS is doing something quite different [almost going] back to the biopharma business. You've got other companies like Merck and Pfizer who have chosen to consolidate, then you've

got Lilly and AstraZeneca, who are really banking on the old model and putting their emphasis very much on research and development to a greater or lesser extent.'

David Redfern, GSK

This polarization of approaches to risk management is a striking variation that will, in time, be selected for or against by both customers and investors. The latter are naturally taking great interest in the diversification versus focus approach since it directly impacts on the risk-return ratio that is fundamentally important to them. As Amit Roy of Nomura observes, however, investors may not allow Chief Executives the freedom to choose between diversification and focus for an indefinite period:

'Should a pharma CEO be the person who diversifies its company amongst drug development, generics distribution, vaccines, biotech, and so on? Or should it be the portfolio manager of investment stocks who takes that diversification position? I would argue that, unless the acquiring company brings something to the target that they're acquiring, some synergy or some skill set that improves it, unless that's the case, I'd argue that the portfolio manager is in the best situation to diversify risk and these companies should get on and do what they do best. And of course, it's the whole agency issue. A company itself would rather like to stay in business, but is that the best use of capital? I'm not a hundred per cent sure.'

Amit Roy, Nomura

From an evolutionary perspective, this variation and polarization of strategy represents an attempt to meet a fitness criterion that applies in all habitats, that of managing risk. As we'll discuss, it's an attempt that will be judged by both the customer and capital markets.

THE EXTENSION OF THE PHARMACEUTICAL VALUE PROPOSITION

The sixth and final type of business model variation to emerge from the research relates to both parts of a firm's strategy: what is offered and to whom. This is a shift away from selling medicines to health systems in order to help them achieve health outcomes, a shift towards directly taking responsibility for those health outcomes. In Chapter 5, we saw that disease patterns, value-seeking payers and new technology converged to create peaks in the landscape that demanded the prevention of disease and the management of the chronically ill. Variations in strategies that seem to be climbing up those peaks were observed in the research, although with a noticeable range of scope. Some of these variations were only limited in scope, an extension of the product and customer support model that has existed for many years. The latter suggested much larger, more radical variation of the value proposition that moved much further up the patient management value chain.

The first, limited, type of variation was described by David Redfern:

'I think in certain disease areas [disease management] may become more important. I see it happening relatively slowly. Take for example, asthma, which is a therapy area [GSK] knows well and has leadership in. In the United Kingdom, over the last five years or so, the interaction we have with GPs and primary healthcare trusts has become much more than about Serotide,

which is our leading medicine for asthma. We work much more with the primary healthcare trusts to help and manage their asthma patients better and that takes all sorts of different forms. We will arrange for specialists to visit the trust and the big GP practices to review their patients and so forth. In services, providing a more added-value approach to scientific information and disease management, I think the industry can have a facilitating role there.'

David Redfern GSK

A similar extended support strategy variation, but adapted for a more specialized therapy, was described by Angus Russell:

'I think there are certain areas that lend themselves to that [disease management approach] but you have to become really expert to do this. Our human genetic therapy business … doesn't only deal with producing therapies for the diseases; we have a very, very tight collaborative relationship with the physicians, the specialists, because they're very few in numbers.'

Angus Russell, Shire

These and other examples that emerged from the research are variations in strategy that appear to be adaptations to habitats where value is created by customer management; but they are relatively limited in scope and seem to represent steps rather than leaps towards new business models.

By contrast, a more significant extension of the pharmaceutical value proposition seems incipient in the approach of Johnson & Johnson:

'We're currently a consumer, diagnostic and medical device and a pharmaceutical business. If I look at the next 10 to 15 years, I would say we'll add two substantial legs to the armamentarium going forward. One will be a broader diagnostic business, not clinical diagnostic, but much more linked to therapeutic diagnostics. The other may well be services for the management of chronic disease. We have signed an agreement with one of the regions in Germany to manage their schizophrenic patients. That's a long term arrangement and it is not about drug management. It's about managing schizophrenic patients, ensuring that they have appropriate access to care, to provide [them with] access to medications, not only ours but in general, provided they have appropriate support mechanisms when they come out of hospitals.'

David Norton, Johnson & Johnson

The possibility of the pharmaceutical value proposition extending in this way towards something more akin to a disease management programme was mentioned by several research respondents. Disease management programmes, after an apparent false start in the 1990s, seem to be maturing into effective tools for managing healthcare costs (8). However, the industry's culture seems to be a hindrance to it climbing this particular fitness peak, as Rolf Badenhoop of ZS Associates points out:

'Another direction of development might well be that of value-added services, which we see more in med tech and diagnostics. This would involve setting up a disease management programme for a specific therapy area and using not only their own products but also others. I've not yet

seen that model emerge in pharma. Companies remain very product oriented and technological innovation is seen as the growth engine.'

Rolf Badenhoop, ZS Associates

Perhaps as a result of this culturally embedded reluctance to move away from product orientation, the most interesting developments in the prevention and management space are observed in the strategy variations of companies outside the research-based pharmaceutical industry. For example, Cisco's work with companies to provide on-site health management integrating technology, disease management and coaching, which showed significant cost savings (9). From a different technological direction but with the same aim is the strategy variation shown by Nestlé, with the establishment of Nestlé Health Science S.A. and the Nestlé Institute of Health Sciences in January 2011. To quote from its press release:

Nestlé today announced the creation of Nestlé Health Science S.A. and the Nestlé Institute of Health Sciences to pioneer a new industry between food and pharma. These two separate organizations will allow Nestlé to develop the innovative area of personalized health science nutrition to prevent and treat health conditions such as diabetes, obesity, cardiovascular disease and Alzheimer's disease, which are placing an unsustainable burden on the world's healthcare systems.'

Nestlé

It is the phrase 'new industry between food and pharmaceuticals' that is telling here, clearly indicating a strategy variation that is trying to fit a new habitat. The same is true of attempts to move beyond simple over the counter products into a new health maintenance space, as GSK is attempting with Alli, its weight loss product. This is an example of a strategy variation, towards prevention and enabled by their customer management capabilities in branding, that may be selected by market habitats that demand health maintenance and trusted brands rather than a technically advanced or low-cost value proposition.

What Cisco, Nestlé and others are doing are not variations in the strategy of pharmaceutical companies; but this does not mean they can't be selected by the environment to become an important part of the pharmaceutical market. It was, as discussed in Chapter 2, variations in the strategy of dye companies that led to the emergence of the modern pharmaceutical industry. In the same way, it seems likely that variations by Cisco, Nestlé or, closer to home, Johnson & Johnson and GSK, might contribute components to the business models of the future pharmaceutical industry.

In evolutionary terms, therefore, what we see are variations that are trying to climb those peaks where value is created by customer management of some kind, as opposed to innovative research or efficient operations. The customer to be managed may be the wealthy, in the case of the Wealthy Well habitat, or institutional buyers, in the case of Chronic Cost Containment or Mass Prophylaxis, or mass consumers, in the case of Get Well and Stay Well habitats.

This overview of observable strategy variations in the pharmaceutical industry is necessarily broad and high level. There are many more examples that could be cited and many lower order variations that could be described. But the six broad classes of strategy variation, restated for clarity in Table 6.1, are those that emerged most strongly from the research. In short, these are the six principle ways in which companies are varying what they do as they attempt to adapt to the changing pharma fitness landscape. It is from these that successful variations will be selected and amplified to form the industry's new business models.

Table 6.1 **The six major themes of strategy variation in the pharmaceutical industry**

Theme	Strategic imperative
The quest for innovation leadership	To create a clearly better clinically outcome
The expansion out of the developed markets	To address the needs of new customer types
The growth of generic approaches	To address the demand for low cost therapies
The drive to demonstrate value	To demonstrate comparative value
The polarization of risk management	To manage the risk associated with innovation
The extension of the pharmaceutical value proposition	To create value beyond that directly attributable to the product

These six broad groups of strategy variation indicate that what is actually happening in the industry is in line with the predictions of evolutionary theory and the fitness landscape. To point out just a couple of correlations, Herceptin is a step up innovation-based peaks – either Lazarus and Narcissus, Advanced State Provision or Pressure State habitat, depending on local context. Johnson & Johnson's ambitions for another leg of their business is a step up the Chronic Cost Containment peak. GSK's Alli weight management product and Nestlé's new pharmaceutical nutrition division are steps up the peak of Stay Well or perhaps Mass Prophylaxis. In short, what we can observe going on correlates to what the theory predicts: the evolution of new strategies that, when accompanied by corresponding capabilities and organizational structures, will amount to new business models adapted to fit the peaks of the fitness landscape.

Synergies and Diseconomies of Scope

We've now assembled almost all the knowledge we need to predict what new business models will evolve to occupy the pharmaceutical market of the future. We have a predicted fitness landscape, which evolutionary theory says should be populated in due course with 'fit' business models that meet its various demands. And we have evidence of variation in existing business models that, for all its complexity, seem to resolve into a number of broad directions of travel, each of which is a migration up one or more peaks of the fitness landscape. Simplistically, we might draw a line from the observed strategy variations to the endpoint implied by the fitness landscape. If we did, we might anticipate the evolution of 11 new pharma business models, each of which fits one and only one of the fitness landscapes' peaks.

However, there is one more tranche of knowledge to add to our deliberations before we predict what pharmaceutical business models will evolve. This is thinking from strategic management literature and it refines the 11 species prediction in a subtle but important way. In particular, we need to factor in what we know about the scale and scope of business models and what that tells us about their limits and design.

Scale, Scope and Synergy, Limits on Business Model Design

Research into why one type of firm works better than another is, literally, centuries old. Famously, Adam Smith's Wealth of Nations, in 1776, examined how and why a pin factory worked (that is, why it was more efficient than a similar number of cottage-based workers) and concluded that it was because of the specialization of workers and integration between different specialized processes. The modern incarnation of these specialization and integration ideas can be traced to the work of Lawrence and Lorsch in the 1960s. Their research into integration in complex organizations (10), again pointed to the need to balance specialization of sub-units with the coordination of those sub-units. Later, Burrell and Morgan's Congruency Hypothesis (11) pointed to the need for and the difficulty of achieving both macro-congruence (the fit of a unit or sub-process with its external, market environment) and micro-congruence (the fit of a process or unit with the rest of the organization). This latter hypothesis, for example, has been used to explain the effectiveness or otherwise of strategy-making processes in medical technology and pharmaceutical companies (12;13). Without taking too much of a digression into systems theory and the contingency approach, as it is called, the bottom line of this work is that the most effective organizations are those that manage to achieve both macro- and micro-congruence, a very difficult trick.

In plain English, this means 'what works is what fits' and by fit we mean fits with both the external market environment (the evolutionary habitat in our terms) and, critically, fits with other parts of the organization, its processes and culture. This is more than an abstract diversion into management research. It tells us that there may be limits to the effective size and scope of a business model as the costs or inefficiencies of coordinating the disparate parts of the organization start to outweigh any benefits of putting them together. The same problem is described by the concepts of economies and diseconomies of scales and scope. Traditional approaches to economics suggest that size is important and that the larger the size of a company the more efficient it is. However, various studies have also indicated that, beyond a certain size (which is context specific), efficiency declines with size. These economies and diseconomies of scale are closely related to the scope – the span of interests – of the company. A company with a narrow scope of interests might achieve economies of scale at a size where a more broadly focussed company might not because the coordination difficulties of the latter are greater than the former. In the pharmaceutical industry, this trade off between scale and scope has been shown in several pieces of research (14 – 16). This is a particularly complex area of research, with no definitive answers and lots of complicating factors, such as the nature of the industry studied, but we can draw a broad conclusion that the likely shape of the industry will be a balance between the drive for economies of scale and the counter veiling diseconomies of scope.

In practice, the balance point between a huge, efficient firm that operates many different business models and a more focussed, highly effective firm that attempts to dominate only one habitat will be determined by the synergy between different parts of the business. As Goold and Campbell described (17), synergy can be either external (derived from shared customers) or internal (derived from shared assets or resources).

Looking across the habitats predicted by evolutionary theory, we can see potential for both kinds. The distinctive competencies for Lazarus & Narcissus, Advanced State Provision and Pressure State habitats all rest on capabilities in innovative product development. The Core State Provision, Chronic Cost Containment and Mass Prophylaxis habitats each share the same institutional payer customers. Get Well and Stay Well habitats rely on brand management competencies and share customers. By contrast, there is little visible synergy between business models aimed at the Limited Choice and Wealthy Well habitats. The realities of what synergies can be achieved, therefore, will lead to business models that attempt to address a number of fitness habitats that are related by either customer type or asset and resource requirements. We might therefore expect neither 11 tightly focussed business models nor just one conglomerate business model but rather a number in between those two extremes, each of which balances scale and scope.

Taken together, the implications of the future pharma fitness landscape, the strategy variations observable today and the balancing forces of realizable synergies give us a good guide to what future business models will evolve to dominate the future of pharma. Each of those models will carry genes – capabilities, organizational routines – that we can trace back to existing business models, in the same way we can trace back our ancestry, but they will be fully adapted to the new world in which they will have to survive.

Seven Species in the Future of Pharma

Pulling together the strands of fact and theory discussed so far in this chapter, we can predict seven new species of pharma business model. Each species will include a number of firms and those firms will differ from other members of their species in detail, but they will be recognizably of the same species sharing similar strategies and capabilities. By contrast, members of different species will be able to look at each and recognize that they differ in strategy and capabilities. In the rest of this chapter, we'll look at what those species are likely to be.

MONSTER IMITATORS

The Monster Imitator is a phrase borrowed from Sidney Winter:

> 'Perhaps most interesting, we discovered quite unexpectedly the phenomenon known informally as "the monster imitator" ... Such a firm avoids the cost burdens of innovation and simply gobbles up what innovators elsewhere have made available.'

Sidney Winter (18)

The Monster Imitator business model will evolve in response to the selection pressures of the Core State Provision habitat and, to a lesser extent, the Limited Choice habitat. For both of these habitats, the need for comparative value translates, in the absence of new therapies that are strongly differentiated from generics, acceptable performance at the lowest possible cost. In the face of these demands, a Monster Innovator's value proposition will be focussed on cost and made possible by hyper-efficient operations economies of scale. This model is foreshadowed by today's generic firms but should not be mistaken for mere extension of them. Monster Imitators are likely to be of a scale that dwarfs even today's largest generic companies and will achieve an efficiency that makes today's lowest cost operations look profligate.

As a result of competition between Monster Imitators, the price of generics will be a small fraction of today's costs and almost negligible next to the cost of advanced, patented products. For firms adopting the Monster Innovator business model, scale will be everything and, operating on a global basis, they are likely to borrow ideas from very lean supply chains in other industries, such as airlines or retailing. Indeed, low cost airlines or Wal-Mart might be indicative of the lean operations and dedication to cost-cutting we might expect to see in Monster Imitator companies.

Offering only adequate quality and service and focussing tightly on the Core State Provision and Limited Choice habitats, we might expect firms operating this business model to hold the majority of the industry's volume by offering nothing more than the lowest possible price. Just like a biological species, this intense adaptation to a low cost market will preclude them from competing in any other habitat. We may already see the early signs of the evolution of Monster Imitators in the growth of Teva and other large, consolidating generics. But it may also be that this model comes to be adopted by a national champion from India, Brazil or China. In any event, the scale economies of Monster Imitators suggest that only a small number of them will dominate their habitat.

GENII

The Genius business model will emerge to meet the fitness criteria of the Advanced State Provision, Pressured State and Lazarus and Narcissus habitats. These three habitats share the need for clearly superior clinical efficacy and, with small adaptations for market access and patient advocacy capabilities, one business model will be able to address all of these habitats. At the core of the Genius value proposition will be clinically superior outcomes made possible by combining advanced biological and other technologies into very productive research and development. The Genius model may look superficially similar to present day research-based companies and biotechs, but the possibilities, challenges and risks associated with the new model are much greater than those of the old. In this business model, inventing, developing and commercializing new therapies will be everything and the way in which it invents and commercializes new products will employ all of the new technological and organizational developments discussed in Chapter 4. However, the extreme focus needed on innovation, and the costs involved, will make it unlikely that this species of business model will be able to survive outside of its high price habitats.

We see the antecedents of Genii in the 'pure-play' research-based strategies of Roche and others but it is by no means certain that Genii will consist only of the descendants of those players. The turbulence and uncertainty created by rapid technological change may lead to the emergence of new technological leaders, just as Amgen emerged from early biotechnologies. Also, conventional strategic wisdom would imply that an attractive and growing habitat will entice new capital into the market and the failure of one of the current research-based companies would create an acquisition target and entry path for such new entrants.

TRUST MANAGERS

The Trust Manager business model will evolve to meet the needs of the Get Well and Stay Well habitats, which demand trust above all else. The similarity of the two habitats will allow one business model to address both, with the differing pattern of customer engagement, episodic for the former and continuous for the latter, requiring only minor adaptation in capabilities. At the core of the Trust Manager business model will be the capability to create and maintain a brand that is trusted by the consumer who faces difficulty in making sense of health information. The forerunners of Trust Managers are OTC companies; but Trust Managers are likely, with the retrenchment of state provision, to greatly extend their range both in terms of therapeutic areas and engagement with the customer. We see the antecedents of Trust Managers in GSK's Alli and Pfizer's OTC Viagra, but also in functional foods and nutraceuticals, such as cholesterol-lowering margarine and fortified breakfast cereals. It is likely, however, that initiatives such as those from Nestlé that I have already described, will lead to a much more clinically oriented set of value propositions in this habitat.

DISEASE MANAGERS

The Disease Manager business model will arise to occupy the Chronic Cost Containment habitat. In this part of the market, the most important fitness criteria will be to minimize the overall cost of managing this large population of patients suffering from diabetes, asthma and cardiovascular diseases but also, increasingly, degenerative diseases such as Alzheimer's.

The core of the Disease Manager model will therefore be the combination of scientific knowledge and customer management capabilities to manage chronically ill patients cost effectively. This combination represents either backward integration by healthcare providers or forward integration by pharmaceutical companies. Both pathways may lead to a future Disease Manager business model that will have some characteristics of each progenitor, but which will be very different from either. We can see the forerunners of the Disease Manager model in what some healthcare organizations do now, but perhaps more importantly in the extended service of GSK in asthma and Shire in genetic therapy.

Johnson & Johnson's strategic ambitions may point to a more radical development of this model and Eli Lilly's cooperation with Boehringer Ingelheim to complete its diabetes portfolio may presage a Disease Manager approach for them. As with other business models, however, the very existence of this large, and potentially lucrative, habitat might lead new players to enter the market by acquisition, or otherwise.

LIFESTYLE MANAGERS

The Lifestyle Manager business model will arise to occupy the Mass Prophylaxis habitat. This part of the market, which demands the prevention of lifestyle related diseases, especially amongst high risk populations, is complementary to the Disease Manager business model, but offers a very different value proposition. At the core of Lifestyle Managers' business will be the combination of analytics, processes and therapies to identify patients, manage their behaviour and treat precursor conditions like hyperlipidaemia.

We can see forerunners of Lifestyle Managers in public health campaigns for improved diet, smoking and exercise; but AstraZeneca's shifting positioning of Crestor, towards metabolic syndrome prevention, might be a more telling lead indicator. More radically still, the Cisco at-office health management programme, which combines information and pharmaceutical technology, might indicate a more innovative Lifestyle Manager approach. Like the Disease Manager model, the Lifestyle Manager business model sits at the junction of other current business models, ranging from health and fitness to weight management and pharmaceuticals; and the new business model is likely to inherit some of its genes from each of them.

VALUE PICKERS

The Value Picker business model will arise to occupy the Value Pockets habitat. This habitat, which will be fragmented but still extensive and lucrative, will demand the creation of comparative value in the gaps left by Monster Imitators, Genii and those following other business models.

At the core of the Value Picker business model will be the ability re-innovate with existing molecules, reformulating them, developing new indications or new ways of combining or administering them so as to create comparative value in the pockets left behind by large scale business models. We can see the forerunners to this in what Norgine does with products like Movicol, for faecal compaction, creating value by re-innovating an existing molecule. However, the potential to find and exploit such value pockets might in future come from entirely new directions, as large scale business models rationalize their focus and new means of customer analytics and targeting allows firms to identify more granular customer needs. Value Pickers may not be able to command the volumes of Monster Imitators, nor the margins of Genii but, by combining reasonable volume, reasonable margins and reasonable business risk, it may be able to sustain a significant number of companies.

HEALTH CONCIERGES

The Health Concierge business model will be an adaptation to the needs of the Wealthy Well habitat. Like the parallel Lazarus and Narcissus habitat, this demands optimal clinical outcome; but, in this case, the outcome is health maintenance rather than cure or management of extant conditions. At the core of the Health Concierge business model will be highly personalized patient management made possible by the combination of genetic technology, patient monitoring, and new therapies, for pre-emptive screening, diagnosis and treatment.

The nearest forerunner to a Health Concierge is the personal physician, but the possibilities opened up by new technology are likely to render this approach susceptible to replacement by a business model that is larger in scale and wider in scope, in a manner analogous to financial services or travel management. We can see the early signs of Health Concierges in the regular screening and health consultations offered by healthcare providers, but the technological challenges and opportunities created by Biology 2.0 and the second therapeutic revolution suggest that their model might be displaced by more knowledge-intensive providers such as pharmaceutical companies.

As with the other business models based on customer management, Health Concierges will look quite different from traditional pharmaceutical companies; but in their use of advanced technologies like biomarkers, genetic screening and preventative therapies, they will be more like pharmaceutical companies than personal physicians.

Interim Species and Umbrella Companies

In the preceding section, I have predicted the evolution of seven new pharmaceutical business models. This prediction is the logical conclusion of combining the theory of evolution, the facts about the social and technological environments shaping the pharmaceutical market and the evidence of variation in current industry business models. Each business model will, like a species, be an adaptation to its environment resulting from a process of variation, selection and amplification. Moreover, each business model will trade off the ability to survive in other habitats in order to meet the demanding fitness criteria of its chosen part of the landscape. Each business model will, like a species, roam its part of the pharma market to the exclusion of other, less fit, models.

This seven species prediction provides a framework, an overarching view of the future of pharma that allows us, in the following chapters, to draw implications for firms seeking to be part of the future. Before doing so, there are some complexities of the model we need briefly to explore and clarify.

The first is that a business model is not the same thing as a firm. A firm may choose to adopt only one business model and in doing so reduce the diseconomies of scope created by operating a multi-business model organization. But that choice necessarily limits the scale of the company and, for the large pharmaceutical companies, the constraints of, say, the Genius model may not match its corporate ambitions. Pharmaceutical companies driven by the need for scale will, therefore, probably attempt to implement several business models at once in order to occupy several habitats and reap the commensurate rewards. This will create problems of coordination, but very large firms may have little choice.

The second is that evolution is a gradual process, even during a spurt that punctuates an episode of equilibrium. Between the eozostrodon of the Triassic era and homo sapiens today lie many generations of intermediate species. In the same way, the evolution of, for example, Monster Imitators with their focus on costs and Genii focussed on innovation will be preceded by numerous, hybrid, intermediate forms that seem to fit neither category. The convergence of generics and research-based models may be an example of this. These interim species will evolve, become extinct or survive through some special case of isolation from selection pressures, much like the duck-billed platypus.

The third is that the boundaries between habitats and species will never be perfectly defined. There will always be a grey area between, for example, whether a treatment fits within Core State Provision or Advanced State Provision, or even where the boundary between state and consumer provision lies. Habitat boundaries will vary with geography and time. As a result, companies will usually compete with the other companies in the business model, but there will be instances where business models compete. We see this now, for example, when generic companies threaten to run comparative health economics outcomes research against advanced branded therapies.

Notwithstanding these complexities, this combination of theory and fact predicts a pharma landscape of hills and troughs occupied by seven major species, mostly occupying their habitats and competing against their cousins, except at the edges of their territory. Even allowing for the inexactitudes of prediction, this picture poses questions for firms wanting to live in that landscape. There are questions to be answered about what capabilities, what DNA will be needed and questions about how to make the evolutionary transition faster and better than other firms. That will be the subject of the remainder of this book.

Reference List

(1)   Gould, S.J. and Eldredge, N. 1977. Punctuated Equilibria: The Tempo and Mode of Evolution Reconsidered. *Paleobiology*; 3(2):115–51.

(2)   Hannah, L. 1999. Marshall's Trees and the Global Forest: Were 'Giant Redwoods' Any Different? in *Learning by Doing, in Markets, Firms and Countries. National Bureau of Economic Research*, edited by N.R. Lamoreaux, , D.M.G. Raff, and P. Temin. Chicago, Ill: University of Chicago Press, pp. 253–294.

(3)   Fligstein, N. 1990. *The Transformation of Corporate Control*. Boston, MA: Harvard University Press.

(4)   Ormerod, P., Johns, H. and Smith, L. 2001. *Marshall's Trees and the Global Forest: The Extinction Pattern of Capitalism's Global Firms*. [online] http://www.volterra.co.uk/2001 Available from: URL: www.volterra.co.uk [accessed: 5 January, 2011].

(5)   Ormerod, P. 2005. *Why Most Things Fail and How to Avoid It*. London: Faber and Faber.

(6)   Simonian, H. 2010. Roche to Slash Staff Numbers by 6%. *Financial Times*. 17 November, 2010.

(7)   Kelley, T. and Cortez, M. 2010. AstraZeneca's Risky Bet on Drug Discovery. *Business Week Online*, 29 December 2010. Available at: http://www.businessweek.com/magazine/content/11_02/b4210020402634.htm [accessed: 5 January 2011].

(8)   Pfizer Seeks More Asia Research Partnerships. 2010. http://in reuters com/article/idINIndia-51534220100916 [accessed: 5 January 2011].

(9)   Weselby, C. *Improving Health at the Office*. 2009. [online] Available at: http://www.cerner.com [accessed: 5 January 2011].

(10)   Lawrence, P.R. and Lorsch, J.W. 1967. Differentiation and Integration in Complex Organisations. *Administrative Science Quarterly*; 12(1):1–47.

(11)   Burrell, G. and Morgan, G. 1979. *Sociological Paradigms and Organizational Analysis*. 1st ed. Beverley Hills:CA: Sage.

(12)   Smith, B.D. 2003. The Effectiveness of Marketing Strategy Making Processes in Medical Markets. *Cranfield School of Management*, PhD Thesis.

(13)   Smith, B.D. 2003. Success and Failure in Marketing Strategy Making: Results of an Empirical Study Across Medical Markets. *International Journal of Medical Marketing*; 3(4):287–315.

(14)   Henderson, R. and Cockburn, I. 1996. Scale, Scope, and Spillovers: The Determinants of Research Productivity in Drug Discovery. *RAND Journal of Economics*; 27(1):32–59.

(15)   Graves, S.B. and Langowitz, N.S. 1992. Innovative Output and Firm Size in the Pharmaceutical Industry. *International Journal of Production Economics*; 27(1):83–90.

(16)   Cockburn, I.M. and Henderson, R.M. 2001. Scale and Scope in Drug Development: Unpacking the Advantages of Size in Pharmaceutical Research. *Journal of Health Economics*; 20(6):1033–57.

(17)   Goold, M. and Campbell, A. 1998. Desperately Seeking Synergy. *Harvard Business Review*; 76(5):131–44.

(18)   Winter, S.G. 2005. Developing Evolutionary Theory for Economics and Management. in *Great Minds in Management: The Theory of Process Development*, edited by K.G. Smith and M.A. Hitt. Oxford: Oxford University Press. pp. 509–46.

PART **III** *A Changed Industry*

7

Sex, Forced Moves and Good Tricks: What New Capabilities Will Be Needed to Survive and Thrive in the Future of Pharma?

'The competitive advantage of firms stems from dynamic capabilities rooted in high performance routines operating inside the firm, embedded in the firm's processes, and conditioned by its history.'

David J. Teece (1)

In his masterly discussion of evolutionary theory, the cognitive scientist Daniel Dennett coined two memorable phrases that have embedded themselves in the vocabulary of the subject (2). He talks of 'Good Tricks', a behavioural talent that protects or enhances dramatically a species' chance of survival. He also talks of 'Forced Moves', a way of behaving that is dictated by reason and to which there is no sensible alternative. This chapter is about the Good Tricks and Forced Moves that pharmaceutical companies will develop as they adapt to the future fitness landscape of their industry.

In Chapters 5 and 6, we saw how a combination of evolutionary theory, observations of current strategy variations in the pharmaceutical market and knowledge from the strategic management literature allows us to predict the evolution of the pharmaceutical industry's business models into seven new, distinct species that will be well adapted to their particular habitats. We then began the process of examining what those new business models will look like. At a broad level, we identified their strategies in terms of what they would offer and to whom. That led logically to what their distinctive competencies would have to be in order to realize these strategies. In doing so, we characterized some but not all components of each of their business models. These are restated in Table 7.1 for the sake of clarity.

Table 7.1 The seven new species of pharmaceutical business model

Name of Business Model	Habitats to which it is adapted	Nature of Value Proposition	Distinctive Competencies
The Monster Imitator	Core Social Provision Limited Choice	Very low cost, off patent drugs at adequate quality and service levels	Identify those products most in demand by institutional payers and poor self-payers then manufacture and distribute those products at the lowest possible cost consistent with minimum quality and service standards.
The Genii	Lazarus and Narcissus Advanced State Provision Pressured State	Advanced therapies that have demonstrably better clinical outcome than very low cost generic alternatives	Identify the most lucrative unmet clinical needs; discover and develop products to meet those needs. Demonstrate their clinical and economic superiority to existing therapies and marshal political support for their provision.
The Trust Manager	Get Well Stay Well	Trusted drugs, nutraceuticals and related programmes that treat minor ailments and enable the maintenance of good health	Identify the most lucrative opportunities to treat minor ailments and maintain health. Provide branded therapies and programmes that are sufficiently effective and trusted to command a market premium compared to very low cost generics.
The Disease Manager	Chronic Cost Containment	Complete therapy provision and management for the effective management of chronic conditions at the lowest cost consistent with adequate quality and service levels	Develop and manage therapies and programmes that are trusted to manage chronic conditions more cost effectively than in-house state provision and at adequate quality standards.
The Lifestyle Manager	Mass Prophylaxis	Provision and management of therapies and programmes that minimize the development of more serious conditions at the lowest cost and adequate quality and service levels	Identify the most lucrative opportunities to reduce state healthcare costs by prevention of lifestyle related conditions. Develop and provide therapies and programmes that prevent these conditions more cost effectively than in-house state provision and at adequate quality standards.
The Value Picker	Value Pockets	Innovative new drugs and adaptations of off patent drugs that provide comparative context specific value when compared to low cost generics	Identify specific clinical or usage contexts in which greater value can be created for institutional payers compared to current therapies. Commercialize new or reformulated therapies that meet the economic and clinical needs of those contexts.
The Health Concierge	Wealthy Well	Provision and management of therapy and programmes that resolve non life-threatening ailments and maintain health more effectively that state provided alternatives	Develop and manage therapies and comprehensive programmes that maintain health and resolve minor conditions more effectively and with a superior patient experience to the state provided alternative.

This characterization of the seven business models is useful, but far from complete; and it is not sufficient if, for example, we want to guide the development of a particular company. There are two major gaps yet to fill. Firstly, the distinctive competencies give only the most superficial, top level view of what a business model must deliver. They say little about the many contributing capabilities that a firm must master in order to make such competency possible. Also, what we have so far says little about how firms might organize themselves to develop and deliver their value propositions in their chosen habitats. What remains therefore, following the definition of a business model given in Chapter 5 (page 93), is to uncover the capabilities required by each business model and the organizational structures associated with them. Organizational structures are the subject of the next chapter but first, in this chapter, I will describe what the research for this book discovered about the necessary capabilities of each business model, both their Forced Moves and their Good Tricks. I will start by clarifying the concept of organizational capabilities because it is a complex area and easy to be misled by the terminology. That clarification reveals that organizational capabilities are best understood as being in three different categories: basic, differentiating and dynamic. I will then use that three category framework to describe the Forced Moves (the capabilities that will be essential for all seven of the business models), and the Good Tricks (the capabilities that will be essential to particular business models). As we will see, the Good Tricks have a further special category of dynamic capabilities, but I will cover that in due course. By the end of this chapter I will have described the capabilities that each of the seven business models will develop and we will understand better what firms will need to do to survive and thrive in the future of pharma.

Core, Differentiating and Dynamic: Understanding Capabilities

The term 'capabilities' has, unlike many terms in management research, a superficial clarity and familiarity; like segmentation, strengths and insights, it seems obvious what it means. But, also like those terms, familiarity can be misleading. If we are really going to understand how firms will live in the new fitness landscape we need to invoke the spirit of Voltaire again and define what exactly we mean by capability. In particular, we need to be clear about four things: Who or what is capable? What is a capability? What are the different varieties of capability? What are capabilities made from? In this section, I will quickly clarify those things, so that we can understand and explain the capabilities of the different business models more effectively.

Firstly, we need to be clear that we are talking about *organizational* capability, the ability of an organization, as distinct from the capability of an individual, to do something well. Although individual capabilities are important and contribute to organizational capabilities, it is the latter that we are examining here. And, by organization, we do not necessarily mean just the business unit or the firm. As I will discuss in Chapter 8, we could mean a network, an alliance or some other set of relationships that creates an entity that acts together. So, by organizational capability, we mean the ability of a collection of people who work together, whatever their contractual relationships, to perform some task.

We also need to be clear that a capability is not the same as the outcome one hopes to get by employing that capability. New drug approvals, low operating costs and high market share are each the result of employing several capabilities together and each of them may amount to a distinctive competency, but they are not organizational capabilities. An organizational capability is a lower level construct than a distinctive competency. For example, designing and running good clinical trials is an organizational capability that contributes to getting new drug approvals. Efficient procurement is an organizational capability that contributes to low operating costs. Key Opinion Leader management is an organizational capability that contributes to high market share. But we have to be careful not to get too reductionist here. Being able to punctuate promotional literature correctly is not usually counted an organizational capability, for example, even though it is important. Prahalad and Hamel (3) considered that a firm might have five or six capabilities that contributed to its competitive strength. Typical of the semantic difficulties academics have, however, they called them core competencies. To be clear, when I use the term organizational capabilities I mean a handful of things that the organization is capable of, which contribute importantly to its competitiveness.

This definition allows us to consider the differences between the three different types of capability. Importantly, different types of capability seem to have different effects on firms' competitiveness. That is not to say that some are more important than others and categorizing capabilities is not the same as ranking them. Rather, capabilities seem to fall into the three distinct categories of core, differentiating and dynamic.

Core capabilities are those that a firm must have just to take part in a market. They are the organizational capability equivalent of Dennett's Forced Moves because, if a firm did not develop them, it would simply die. Collis called them:

'those that reflect the ability of a firm to perform its basic activities.'

Collis (4)

In the pharmaceutical industry, manufacturing to high quality standards and sticking to international rules about clinical trials are examples of core capabilities. As those examples illustrate, core capabilities are often the things that firms outsource first, if they can, because specialized suppliers can be more efficient and effective than an in-house operation. Core capabilities, if done well, may contribute to efficiency but even when done excellently they contribute little to competitiveness because everybody in the market is already doing this particular thing well enough. As Michael Porter famously said, operational effectiveness is not the same as competitive advantage (5).

On the other hand, messing up core capabilities can get a firm into serious trouble. To take one example of many in the industry, Genzyme's manufacturing problems at its Allston plant in 2009/10 led to a large fine and shortages of its Gaucher's disease treatment Cerezyme, which was the only approved treatment option available at the time. From the customers' point of view, core capabilities are those that meet what Herzberg called hygiene needs. By that, he meant needs that do not satisfy us when they are met, but which make us dissatisfied when they are unmet, such as, for example, our need for food, water and shelter. Typically, hygiene needs and, therefore, core capabilities do not vary much between customers, so they tend to be similar in all business models. However, core capabilities change as the environment changes, as we will discuss shortly.

Differentiating capabilities are the equivalent of Dennett's Good Tricks, because they greatly enhance the ability of a business model to survive and enable a firm's competitive strength. Dosi and his co-authors expressed it well:

'We then arrive at the idea that a successful large corporation derives its competitive strength from a small number of capability clusters where it can sustain a leadership position.'

Dosi, Nelson and Winter (6)

In Herzberg's terms, differentiating capabilities are those that address a customer's higher needs, the ones that drive their purchasing behaviour. Since these tend to differ by customer type, the differentiating capabilities needed by one business model are often different from those required by another. Being superior to the competition with respect to a differentiating capability is the source (along with dynamic capabilities, discussed later) of a firm's competitive advantage. For that reason, differentiating capabilities tend not to be outsourced so readily as core capabilities, in case this allows them to be copied by rivals. Examples of differentiating capabilities include Roche's capability to co-develop oncology drugs and therapeutics, or Almirall's capability to form complementary distribution relationships with other speciality pharmaceutical companies.

Interestingly, capabilities that are initially differentiating capabilities tend slowly to become core capabilities as a market matures. At one time, performing clinical trials that met international standards was a differentiator in the pharmaceutical market. Now, with the help of specialist suppliers, it is an important but core capability. The ability to manufacture biologics is presently a differentiating capability, but shows every sign of soon becoming a core capability.

Dennett's ideas of Forced Moves and Good Tricks fit well onto what we know about organizational capabilities being either core or differentiating; but he also introduced a third idea that is very useful in understanding how business models evolve. He described how, in most examples of evolution, the process is slow, its pace limited by the gradual accumulation of small variations that are selected by the environment one by one. He paints a picture of a slow, wandering ascent up the fitness peak, but then he introduces the idea of metaphorical cranes that can quickly pick up a species and put it up on higher ground. In reality, a crane would be some trait that allowed species to vary quicker by taking on board new genes rather than waiting for the existing ones to mutate. And, of course, biological evolution has developed a marvellous crane that does just that, we call it sex. The third and final category of capabilities, which the management researchers call dynamic capabilities, is the equivalent of sex; they allow business models to adapt much more quickly than by simple mutation of their existing capabilities.

Dynamic capabilities is a term that often misleads, so it needs a little explaining. Dynamic capabilities are those that allow a firm to be dynamic, in other words, to adapt and change. The concept was first defined by David Teece and his co-workers who described dynamic capabilities as:

'the firm's ability to build, integrate and reconfigure internal and external competencies to address rapidly changing environments.'

Teece, Pisano and Shuen (7)

Because we are examining the evolution of pharmaceutical business models in rapidly changing environments, this definition is important and tells us a lot. Dynamic capabilities are processes that act on other capabilities to change them and create new differentiating capabilities. In Dennet's terms, dynamic capabilities allow business models to develop Good Tricks. For example, Veronique Ambrosini and her colleagues described dynamic capabilities as a four part process of reconfiguration, leveraging, learning and creative integration of other assets, resources and capabilities (8). Other researcher have described how they arise from the history of the organization (9) and cannot be bought in, only developed in-house (10) so they become 'embedded in the firm'(11).

Unlike differentiating capabilities, dynamic capabilities do not act on the customer directly; instead they act on the organization, reshaping it and allowing it to develop new differentiating capabilities. Examples of dynamic capabilities are much rarer than those of differentiating capabilities, which might explain why so many firms become extinct rather than survive in periods of rapid change. Those dynamic capabilities that do exist involve making sense of environmental changes, developing new or transforming old capabilities to match the new environment and then employing them. We might for instance, see some of the examples of strategy variation that I described in Chapter 6 as examples of dynamic capabilities at work. Sensing that emerging market consumers will buy their own drugs is the result of some market understanding capability. Similarly, when a western big pharma company develops branded generics for those markets and creates joint ventures with local companies to distribute them, they are showing the outward signs of dynamic capabilities working inside the company.

Having clarified what we mean by organizational capabilities and distinguished between the different categories of capabilities, I can complete this section by answering the last of the four questions I raised earlier: What are organizational capabilities made from?

The answer takes us back, briefly, to Chapter 2, the theories of evolutionary economics and the work of Nelson and Winter. Organizational capabilities, whether they are basic, differentiating or dynamic, arise from activity. More particularly, being organizational rather than individual, they arise from some pattern of interaction between different individuals and between parts of the organization. These patterns need not be fixed in stone; they can and do vary to meet specific circumstances. But, although they can vary, they are repeated patterns of interaction and they are neither ad hoc nor random. They are sometimes tacit and unwritten, sometimes explicit and codified, most often a mixture of the two. Academics call these semi-codified patterns of variable but repeated interaction 'organizational routines'. In business, we tend to look at larger, structured aggregates of organizational routines and call them business processes.

Organizational routines are analogous to the genes of an organization, acting as stores of knowledge about how to do things and making the process of doing things, if not automatic then, to some degree, mindless. In other words, organizational capabilities are made from a collection of organizational routines. We can unravel this chain further to make the role of organizational routines and capabilities even clearer. As shown in Figure 7.1, a firm's success depends on it being able to create customer preference. A firm creates customer preference by offering the customer a value proposition that is superior to that the competition. The ability to make such a proposition depends on the firm having the appropriate and necessary distinctive competency. The distinctive competency is the result of a conjunction of a set of appropriate organizational capabilities, both core and differentiating. Each organizational capability is the result of a number of organizational routines. This important, if slightly obvious, connectivity is what David Teece is explaining in the quote at the head of this chapter.

Figure 7.1 The link between organizational success and organizational routines

This whistle stop review of what we know about organizational capabilities helps us to know what we are looking for in the capabilities of new pharmaceutical business models. What we need to identify are three distinct kinds of capability:

- Core capabilities: the 'Forced Moves' that, if not performed well, will condemn a firm to failure.
- Differentiating capabilities: the 'Good Tricks' that, if performed well, will enable a firm to perform better than its competitors in its chosen habitat.
- Dynamic capabilities: the 'Cranes' that, if used well, will enable a firm to evolve faster and better than its rivals.

Identifying these capabilities is the task of the remainder of this chapter. Once done, it will prompt the question of what to do about developing any capabilities that we currently lack but need for the future. As we now know, capability development is about identifying, building and assembling new organizational routines. That will be covered in Chapter 9.

Core Capabilities

Clearly, there are perhaps tens or hundreds of things that might '*reflect the ability of a firm to perform its basic activities*', to use Collis's words, cited earlier. These include capabilities to set up and run a functioning company and perform the many basic but essential tasks associated with inventing, making and commercializing a pharmaceutical value proposition in a mature, competitive and regulated market.

The vast majority of these core capabilities will almost certainly not change in the pharmaceutical market of the future. Firms will still need to recruit, retain and develop staff, keep accounts and myriad other tasks; but they will either have these capabilities or acquire them relatively easily. Much more important and interesting for our purposes are core capabilities that will be significantly different from today and which, if not developed well, will lead to the extinction of the company. In fact, the research revealed four of these newly critical core capabilities, and these are described overleaf.

ADVANCED REGULATORY AND QUALITY CAPABILITIES

The commercialization of new drugs has, since the advent of regulation in the 1960s, always entailed overcoming what the industry sometimes refers to as the three regulatory hurdles of safety, quality and efficacy. Without the core capability to prove that its products meet the mandated standards for all three of those requirements, a pharmaceutical business model is not viable. These requirements have spread internationally to create the present situation, where no significant market is accessible without overcoming these hurdles.

The capabilities needed to overcome these three hurdles will not lessen and, in most cases, will increase quite significantly for three mutually reinforcing reasons. The first is that the height of these hurdles reflects, in part, a society's level of risk aversion, as discussed in Chapter 3. As our societies become more litigious and more risk averse, the safety, quality and efficacy standards required by regulatory authorities are increasing all the time. The second factor is the growth in importance of emerging markets, which implies the need to overcome regulatory barriers in those newly important countries, often with data that recognizes local population genotypes. That is not in any way to imply the prior dumping of unsafe products on poor countries, rather to recognize that they are now important markets that must be addressed. The third, and perhaps most significant, factor is the increasing complexity of the products being developed and claims being made. Consider, for example, the regulatory burden for a new treatment for Alzheimer's that combined a therapeutic diagnostic, a biologic molecule and a novel, nanotechnology-based delivery mechanism.

Taken together, therefore, these three factors mean that the core regulatory capability required to operate a pharmaceutical company is shifting quite fundamentally. We might summarize that as being a shift from: gaining approval for a small molecule, with modest claims, in a smallish number of similar markets with reasonable risk tolerance, to: gaining approval for a big molecule, with strong claims, in a large number of differing markets with very high risk aversion.

Developing such a capability will, for existing pharma companies, be an incremental process of building on current core capabilities. But, even with a strong base, the difference between former and future regulatory demands will make it challenging for pharmaceutical companies to support these core capabilities.

REPUTATION AND TRUST MANAGEMENT

For three obvious reasons, how the pharmaceutical industry is seen by outsiders has always been even more important than for other major industries. Firstly, the industry deals – quite literally – in life and death, so trust is very important. Secondly, the industry is particularly susceptible to public policy and public spending choices. Finally, the scale and capital intensiveness of the industry means that outside investors are usually very important. These three factors are significant because two of the social shifts described in Chapter 3 relate to the pharmaceutical industry's relationships with two of its major constituencies, the public and its investors. Contemplative investors and an informed, sceptical, proactive public imply that, in the future, those relationships will be both more important and more problematic.

The burgeoning importance of the relationship with the public is both direct and indirect. Directly, the public will make the purchase decision in four of the habitats and influence it in the others. Indirectly, the public will, through their politicians, direct government policy in areas such as intellectual property protection, regulatory approval, health budgets and priorities, and sales and marketing practices. Because of this influence, it is important that a vociferous group of industry critics has developed that seek to influence the public's view. As an early prototype of this group, the Australian academic John Braithwaite may sound extreme but he is not atypical of his peers:

'Every scholar who has surveyed the comparative evidence on bribery in international trade has concluded that pharmaceuticals is one of the most corrupt, if not the most corrupt, of industries.'

John Braithwaite (12)

It is not difficult to anticipate the impact a public influenced by Dr Braithwaite or his apologists might have on the industry. Even without this influence, the nature of the relationship between the industry and the public might become problematic as the public becomes more sceptical, internet informed and proactive, at the same time as the complexity of the clinical and health economic decisions increases. The media-fuelled activism about BioMarin's Firdapse for Lambert-Eaton Myasthenic Syndrome is but a small example of that.

At the same time, investors are reexamining the position in their portfolio of pharmaceutical companies and becoming more active, as Carl Icahn's intervention in Genzyme illustrates. Given turbulent market conditions, variable financial performance and significant turnover of pharma companies CEOs, managing contemplative and active investors will become even more important than before. Taken together, these factors mean that the industry's previous core capability in reputation management will, like that in regulatory, need to improve markedly. That improvement in capability might be summarized as going from: maintaining a good relationship with a relatively passive and well-disposed public and investor base, to: improving the relationship with an active and sceptical set of investors and public. Achieving such a capability will require pharma companies to engage with the public and investors in a way that is much more effective than they do today. It will be sufficiently different from the present to be a new core capability in reputation and trust management.

DEALING WITH MARKET HETEROGENEITY

The very term 'the pharmaceutical market' implies a single market, but has always been something of a misnomer; the industry consists of many sectors that differ from each other.

Traditionally, the industry has described and managed that heterogeneity by categorization of market areas, for example, by primary or secondary care, therapy areas or geographies. However, for all their differences, these different parts of the market shared enough similarities to allow them to be managed by one organizational structure with minor sub-divisions.

However, fitness landscape and business models described in Chapters 5 and 6 reveal a fragmentation of the pharmaceutical market at both a strategic and operational level. We will discuss the strategic implications of this later in this chapter (under the section about dynamic capabilities), but the operational fragmentation implies a new core capability. As we discussed in Chapter 3, the buying context of pharmaceutical markets is becoming more variable. Different customers, with different commercial arrangements that change over time and according to different clinical, geographical and economic contexts, all suggest that the core capabilities embedded in pharmaceutical commercial models will need to change.

This might be summarized as moving from: dealing with a large number of organizational customers whose commercial arrangement varied a little along a few dimensions, to: dealing with a huge number of customers, organizational, individual and hybrids of the two, whose commercial arrangements will vary greatly along multiple dimensions. Achieving such a capability will require pharma companies to understand and respond to this fragmentation, probably employing sophisticated analytics. It will be so different from their present practices that it will be a new core capability in dealing with market heterogeneity.

FRUGALITY

The core capabilities in regulatory and quality, trust and reputation management and managing market heterogeneity will all raise the bar for what is needed just to stay in the pharmaceutical game. It is worth pausing for a moment to reflect that all the effort required to build these new core capabilities will add only to operational effectiveness and not at all to competitive advantage. The necessary capability development work will make heavy demands on the leadership and resources of the industry. However, those demands will be amplified by the emergence of a fourth new core capability, frugality.

Historically, few would have applied the adjective 'frugal' to the pharmaceutical industry and, whilst not suggesting it is spendthrift, the industry's spend in all parts of its value chain has been commensurate with the large gross margins it has been able to command. This is less true for the generic part of the industry, of course, but even that area, with its comparators set by prices of research-based companies, is not the acme of parsimony. As customer value becomes the primary fitness criteria for pharmaceutical business models, frugality will become a core capability. This will be true to an extreme degree in those habitats such as Core State Provision and Limited Choice. But even in areas where innovation and service allow differentiation, such as advanced state provision and chronic cost containment, the comparator will be the ultra-low, commodity pricing of the Monster Imitators, rendering a degree of frugality imperative. Brian McNamee put it well during the research interviews. Asked about what will be the most notable changes in the industry, he said:

'Well, I think frugality. It's going to be a lot leaner in the future. I think that people are going to have to learn to prosper in an environment where there's less money available, whether it be in the commercial spend or in other areas. I think that people will need to make much clearer decisions about their portfolio, so they don't have duplicate programmes, or drop programmes

if they're not an early leader in the field. I think also it's going to be the era where there's going to be less money overall spent on research and development than there has been historically.'

Brian McNamee, CSL

The same idea cropped up as one of the scenarios that Merck foresees as a possible future aspect of the market:

'... you could think about a world – the world that we call frugality – which is, that costs become the absolute dominant factor in our industry and innovation fundamentally is not rewarded.'

Merv Turner, Merck

Frugality will be a core capability of all the business models we have described, but will undoubtedly be more significant to those, like Monster Imitators, that do not involve scientific or customer management innovation. We can summarize the shift in this capability as being from: a world in which frugality was only a secondary consideration, for part of the industry, to: one in which frugality is an important core capability, even for the whole industry.

Dennett's term Forced Moves is a good one for these four core capabilities. Each of them will be forced on the industry by its changing social and technological environment. Whilst recognizable as descendants of what firms do today, each of them will be sufficiently different from the core capabilities of today's pharma business models to be called new requirements. Each of them will be difficult enough to achieve but, as is the nature of core capabilities, employing them will be necessary but not sufficient to survive in the future of pharma. Making these Forced Moves will merely set the scene for the development and employment of the differentiating capabilities that are necessary to competitive advantage. It is these that we turn to next.

Differentiating Capabilities

By their very nature, the seven new business models will differ in the cluster of differentiating capabilities they need. For each, this will be dictated by strategy and the distinctive competency needed to address its habitat. Importantly, whilst each of the business models will focus on creating value either through innovative product development, efficient operations and supply chain or customer management, they will need to differentiate across the whole length of the value chain. Our research found that, whilst differentiating capabilities are emerging primarily in that part of the value chain on which the business model is focussed, other parts of the value chain are evolving too. The picture that emerges is of really quite dramatic developments in differentiating capabilities and these are described below, structured by individual business model type.

MONSTER IMITATORS

The distinctive competency of the Monster Imitator is, as we've discussed, being able to identify those products most in demand by institutional payers and poor self-payers and then to manufacture and distribute those products at the lowest possible cost consistent with minimum quality and service standards. To do this in a way that is competitively superior to the competition will require four differentiating capabilities:

Spotting big fish

The first differentiating capability for a Monster Imitator will be to identify which products to imitate. The lean nature of the business model allows little room for experimentation or for being a market follower. This means that the firm must be capable of analysing the market potential of products long before they lose patent protected exclusivity. Further, they must be able to make sound judgements about the commercial risk associated with imitating each potential product. The desired differentiating capability will be to identify those products that combine high potential returns with a low commercial risk.

Patent busting

Complementing the 'winner spotting' capability will be a differentiating capability to break intellectual property protection as early as possible. Again, the lean nature of the business model allows little room for speculative challenges that waste money and legal resources. Instead, Monster Imitators will become patent busters extraordinaire. As we'll discuss later, this will inevitably become a legal arms race between the patent lawyers of the Monster Imitators and those of the Genii, and the Imitators who win this race will have a competitive advantage. The desired differentiating capability will be to identify those legal challenges that are worth making and then overcoming the defensive tactics of the patent holding Genii.

Ultra efficient operations

Once a winning target has been identified and the legal battle won, a third differentiating capability will become important, this time in the operations area. Particularly when imitating more complex products, biosimilars for example, it will be very important to assimilate manufacturing techniques quickly, whilst driving costs out of the process. Again, the business model leaves little room for learning by trial and error. Some Monster Imitators will choose to outsource manufacturing, in which the challenge will be to find and work with appropriate suppliers. In either case, the desired differentiating capability will be to make the product cheaper than any other, whilst meeting the minimum quality and service level standards.

Strategic account management

Alongside identifying and producing the product, the remaining differentiating capability of Monster Imitators will be to commercialize it in a way that optimizes share and margin. Whilst this is the same challenge facing other business models, the detail of this capability will be very different for the Monster Imitator. It will involve pushing volume through commercial arrangements with payers and not creating 'pull' through sales forces. The desired differentiating capability, therefore, will be to understand how to drive market penetration through large customers.

These four differentiating capabilities can all be seen in their embryonic form in the current business models of present day generics firms. However, as previously discussed, it would be a mistake to see the Monster Imitator as a mere extrapolation of today's generic companies. The alacrity with which they will deploy these differentiating capabilities will be an order of magnitude higher than present day generic companies. Winner spotting and patent busting will be more aggressive and will be aided by cost conscious payers. Operating efficiency, enabled by scale and new technology, will be much higher than today. Commercial operations, enabled by new sales and marketing processes, will be much leaner and yet more aggressive than a typical generic firm. The firms that implement the Monster Imitator business model will make even the best of today's generic companies look like gentle minnows. They will be fearsome competitors.

GENII

The distinctive competency of the Genii will be to identify the most lucrative unmet clinical needs and then bring products that meet those needs to the market. When operating in the Advanced State Provision habitat, they will also need to demonstrate their clinical and economic superiority to ultra low cost generics therapies and, in the Pressured State habitat, marshal political support for their provision. To do this in a way that is competitively superior to the competition will require four differentiating capabilities:

Spotting viable markets

An essential differentiating capability for the Genius business model will be to 'pick winners'. However, the nature of this capability will be very different from the analogous capability in Monster Imitators. It will, like the Monster Imitator model, combine the assessment of market attractiveness and success probability, but the components of those two factors will be very different. Market attractiveness for innovative treatments will be difficult to assess, involving estimates of penetration into novel markets and judgements about price elasticity and competitive activity. Success probability will be equally problematic, combining assessments of technical, clinical and commercial risk. The nature of the business model employed by Genii is that failure will be costly, so firms who can 'pick winners' well will have considerable competitive advantage. The desired capability will be to accurately judge the risk-adjusted return on investment for each new product development.

New product commercialization

The most obvious differentiating capability for the Genius business model will be the ability to invent and commercialize new products. Invention capabilities may be in-house, acquired from outside or, perhaps most commonly, a combination of both. When innovation is in-house, it will require solving the problems of research and development productivity that hinder current business models, enhancing creativity, reducing bureaucratic barriers and enabling the 'early, cheap fail' of molecules in development. When the innovation is externalized, it will require effective scanning of the discovery environment to spot potential products early. It will also require the ability to make the firm an appealing partner to attractive discoverers who, inevitably, will have their choice of suitors. In either case, future innovation capability will be wider than the pharmaceutical expertise of traditional research-based pharma. It will require the synthesis of several streams of knowledge, including pharmaceutical, diagnostics, materials and broader scientific understanding. The desired differentiating capability will be to bring to market new products of incomparable efficacy.

Intellectual property defence

The Genius model, when executed well, will create molecules of huge commercial potential. This will, unavoidably, attract the attention of fast following Monster Imitators and so it requires the development of a third differentiating capability in intellectual property defence. To counter the Monster Imitators' 'patent busting' capability, Genii will need the differentiating capability of making imitation as difficult as possible for as long as possible.

Intelligent operational strategy

Whilst efficient operations will not be the focus of the Genii, operations strategy will be the source of at least one differentiating capability. Even the high margins commanded by truly innovative products will not, in the context of a value driven market, make operational efficiency irrelevant. Firms operating the Genius business model will always face the challenge of optimizing operational efficiency, whilst both maintaining quality standards and avoiding leakage of proprietary knowledge, especially when the product is technically complex. In practical terms this may often involve the choice between relatively costly in-house operations and outsourcing, with less direct control over quality and intellectual property protection. Firms that make this judgement well will have a competitive advantage over their rivals. The desired capability will be to select and execute operations and supply chain strategies that are appropriate to the cost, quality and intellectual property context.

Value proposition development

The fact that Genii will need to address three habitats implies the need for a triad of differentiating capabilities in the customer management part of the value chain. The Lazarus and Narcissus habitat will demand capabilities in developing channels to market and marketing strategies for this new end user group. The Advanced State Provision habitat will require capabilities in demonstrating comparative value and working with market access authorities against the background of very low cost generics. The Pressured State habitat will demand capabilities in working with patient advocacy groups and in political lobbying in order to open and widen market opportunities. The desired capabilities for Genii in customer management are therefore complicated by the needs of the three habitats, but they may be summarized as the ability to translate an innovative product into a compelling value proposition.

These four differentiating capabilities of Genii can all be seen developing in the current business models of present day research-based firms. However, as previously discussed, it would be a mistake to see the Genii as a simple extrapolation of today's innovative companies. The potential benefits and the risks of failure associated with the Genius model are much greater than even the most innovative of today's companies. For that reason, innovation management, operations and customer management will each have to face different, more extreme challenges than those by a typical research-based firm today. However, firms that successfully execute the Genius business model will indeed have little to fear from other business models.

TRUST MANAGERS

The distinctive competency of the Trust Manager business model will be to identify the most lucrative opportunities to treat minor ailments and maintain health, then to provide branded therapies and programmes that are sufficiently effective and trusted to command a market premium, compared to very low cost generics. Trust Managers will need to allow for the demands of both the Get Well and the Stay Well habitats, but the needs of these two will be sufficiently similar to be met by variations within one Trust Manager business model. To compete effectively, Trust Managers will require five differentiating capabilities:

Market creation

The first differentiating capability of the Trust Manager model will be to identify overt and latent parts of the market where a high-trust customer relationship can create value in either health maintenance or managing minor ailments. Since the Get Well and Stay Well habitats will occupy a space between retreating state provision, simple OTC markets and functional food, this will mean developing new markets. It will involve deep understanding of consumers' extant and, more especially, latent health needs and judging the viability of those market opportunities. The desired capability, therefore, will be to create and build on genuine market insight into consumer health needs.

Branded proposition development

Having gained valuable insight into the needs of the Stay Well or Get Well habitats, the second differentiating capability of Trust Managers will be to develop compelling value propositions based upon those insights. These will include on new or adapted molecules, novel formulations and delivery vehicles and ICT enabled support programmes. In any case, the desired capability will be to create a value proposition that effectively restores or maintains health and is trusted to do so to such a degree that it commands a premium over its OTC comparators.

Intelligent operational strategy

Given market creation and a novel, differentiated value proposition, the third differentiating capability of the Trust Manager business model will be in the operational area. Operational challenges will be similar to those facing the Genii, in that they will require balancing the needs of low-cost operations against the need to maintain quality and uniqueness. This will demand careful judgement as to when to outsource, and when not to do so. As with Genii, the desired capability will be to select and execute operations and supply chain strategies that are appropriate to the cost, quality and intellectual property context, albeit within a very different scientific and cost environment from habitats occupied by the Genii.

Channel management

Get Well and Stay Well habitats will both require channels to access consumers, whether via traditional retail channels, online channels or both. Whatever the details of channel strategy, the ability to establish and manage channels to market effectively will be a differentiating capability. The desired capability, therefore, will be to establish and manage appropriate and profitable routes to market.

Brand management

The strength of corporate and product brands will be essential to the competitiveness of the Trust Manager business model and so building and maintaining brands will be the differentiating capability arguably most central to the model. This will involve deep customer insight and effective marketing communications management. The desired capability will be to build a brand that is trusted sufficiently by consumers to command strong customer preference.

These five differentiating capabilities of Trust Managers are less visible in current pharmaceutical business models than those of Market Imitators or Genii. Their precursors are only partly observable in current OTC business models and, to a limited extent, the fitness industry. The Trust Managers' dependence on pharmaceutical science as the basis of their value proposition will, however, mean that it is still a species of pharmaceutical company. This will, indeed, be a market habitat situated between traditional pharma, food and the fitness industry and will require differentiating capabilities that are significant developments of those currently seen in all of those three sectors. But, in carving out that new space, firms that successfully adopt the Trust Manager business model will be largely immune from competition from other business models.

DISEASE MANAGERS

The distinctive competency of the Disease Manager business model will be to develop and manage therapies and programmes that are trusted to manage chronic conditions more cost effectively than in-house state provision and at adequate quality standards. To compete effectively, a firm operating a Disease Manager business model would need to develop and employ three differentiating capabilities:

Actuarial capabilities

The first differentiating capability of an effective Disease Manager will be to identify where it can create value at a profit. Since the model involves taking on the risk associated with a chronically ill population, this will mean combining clinical and actuarial knowledge to select what business to take and to structure commercial arrangements. The desired differentiating capability will be to select disease areas and treatment contexts that are financially attractive and which are a good fit with the firm's particular strengths.

Combined product and service design

An effective Disease Manager would need to construct a value proposition that was both compelling to the payer and had a high probability of generating a good return for the firm. This would be a complex product and service development task, including clinical considerations but also factoring in many commercial risk factors, such as variation in patient population profiles and the political risk of adverse events. The desired differentiating capability would be to design a product and service offer that created customer preference whilst generating a viable risk adjusted return on investment.

Service execution

An important differentiating capability of a Disease Manager will be that of executing efficiently and ethically against a comparator of a state provider. This would involve complex clinical considerations, process management and the ability to tailor the service to both payer and patient needs. Further, it would require careful management of reputation risk. The desired differentiating capability is to deliver good patient outcomes at an appropriate rate of return.

These three differentiating capabilities can only be observed to a very limited extent in current pharmaceutical business models. Prototypes can be seen in some medical technology markets, in dialysis management and of course, in healthcare providers. However, the differentiating capability profile of Disease Managers is more likely to be a blend of pharma company and healthcare provider, with the scientific knowledge of the former making it a species of pharmaceutical company rather than a variant of a healthcare provider. Implemented well, the Disease Manager business model greatly reduces the costs of chronic care and so creates a large profit pool of a level currently unavailable to product only pharmaceutical companies. Its combination of product and service capabilities will make it very hard for companies using other business models to compete.

LIFESTYLE MANAGERS

The distinctive competency of the Lifestyle Manager business model will be to identify the most lucrative opportunities in preventative healthcare and then provide therapeutic programmes that prevent these conditions more cost effectively than in-house state provision and at adequate quality standards. To compete effectively, a Lifestyle Manager firm would need to develop and employ four differentiating capabilities:

Distinguish manageable opportunities

The first differentiating capability of the Lifestyle Manager will be the ability to separate out, from the complexity of lifestyle related health issues, opportunities to improve public health. This will involve combining biological, sociological and other knowledge sources to identify those patient populations that are both at risk and amenable to prophylactic treatment. The desired differentiating capability will be to identify patient populations where preventative intervention generates the greatest return.

Combined product development

Central to the Lifestyle Manager business model will be a value proposition that includes therapeutic products capable of preventing or delaying serious diseases. The value proposition may also include delivery technology and behaviour management processes based on information technology. The desired differentiating capability will be to create products that greatly reduce lifestyle-related diseases amongst the targeted populations.

Patient engagement

The success of the Lifestyle Manager business model will depend on the ability to develop committed engagement, over long periods of time, of target patients. This will involve expertise from social marketing and knowledge of customer relationship management processes. It will be characterized by high levels of patient compliance and low levels of patient dropout. The desired capability will be to ensure long term, committed patient compliance with preventative health programmes.

Value demonstration

The long term nature of the Lifestyle Manager value proposition means that the value it creates will be large but difficult to demonstrate and quantify compared to short term acute therapies. In order to win and retain payers, effective Lifestyle Managers will, therefore, need to gather and use epidemiological and outcome data to demonstrate the continual value created by their activity. The desired capability will be to demonstrate the comparative value to payers.

The Lifestyle Manager business model is a novel application of the pharmaceutical industry's knowledge assets and, with the exception of the pharmacological part of the product development process, these four differentiating capabilities are as yet barely present in the industry. Some precursors can be seen in current clinical trial activity and in patient compliance programmes. Outside the industry, some early forms of the necessary capabilities are seen in public health programmes such as smoking cessation. The great strength of Lifestyle Managers will lie in the combination of these capability clusters. With good execution, the Lifestyle Manager business model will make a dramatic difference to health, happiness and wealth of many societies. By addressing a habitat not currently well addressed by either governments or the industry, it will create value and a profit pool that other business models will find hard to access.

VALUE PICKERS

The distinctive competency of the Value Picker business model will be to identify specific clinical or usage contexts in which greater value can be created for institutional payers, compared to current therapies. Having done so, they will then need to commercialize new or reformulated therapies that meet the economic and clinical needs of those contexts. To be effective, Value Pickers will employ four differentiating capabilities:

Niche opening

The initial differentiating capability development of the Value Picker business model will be its ability to identify value pockets which, by definition, will be hidden in the nooks and crannies between the other, much larger scale, business models. This will involve matching unmet patient and payer needs with the untapped potential of product combinations, reformulations and delivery methods. The desired differentiating capability will be to spot junctures between customer needs and technical possibilities that others have failed to spot.

Agile and parsimonious development

The nature of the Value Picker business model, with its relatively small-scale value pockets, will make it necessary for companies employing that model to develop products in a different way to those following other business models. This will involve development processes that are less technically advanced but more agile and parsimonious than those of other business models. The desired differentiating capability will be to reconfigure existing knowledge into a new value proposition quickly and relatively cheaply.

Asymmetric marketing

The competitive context of the Value Picker business model, operating in the gaps between much larger scale models, means that making itself heard against the noise of other larger players, will be an important differentiating capability. It will involve mastering a range of indirect marketing channels and maximizing word-of-mouth effects, rather than competing for share of voice through traditional marketing channels. The desired differentiating capability will be to communicate to customers with an effectiveness that is disproportionate to the resources available.

Astute differentiation maintenance

In order to maintain the differentiation of its value proposition, the Value Picker will need to defend its intellectual property rights. Given the nature of its innovation, this is likely through a subtle combination of patent, copyright, branding and other methods rather than relying heavily on strong patents alone. The desired differentiating capability will be to make copying not worth the effort involved.

Although their development is as yet incomplete, many of the differentiating capabilities of the Value Picker business model can be observed in the activity of current pharma business models, particularly in late stage life cycle management. But the well-developed Value Picker, with these capabilities refined to be much more effective than present day practice, will be a strong business model, capable of generating significant value and relatively protected from competition from other business models.

HEALTH CONCIERGES

The distinctive competency of the Health Concierge business model will be to develop and manage therapies and comprehensive programmes that maintain health and resolve minor conditions more effectively and with a superior patient experience than the state provided alternative. It will achieve this by employing four differentiating capabilities.

Value aggregation

The nature of the Health Concierge business model is that it will need to create value across a very wide range of clinical, patient and usage contexts. As a consequence, an important differentiating capability will be combining the capabilities of multiple partners to create a comprehensive service and therapy value proposition. This will involve synthesizing several knowledge assets, including biological, information technology and service provision. The desired differentiating capability will be to create a comprehensive range of health management solutions from a complementary but disparate network of assets.

Value customization

The essence of the Health Concierge business model will be its ability to customize its service to its individual customers, however their needs vary over time. This will involve maintaining a deep, intimate knowledge of each patient's situation over a long period and constructing a service and product package that meets almost all of the patients' needs. The desired differentiating capability will be to deliver a comprehensive care package that is demonstrably better than any alternative.

Aspirational brand management

The Health Concierge business model will rely on a strong brand image with values that include implicit trust and status. Creating and maintaining such a brand will involve understanding the motivations of target customers as well as effective brand management processes. The desired outcome will be to be seen as a brand that customers trust unreservedly and to which non-customers aspire. The desired differentiating capability will be to create a brand to which all potential customers aspire.

Customer experience excellence

Customer perception of and preference for the Health Concierge business model will depend as much on their experience of it as on the clinical outcomes. Achieving an appropriate customer experience will involve understanding the customer journey and the ability to manage the entire process to a consistently high standard. The desired capability will be to create a flawless, comforting experience that far exceeds other healthcare experiences.

Since the Health Concierge business model is an extensive evolution from existing pharma models, these four differentiating capabilities are not obvious in present day practice. Some of them can be observed in premium health services and others in luxury goods companies, but the Health Concierge business model will combine those with the scientific expertise of a research-based pharmaceutical company, making it different from all three current business models. When this combination of differentiating capabilities is employed well, companies operating the Health Concierge model will become the unassailable preference for patients in the Wealthy Well habitat.

Dynamic Capabilities

We have so far identified that all pharmaceutical business models will have to make some Forced Moves and develop the four core capabilities described above just to exist in the pharmaceutical market of the future. We have also drawn out the Good Tricks, the various differentiating capabilities that will be characteristic of each of the seven new business models. Both core and differentiating capabilities will be necessary for a firm to survive and exist in its chosen habitat or habitats.

However, we have also noted that these capabilities do not currently exist in pharmaceutical companies or indeed in any other companies. We can observe prototypical forms of them in existing pharma business models. We see embryonic frugality in the consolidating generics companies, nascent commercialization of advanced therapies in the value-based pricing of some research-based companies and budding niche opening in some speciality pharma companies. Just as significantly, we see good examples of channel management capabilities in consumer goods companies, actuarial capabilities in health insurance companies and aspirational brand management in some luxury goods companies. But the evolution of old pharma business models to new ones is likely to be very slow, too slow, if it relies on the random variation of firms' internal organizational routines. To make that evolution possible at a pace commensurate with environmental change, and so avoid extinction, firms will need a crane to help them climb the fitness peaks. In other words, they are going to need some dynamic capabilities.

To use Ambrosini's words (see page 128) companies that wish to adapt successfully to the future of pharma will have to reconfigure, leverage, learn and creatively integrate their existing resources as well as those of other firms to create these new core and differentiating capabilities. The exact blend and nature of these will vary depending on what organizational capabilities a firm already has and what it needs to develop, but the research unearthed five main dynamic capabilities that will be required.

MARKET INSIGHT CREATION

As a starting point for developing new core and differentiating capabilities, firms will need the ability to create market insight. This much-abused term refers to knowledge about the market that is valuable, rare, hard to copy and upon which organization can act (13). It is not the same as the mountains of data, information and operational knowledge that many firms have and which gives them little competitive advantage. Creating market insight involves synthesizing multiple sources of information, using a combination of inductive and deductive methods to transform that knowledge into true insight then using that insight to direct strategy. It is, therefore, a dynamic capability, acting on the internal resources of the firm and enabling adaptation.

STRATEGY-MAKING CAPABILITIES

The development of new capabilities will inevitably require resources that, equally inevitably, will be constrained. So, a necessary precursor to developing new capabilities will be a firm's ability to allocate resources effectively. Since the pattern of a firm's resource allocation decisions is what we call strategy, firms will need strong strategy-making capabilities before they can develop their organizational capabilities. This does not simply mean they have to be good at formal planning. Strong strategy usually emerges from a mixture of planning, incrementalism and external forces that is congruent to the firm's specific context (14). To adapt their organizational capabilities successfully, companies will need to develop the ability to craft a mixture of strategy-making processes that fit context, rather than blindly mimicking the strategic planning textbook or consultant's 'best practice'. Because that congruent process will act on the internal resources of the firm and enables it to adapt to change, it is a dynamic capability.

STRATEGY EXECUTION CAPABILITIES

Core and differentiating capabilities only become important when they are brought to bear on the market via the implementation of strategy. Unfortunately, we know that strategy implementation is problematic in many companies and is hindered by many internal constraints, particularly intra-organizational conflict and individual motivation and commitment (15;16). To ensure employment of their new core and differentiating capabilities, firms will need the ability to predict and pre-empt barriers to strategy implementation. Because this ability will act on internal factors and will enable adaptation, it is a dynamic capability.

ORGANIZATIONAL LEARNING CAPABILITIES

The development and employment of new organizational capabilities, both core and differentiating, will be built on the firm's knowledge assets. To ensure that its capabilities will keep pace with its competition and the market's demands, firms will need to ensure that its stock of knowledge is maintained and expanded continually. This knowledge accumulation process, commonly called organizational learning, occurs via a spiral of assumption testing, revision and retesting (17) and is hindered by numerous tangible and intangible organizational traits and behaviours. To enable organizational learning, firms will need to develop their learning spiral processes and manage its barriers. Since organization learning acts upon internal knowledge assets and resources, it is a dynamic capability.

MULTIPLE BUSINESS COORDINATION CAPABILITIES

For some larger firms, realizing their corporate goals will not be possible within the constraints of a single habitat or business model. They will therefore need to manage a business that incorporates two or more business models, with the inherent antagonism and risk of diluting or blurring capabilities. This will involve managing antagonism, realizing synergy and avoiding the dilution of capabilities (18–20). Since all of these activities act upon the internal processes of the firms multiple business models, this is a dynamic capability.

These five dynamic capabilities can all be observed in current pharmaceutical industry business models, but the performance of the industry during the first decade of the 21st Century suggests that it is not able to adapt to the changing market conditions with sufficient speed and sensitivity. This strongly implies that the dynamic capabilities of the industry are inadequate in the context of a rapidly and fundamentally changing social and technological environment. The corollary of that inadequacy is, of course, that pharmaceutical companies will need to improve their dynamic capabilities or risk extinction.

A Step Forward in Understanding the Seven Business Models

At the beginning of this chapter, I promised to describe the capabilities that each of the seven business models will develop and so improve our understanding of what firms will need to do to survive and thrive in the future of pharma. By elaborating on the nature of organizational capabilities and then specifying the core, differentiating and dynamic capabilities implied by the new business models, I hope I have fulfilled that promise. For the sake of clarity, the organizational capabilities described are summarized in Figure 7.2. With this explication of necessary capabilities, we are now left with one other component of the new business models to discuss, that of organizational structures. That is the subject of Chapter 8.

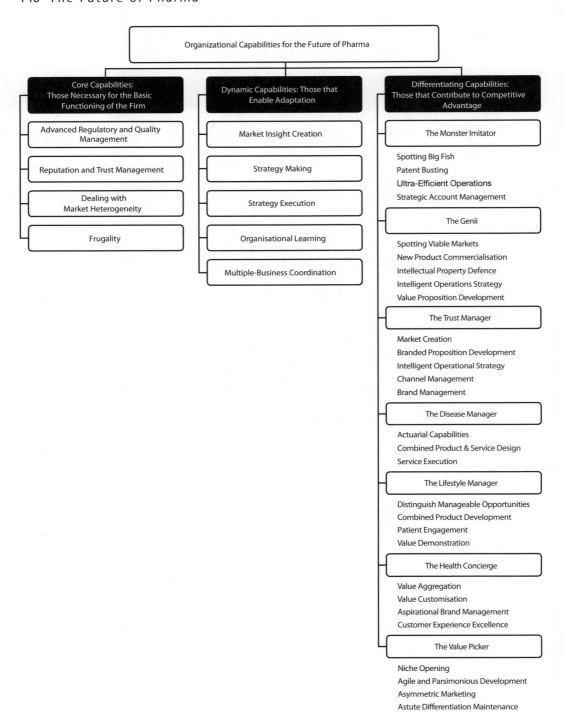

Figure 7.2   The organizational capabilities needed in the future of pharma

References

(1)   Teece, D. and Pisano, G. 1994. The Dynamic Capabilities of Firms: An Introduction. *Industrial & Corporate Change*; 3(3):537–56.

(2)   Dennett, D.C. 1995. *Darwin's Dangerous Idea*. London: Allen Lane.

(3)   Prahalad, C.K. and Hamel, G. 1990. The Core Competence of the Corporation. *Harvard Business Review*, 68(3):79–91.

(4)   Collis, D.J. 1994. Research Note: How Valuable are Organizational Capabilities? *Strategic Management Journal*; 15:143–52.

(5)   Porter, M.E. 1996. What is Strategy? *Harvard Business Review*; 74(6):61–78.

(6)   Dosi, G., Nelson, R.R. and Winter, S.G. 2010. *The Nature and Dynamics of Organizational Capabilitie*s. 1st edition. Oxford: Oxford University Press.

(7)   Teece, D.J., Pisano, G.P. and Shuen, A. 1997. Dynamic Capabilities and Strategic Management. *Strategic Management Journal*; 18(7):509–33.

(8)   Ambrosini, V., Bowman, C. and Collier, N. 2009. Dynamic Capabilities: An Exploration of How Firms Renew their Resource Base. *British Journal of Management*; 20:S9–S24.

(9)   Zollo, M. and Winter, S.G. 2002. Deliberate Learning and the Evolution of Dynamic Capabilities. *Organization Science*; 13(3):339–51.

(10)   Makadok, R. 2001. Towards a Synthesis of the Resource-based and Dynamic Capability Views of the Rent Creation. *Strategic Management Journal*; 22(5):387.

(11)   Eisenhardt, K.M. and Martin, J.A. Dynamic Capabilities: What are They? *Strategic Management Journal*; 21(10/11):1105.

(12)   Braithwaite, J. 1986. The Corrupt Industry. *New Internationalist*; November 1986(165).

(13)   Smith, B.D. and Raspin, P.J. 2008. *Creating Market Insight*. 1st ed. London: Wiley.

(14)   Smith, B.D. 2005. *Making Marketing Happen*. Oxford: Elsevier.

(15)   Smith, B.D. 2009. Maybe I Will, Maybe I Won't: What the Connected Perspectives of Motivation Theory and Organizational Commitment May Contribute to our Understanding of Strategy Implementation. *Journal of Strategic Marketing*; 17(6):469–81.

(16)   Smith, B.D. 2011. Turf Wars: What the Intraorganizational Conflict Literature May Contribute to Our Understanding of Marketing Strategy Literature Implementation. *Journal of Strategic Marketing*; 19(1):25–42.

(17)   Nonaka, I. 1994. A Dynamic Theory of Organizational Knowledge Creation. *Organization Science*; 5(1):14–24.

(18)   Martin, J.A. and Eisenhardt, K.M. 2001. Exploring Cross-Business Synergies. *Academy of Management Proceedings*; p. H1-H6.

(19)   Martin, J.A. and Eisenhardt, K.M. 2003. Cross-Business Synergy: Recombination, Modularity and the Multibusiness Team. *Academy of Management Journal*; 1–6.

(20)   Martin, J.A. and Eisenhardt, K.M. 2010. Rewiring: Cross-Business Unit Collaborations in Multi-Business Organizations. *Academy of Management Journal*; 53(2):265–301.

8 *Flat, Focussed Tribes: Organizational Structures in the Future of Pharma*

'The corporation as we know it is unlikely to survive in the next 25 years. Legally and financially, yes. But not structurally and economically.'

Peter Drucker (1)

In this book, we have made good use of the analogies between the biological evolution of species and the economic evolution of business models. Both evolve in response to environmental change. In both cases, variation, selection and replication lead to the climbing of 'fitness peaks', which we observe as exquisite adaptation to a particular habitat. Looking for the detailed mechanism, we observe that both genes and organizational routines are replicators that drive the behaviour of their interactor, either an organism or a business model. Both genes and organizational routines act indirectly, expressing themselves through either proteins or organizational capabilities respectively. Ultimately, this is reflected in the characteristics of the organism or firm that allow it to survive in its chosen habitat, which biologists call the phenotype and management scientists call the business model. In biology, we describe these characteristics in terms of the organism's physical and behavioural characteristics.

So far, we have described the survival-enabling behavioural characteristics of the business model, which we called distinctive competencies. But the observant reader will have noticed that we've said nothing about the physical characteristics, the shape and form, of the business model. In other words, we have yet to examine what biologists call morphology and management scientists call organizational structure.

To address that gap we will discuss in this chapter how the structure of pharmaceutical business models will adapt to the environment. Since we have already discussed the strategy and capabilities of these models, this will complete the description of the business model as we defined it earlier in Chapter 5 (page 93). Obviously, this structural adaptation will be needed in order to allow firms to develop and employ their organizational routines and organizational capabilities and so bring their distinctive competencies to bear.

In particular, we will answer the four key questions about the structure of organizations. The first of these is about the nature of the firm. Which of the business models are worth us considering? This is a textbook question of corporate level strategy and the answer is of fundamental importance to the future of the business. We see firms grapple with this decision when firms like Procter and Gamble and AkzoNobel decide to divest their pharmaceutical interests whilst others, like Nestlé or the many new biotech start-ups and spin-offs, begin to enter it.

The second question is about the breadth of the firm. How many of these business models should a firm attempt to operate at once? In management science, this is a question about horizontal integration and getting the answer right and will be critical to the success of large pharmaceutical companies in particular. We can see pharmaceutical companies struggle with this question today as we observe the divergence between those, like GSK, Pfizer and Sanofi-aventis, who are spreading their businesses across several habitats and those, like Roche, AstraZeneca and Lilly, who seem to be focussing more on the Genius model alone.

The third question is about boundaries of the firm. How much of the business model should be done by the firm itself rather than by partners and suppliers? This is a question of vertical integration and getting the answer right will determine the speed and effectiveness with which a firm will be able to build and deploy its chosen business model. We see firms experimenting with the answer to this question today as they outsource some functions, form alliances and partnerships to do some things but chose to keep some activities in-house.

The final question is about excellence. How should firms organize the core of their organization – what they do themselves rather than outsource – so that they are able to meet the fitness criteria of their habitat faster and better than their rivals? This involves questions of intra-organizational structure and getting the answer right will be fundamental to firm performance. We see firms trying to answer this question as they restructure their research and development teams into specialized units and their sales teams into key account teams.

Clearly, the answers to these four questions are sequential; the answer to the first influences the second, and so on, until the combined set of answers provides an insight into the organizational structure of firms in the future of pharma. The rest of this chapter will follow this four question arrangement, discussing the considerations inherent in each question and answer before, at the end of the chapter, coming to some general conclusions about the way pharmaceutical business models will adapt their structures and organizational forms. The conclusion will suggest (not for the first time!) that Peter Drucker had remarkable foresight.

The Direction Question: Which Pharmaceutical Business Models Are Worth Considering?

The direction question is one of textbook corporate strategy and the standard approach is a portfolio methodology using a tool such as directional policy matrix (2;3). In this method, two independent considerations – the attractiveness of the business and the probability of winning it – are combined to guide allocation of resources between the businesses. The two considerations are of course multifactorial. Attractiveness combines issues such as market size, growth rates and profitability, whilst probability of winning depends on the fit between the firm's various current (or possible) capabilities and what the market requires. The result of a well-executed directional policy matrix is not a binary yes/no decision; it is a spectrum of resource allocation decisions, ranging from invest to divest, across the various business options. This seems the obvious way to approach choosing which business model to adopt, but research suggests that pharmaceutical companies are finding it of limited use in practice.

For the purposes of adapting to the future of pharma, directional policy matrix and similar portfolio tools are crude and show the limitations of their origins. They grew from early techniques, like the famous Boston Consulting Group matrix with its familiar 'cash cows' and 'dogs', that were developed to differentiate *between* mature markets rather than emerging habitats or divisions *within* markets. This history has two implications in our context. First of all, most companies already in the pharmaceutical market, or considering entry into it, have capabilities that have some fit with the business models but also have big gaps. This means that, except at the extremes, there are only relatively subtle differences between the probabilities of each company winning in each business habitat.

Secondly, in a period of market turbulence like that facing the pharmaceutical industry, it is very hard to estimate their size, growth, margins and other attractiveness factors. This means that each of the business models may differ in attractiveness, but the margin of error is so large that they overlap greatly. The upshot of this is that, in most cases, pharmaceutical companies applying portfolio management tools in the context of this single, fragmenting and turbulent market find that they provide little practical guidance; what they get is a picture where most of the business models cluster in the middle of the two-by-two matrix. This isn't universally true. Even with the problems associated with its implementation, the directional policy matrix helps companies to rule out the most extreme options. It would tell a small, specialist pharma company with strong intellectual property assets in, say, oncology that the Genius model was a better short term investment than, say, the Monster Imitator model. Similarly, it might tell a large generic company that developing a Trust Manager model would be a long-term strategy option but not a short-term fix. But, by and large, the portfolio management techniques have limited utility when applied within a market that is going through an evolutionary spurt.

These limitations of the standard strategic management tool mean that it usually only gives us a rough starting point for how to design the firm. It will rule out some options but still leave us with a broad range of possible models to follow. That is part of the reason why we observe many pharmaceutical companies spreading their bets; it is a way of 'buying options' in business models that might or might not be worthwhile. This allows firms, as things become clearer, to increase or decrease their commitment to that model relatively easily and, more importantly, it keeps strategic options open. This ambiguity of the corporate strategy decision is an understandable artefact of the turbulent market and makes it all the more important that we consider carefully the second question about business breadth.

The Breadth Question: How Many Business Models Shall We Adopt?

Is it better for a business to encompass several business models or for them to focus on one, or something in between? The horizontal integration question is one of the most fundamental questions asked in management research so, before we explore the specifics of horizontal integration in the future of pharma, we need to understand what is known about that decision.

The question of whether to build a business from multiple business models or focus on just one is of much more than academic interest. The concept of a conglomerate discount, when firms that adopt multiple business models are consistently undervalued by investors in comparison to firms that follow a single business model, is well accepted and is a clear vote by investors against a multiple business model firm. Conglomerate discounts are often explained in terms of Agency Theory that, in essence, suggests that investors suspect the motives of executives. They think that firms expand across businesses for reasons of executive vanity or self-interest, rather than for reasons of good shareholder value (see for example (4;5)). Investors have some reason to be sceptical, since most empirical evidence suggests that conglomeration destroys value (see for example (6;7)). On the other hand, there are arguments for firms to adopt a multiple business model. These arguments include the creation of economies of scale and scope (8), making better use of organizational capabilities (9), and improving market power (10). Taken overall, the consensus view seems to be that whilst most multiple business model firms destroy value in relative terms, well focussed firms made up of related business models do create value, but only if they manage to maximize the advantages and minimize the disadvantages of the diversified approach.

If we apply this knowledge about horizontal integration to our question in the context of pharma business models, we begin to get a conditional answer and a new question. Echoing Amit Roy's thoughts (see page 109 in Chapter 6), firms should restrict themselves to one business model and leave the choice of business to invest in to the investor. We should expect investor pressure, whatever the ownership structure, to create an evolutionary selection pressure towards single business models. However, if executives can demonstrate that, by running two or more business models in one firm, they can create economies, leverage competencies, increase market power or create value in some other way then they should develop just such a multi-business model firm. This raises an important, new question: How might that value creation be done in a firm containing more than one of our seven business models, some of which themselves are already addressing more than one habitat? To gain some insight into that practically important question, we need to refer back to the ideas about synergy, by Goold and others, that we first mentioned in Chapter 6. Taking as a guide Goold's ideas of internal and external synergy and its converse of antagonism, the research for this book identified four principal value creating and destroying mechanisms. These are shown in Figure 8.1 and explicated below.

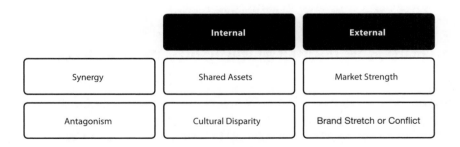

Figure 8.1   Value-creating synergies and value-destroying antagonisms between business models

SHARED ASSETS

If the operation of more than one business model allows tangible or intangible assets to be used across more markets, then it is likely to create value by reducing unit costs. For example, if a Monster Imitator could use its expertise in operations and supply chain to provide drugs via a Lifestyle Manager company then that would represent an internally generated synergy. The same could be said of a Genius firm that is able to utilize its intellectually property gained, for example, in diabetes, to create a more powerful value proposition via a Disease Manager model.

CULTURAL DISPARITY

If the shared assumptions, values and behaviours of two or more business models are not similar, they are likely to destroy value by either creating intra-organizational conflict or by inducing behaviour that is inappropriate for one or more of the business models. For example, the appropriate culture for a Health Concierge may include beliefs and behaviours consistent with personalized service and individual autonomy, whilst that for a Disease Manager may value process consistency and cost control. Cultural disparities like this lead to internally generated antagonisms. For example, we observe that the research and development management processes of big pharma seem often to clash with those of acquired or partnering biotechs.

MARKET STRENGTH

When customer groups overlap or interact in some way, the combined market strength of a multiple business model firm can be greater than the sum of the individual models for a number of reasons. Corporate and product brand recognition, bargaining power and product combination can all contribute to this strength to create an externally generated synergy. For example, a Genius's brand recognition in Advanced State Provision may reinforce a brand perception of efficacy in the Stay Well or Get Well habitats and may confer increased bargaining power in the Core State Provision habitat. A form of this brand recognition and reputation phenomenon is already observed when research-based pharma operate in present day OTC markets. Similarly, the 'bundling' of products in tender-based contracts is another example of market strength that we can see in today's market.

BRAND STRETCH OR CONFLICT

Since customers from one business model will frequently have knowledge of the activity of other models, perceptions of corporate and product brands will frequently 'spill over' (11). For example, firms operating the Monster Imitator model will develop a low cost brand perception that will make it difficult to be accepted in Wealthy Well or Lazarus and Narcissus habitats. We see a precursor of this in today's market when firms with no established reputation in their targeted speciality face difficulties in being accepted by opinion leaders in that field. Brand stretch or conflict is an externally generated antagonism.

These synergies or antagonisms are, of course, only broad umbrella terms. Each may incorporate a range of detailed, context specific phenomena that will either create or destroy value in multiple business model organizations. But they do allow us to gain some insight into when a multiple business model might be the best structure and how those structures might be managed to create value. They help us form a practical answer to our question about how many business models to incorporate into our firm. In short, an organization choosing the multiple business model is only likely be viable if it can create synergy via its brands or asset utilization, and avoid antagonism of brand conflict or cultural disparity.

In terms of our seven business models, these synergies and antagonisms suggest some possibilities of viable business model conglomerates and some others that should be treated with great caution. For example, Genii may be able to realize synergies of both kinds with Health Concierge or Trust Manager models but we might predict strong antagonism between Genii and Monster Imitators. As a rule of thumb, addressing nearby habitats might work, addressing very different habitats almost certainly won't. Once again, drawing a biological analogy helps make the point. Common red foxes, with their ideal habitat of fields and woodland, might be able to survive well in suburban gardens, but they would struggle in the desert or the arctic.

Taken together, this consideration of horizontal integration allows us to add a little more detail onto our prediction of future business models. The majority of firms will adopt a single business model, but some, probably only a small number, will form horizontally integrated conglomerates with the aim of addressing several habitats. To succeed, these conglomerates will need to develop some additional dynamic capabilities that fit under the multiple business coordination capabilities mentioned in Chapter 7. In particular, these capabilities will involve maximizing brand and asset utilization synergies and minimizing antagonism that results from brand stretch and cultural disparity.

This refined prediction throws up some questions about the multiple business model firms we see today, such as Novartis, Pfizer, Sanofi-Aventis and even Teva, with its developing innovative business. If they are evolving (as they seem to be) into the conglomerates we predict, it suggests one of two things. The first possibility is that, behind the scenes, they are developing the capabilities needed by a successful conglomerate. The Novartis/Sandoz structural separation might be an indication of that, as might Teva's attempts at imposing cultural homogeneity across the firm. Alternatively, the diversified firms we see today might be only transitional forms, short term attempts to spread risk that will, in time, revert to more focussed models. Most likely, both these possibilities are correct and some, but not all, of the diversified firms we see today will evolve into successful conglomerates whilst others will either evolve back into focussed firms or become extinct.

Whatever business models a firm chooses and, whether it adopts a focussed or diversified structure, success will still depend on being both more effective and more efficient than rivals in its chosen habitat. Whilst that will partly depend on the horizontal integration questions we have just discussed, it will also depend on the other organizational structure decisions the company makes, as discussed in the next two sections.

The Firm Boundaries Question: What Capabilities Shall We Make and What Shall We Buy?

If a new business model requires the development of a wide range of new organizational capabilities in a relatively short period of time, is it best to develop most of that capability within the firm or through a network of partners and suppliers? This vertical integration question has a long history in management science and, in order to consider it in a specifically pharmaceutical context, it's appropriate to spend a little time reviewing what we know from previous research.

Although it seems a 21st Century issue to ask where the boundaries of a firm should lie and how much goes on within and without those boundaries, the question was first asked in the 1930s in the work of Ronald Coase (12); it was then expanded on by Oliver Williamson (13). These men, each of whom received a Nobel Prize for their work, explored the question of whether it was more efficient for a firm to do everything itself, internally, or to contract some activity out. This has become known as the 'make or buy' decision. It lies behind the outsourcing we see in many industries, including pharma and, in its extreme form, implies the idea of the 'virtual company' (see for example (14)).Without going into the detail of this huge body of work, the consensus view is usually that it is usually best to buy in capabilities unless there is a good reason not to do so. According the theories of Transaction Cost Economics, this is because the market is usually more efficient at allocating resources than most internal hierarchies. The main reasons not to buy in capabilities are when that might involve losing control of some important intellectual property or if, by doing things in-house, the firm can create some synergy between activities. Within the libraries of research that Transaction Cost Economics has produced is quite a substantial body of work that relates specifically to the pharmaceutical industry. Unfortunately, that work is as narrow as it is deep and only really looks at the outsourcing decision with respect to research and development and pays scant attention to other parts of the value chain. What it does tell us, however, is quite useful and has ramifications for the vertical integration question outside research and development. When combined with research into the 'make or buy' decision in other knowledge intensive industries, it allows us to draw some broad conclusions.

Outsourcing research and development in pharma is, from the evolutionary perspective, a form of sex, in that it brings in organizational routines and capabilities (genes) that were developed outside the company. It has a history much longer than the current challenges facing the industry and research in this field goes back to the 1980s. That work mostly says that research and development activity is best managed in-house rather than outsourced, for a number of reasons (15). First amongst these is the issue of appropriability, the problem of owning and making a profit from any intellectual property developed outside the company (16). But there are other issues too. When both upstream activities (such as patent filing) and their complementary downstream activities (such as patent litigation) are both done in-house, the downstream activity often costs less, an important lesson that is sometimes forgotten when outsourcing considerations are evaluated (17). Keeping things in-house also seems to help innovation by providing a stronger link or 'connectedness' to the market place (18) (19). Overall, research in this field suggests that outsourcing or 'vitualization' of research and development, and perhaps of other processes too, is not the panacea some have hoped for.

However, pharmaceutical companies have still needed to import research and development 'genes' and the research evidence is that they are finding ways to do that and solve the appropriation, complementarity and connectedness problems described above. For instance, they are selecting their partners, designing governance structures and limiting the scope of alliances to prevent or limit the misappropriation of intellectual property (20). They are also carefully balancing in-house research and development with outsourced research and development (21) so as to maintain the advanced knowledge they need to manage partners. As a result of this careful selection of partners to complement internal research and development, a variety of partnering models are emerging. For example, traditional, established companies are looking for partnerships that provide new competencies, whilst smaller firms seek to reduce costs or increase capacity (22). Similarly, different modes of research and development collaboration are developing, based on variations in who defines the problem, who chooses the solution and how open or closed the collaborations are (23).

To draw wider lessons from this work, we have to remember that research and development has been the primary mode of value creation for the industry in the past but that it will be augmented in the future much more by operational efficiency and customer management, with different firms focussing on different parts of the value chain. That means that lessons learned from contexts where the value creation process was research and development can be generalized, with caution, to contexts where the principal value creation mode is operational efficiency or customer management. Such generalization allows us to extrapolate from what pharma companies have done in research and development and we can make predictions about how the new pharmaceutical business models will address the vertical integration question in all three value creation modes in the future. In essence, it seems likely that the firm boundaries of future pharmaceutical companies will be drawn using four guidelines.

OUTSOURCE CORE CAPABILITIES AS MUCH AS POSSIBLE

It seems obvious that basic tasks requiring core, non-differentiating capabilities will be disintegrated as much and as quickly as possible, in order to reduce costs and improve flexibility. We see this already in the outsourcing of manufacturing and some clinical development, but in future it will be extended to many more activities in all parts of the value chain, including drug discovery and customer management.

KEEP DIFFERENTIATING CAPABILITIES IN-HOUSE AS MUCH AS POSSIBLE

The threats of appropriation of intellectual property, the costs of disconnecting complementary activities and the need to maintain a connectedness to the market will make firms keep their differentiating activities in-house as much as possible. What is kept in-house will of course vary by business model. Genii will guard jealously much of drug discovery and parts of development and commercialization. Monster Imitators, whilst outsourcing most things for the sake of efficiency, will control the supply chain management processes that hold their business model together. Trust Managers will ensure that their customer insight and brand management processes stay in-house, whilst being willing to outsource much else. In general terms, the differentiating capabilities identified in Chapter 7 will be those kept within the firm boundary and the core capabilities will be outsourced. This, in early form, is what we see now with the rise of outsourcers in development, manufacturing and sales at the same time as firms invest in other parts research and development, strengthen their quality management processes and develop specialist sales teams. Over time, we might expect this polarization to continue and boundaries between in-house and outsourced capabilities to become more predictable.

SEEK OUT AND DELIBERATELY ACQUIRE NEW DIFFERENTIATING CAPABILITIES

Despite the desire to keep differentiating capabilities in-house as much as possible, firms will still find it necessary to form partnerships in order to fill critical gaps in their differentiating capabilities quickly. We see this already in research and development, with extensive partnerships, academic relationships, in-licensing and acquisitions. In future, we will see the same pattern in other parts of the value chain, as firms try to build capabilities in disease management, channel management or brand building, for example. At present, a pharmaceutical company's most likely partnership is likely to be a biotech or other life-science knowledge-based organization. In the future, analogous partnerships are just as likely to arise with retailers, healthcare providers, information technology companies, consumer goods companies and others.

FORM SEMI-PERMANENT RELATIONSHIP NETWORKS

In order to manage the risks associated with buying rather than making capabilities, firms will select and manage relationships in a careful way, perhaps operating in relatively closed, more long lasting collaborative networks analogous to Korean chaebols or the informal networks in the German Mittelstand. Whilst partner selection will still be based on what capabilities will be gained, the need to stay connected to the market, ensure appropriability and reduce risks will be become important factors and will make relationships longer lasting and less ad hoc.

So the business models of the future of pharma will be shaped by these four guidelines, each of which implies a characteristic of the future industry's structure. Outsourcing of core capabilities will mean pharmaceutical firms, or at least their centres, will become relatively smaller in headcount, maintaining only enough core capability staff to manage suppliers and partners. Focus on differentiating capabilities will mean that the balance of functions will change. Most people employed in the core of the organization will be involved in differentiating capabilities, although the balance of these will vary by business model. Genii will have proportionately more scientists; Trust Managers will employ proportionately more marketers; Monster Imitators will require proportionately more supply chain experts. The need to buy in certain differentiating capabilities will mean that firms will operate in symbiotic, chaebol-like, networks and the need to make those networks work well will mean that they are likely to be stable rather than ad hoc and opportunistic.

As we should expect from an evolutionary process, we can point to the antecedents of this new, vertically disintegrated structure. We can see it in the way that pharmaceutical research and development is increasingly carried out by networks. To a lesser extent, we can also see it in manufacturing and supply chains. But the future will be a much broader, more extensive version of this, spread across the whole value chain and encompassing much more than scientific capabilities. However, the redrawing of the firm's boundaries will not go as far as creating completely virtual companies because of the risks of that approach already presaged in the research about outsourcing research and development. The need to maintain differentiating capabilities will mean a strong, competent centre will remain.

If we are looking for a biological analogy for this new industry morphology, it might be lichen, a complex, obligate-symbiotic ecosystem in which numerous species of pharmaceutical company co-exist with a large variety of suppliers of core capabilities and partners providing differentiating capabilities. To an outside observer, it may be technically possible to separate out the component parts of this entity but, in practice, they would have many of the characteristics of a single organism.

In answering the preceding three questions, I have painted a picture of the future, in which a few firms create conglomerate business models to address several habitats, but where more firms concentrate on a single, more focussed business model that is well adapted to one area of the fitness landscape. Such firms will outsource basic activity and hoard their differentiating activity unless they must get it from outside. To the extent that they do outsource, they will operate in chaebol-like networks that will aggregate into an industry that, if it has an organic parallel, is more like lichen than an ecosystem of distinct creatures.

However, while these questions of corporate strategy, horizontal integration and firm boundaries will be very important to the industry's leaders, it will not be uppermost in the minds of most of the people who work in and with the pharmaceutical industry. For the majority, the central issue will be lower, but no less important – how to organize departments and business units to meet the unforgiving demands of their habitat. That is the subject of the next section.

The Excellence Question: How Should We Do What We Do Excellently

As the preceding sections have described, the pharmaceutical company of the future will be very different from its ancestors of the late-20th and early-21st Centuries. It will have a smaller core and will depend more on its partners and suppliers for its capabilities. But it will still have a core, a group of people responsible for identifying, creating and employing its differentiating capabilities and so delivering its distinctive competency, whatever that is. Moreover, that core will need to be significantly better at realising that distinctive competency than the core of other firms trying to deliver the same business model. Just as important for every business model other than the Monster Imitator, the core will need to create sufficient customer perceived value to pull customers away from the very low, almost negligible, cost products offered by the Monster Imitator model. In the true sense of the word, the core of the organization will have to do what it does excellently.

It is that need for excellence that will shape the structure of the firm's core. Excellence will mean something different for every different business model, because differentiating capabilities are specific to each model, but there is a common theme. Every model's capabilities fit into one box or another of the value creating process, as shown in Figure 8.2. In other words, every differentiating capability is a contextualized, model specific version of understanding the environment, creating strategy, delivering value or organizational learning. That means that the structure of the core organization will have to adapt to allow excellence in those four things. This in turn means that, by considering what we know about how organizational design helps and hinders those four value creating steps, we can predict how the core structure of the business model will adapt and evolve to the demands of the environment.

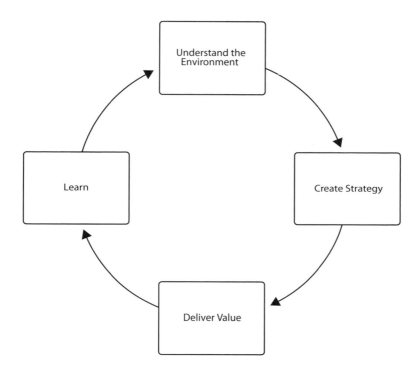

Figure 8.2   The value creation process

UNDERSTANDING THE ENVIRONMENT

This is the primary task of the core organization, since strategy creation, value delivery and organizational learning all flow from it. The results of market understanding are two kinds of knowledge; quite large amounts of operational knowledge and tiny amounts of exquisite market insight (24). The former is basic but important knowledge that is needed just to run the business, knowledge about who the customer is, for example. The latter is knowledge that can be used to create competitive advantage, knowledge about what drives customer preference, for instance. What we know about how market insight is created tells us quite a lot about those organizational structures that are likely to be excellent at it. For example, we know that insight creation is very much a process of synthesis rather than analysis, depending on information flow across intra-organizational boundaries (25). The same work tells us that overly formal processes and over reliance on positivistic, hard data hinders insight creation and that insight often comes from subtle glimpses into small details of the market environment. All of this implies two things about what kind of core organization structure will facilitate excellence in market understanding. The first is that it will be in intimate proximity with both the technological and social environment; it will be the antithesis of an ivory tower. The second is that it will have few internal barriers to information flow, particularly flow of soft, tacit knowledge; what internal borders it has will be porous to knowledge.

CREATING STRATEGY

The second thing the core organization must do is to create a strong strategy, and we know that, whilst market insight is a necessary component of this, it is not the only factor that is important. In particular, we know that a strong, coherent organizational culture is an important enabler of strategy creation, whilst a weak, fragmented organizational culture often hinders strategizing (26). We also know strategy making is not a purely rational process, located neatly in the leadership team. Rather, it is a messy hybrid of planning, vision and 'muddling through' that is dispersed across the organization (27). What this implies for the structure of the core organization is that, to create strong strategy, it should be small enough to allow the members of the organization to share common values and assumptions, which are the foundation of organizational culture. In other words, it will not be a large, multilayered and divisionalized structure.

DELIVER VALUE

We know that even the best strategy cannot deliver value until it is implemented and we know a remarkable amount about what it is that prevents strategies from being executed as planned. For example, we know that tight measurement and control is not enough to ensure implementation because, in knowledge-based firms, the most important activities are 'discretionary', meaning they cannot easily be measured and rewarded (28). We also know that there are broadly two categories of reasons that discretionary activities are not implemented well. Either they are subverted by individual who see those strategic actions as being against their own, personal interests (29) or they fall victim to intra-organizational conflict between functions, conflict that seems to be an instinctive psychological reaction whenever an organizational structure differentiates between two or more groups of people (30). What this implies for organizational design runs counter to the way many traditional organizations are structured. It suggests that departmental structures and 'stick and carrot' control methods do not and will not enable effective value delivery in a knowledge-based organization. Instead, organizations have to allow human groups to have shared rather than conflicting, interests and they have to remove, as far as possible, the functional structures that engender internal conflict. In other words, value is unlikely to be delivered by a traditional looking organization chart and a conventional reliance on metrics, incentives and sanctions.

ORGANIZATIONAL LEARNING

We know that any sequence of market understanding, strategy creating and value delivery will be imperfect and that continuing effectiveness depends on an organization's ability to assess what it has done and learn for the future (31). We also know that the basis of effective organizational learning is hypothesizing and testing. In other words, a process of 'if what we believe is true, then we should see this in reality'(see for example (32) (33)). Rather like the market understanding that it feeds into, organizational learning requires closeness to the market and, like strategy making and value delivery, it is hindered by internal conflict. This means that, from the point of view of organizational learning, an effective organizational structure is small enough to be 'customer intimate' and will lack the departmental demarcation that encourages politicking. In other words, it will be more collaborative than conflicting and it will enable critique rather than censure.

Taken as a whole, this overview of how organizational structure helps and hinders differentiating capabilities points consistently towards smaller, culturally coherent core organizations that are close to their market environment and away from large, bureaucratic and internally fragmented companies who analyse their market at a distance. It implies that the optimal core organization would be a relatively small one, small enough to be led and to share a common culture. Further, it implies that, as far as possible, internal structure of the core will minimize departmental and other divisions. And if the core organization needs to exceed this manageable, communal size then it will sub-divide into units that meet these criteria and which are sufficiently autonomous to require little coordination and control.

What might that number be? In group dynamics and anthropology, the number 150 is usually quoted as the magic number. The British anthropologist Robin Dunbar cites that number as being common in everything from military groups to primitive tribes and suggests that group size coevolved with the human brain and language abilities (34). In his famous book '*The Tipping Point*', Malcolm Gladwell (35) describes how W L Gore and Associates, makers of Gore-Tex, run their 2.5 billion dollar, 9,000 employee company with a core of about 150 people. He quotes Bill Gore as saying, 'We found again and again that things get clumsy when group numbers exceed a hundred and fifty.' Interestingly, and relevant to the discussion about how structure effects market understanding and organizational learning, academic research suggests that 150 is the critical number beyond which knowledge flows within organizations starts to break down (36).

In practical terms, this suggests that pharmaceutical business models will evolve, driven by the need to be excellent, to a have a smallish organizational core of around 150 people or, if it requires more, multiple but relatively autonomous 'tribes' of 150 people. In order to minimize internal barriers and the need for coordination with other tribes, these groups will not be sub-structured around traditional departments, but the whole group will be focussed upon that part of the environment with which it must be well connected. In some business models, that will be a disease type or a scientific area; in others, it will be a customer segment; in others, a supply chain. Whatever the entity around which the group is focussed, it will contain just about everyone it needs to develop and employ its required differentiating capabilities and it will be embedded in a network of suppliers and partners that will supply its core capabilities and perhaps, if absolutely necessary, some differentiating capabilities. Of course, this market-centred, self-contained tribe model is very different from the traditionally structured pharmaceutical company, but we see early evidence of this evolutionary trend when we observe the way GSK has restructured its research and development (37) or perhaps the way that Johnson & Johnson maintains its structure of small, autonomous sub-units.

The Trouble with Lichen

At the beginning of this chapter, I promised some general conclusions about the way pharmaceutical companies will be structured in the future. On our way to those conclusions, we have made four important stopovers en route. First, we considered the corporate strategy decision about which business models to choose. We concluded that, once each company had excluded the obvious, what remained, however far-fetched, was possible. Next we examined the breadth of the pharmaceutical organization and concluded that they would stay narrowly focussed on one of our seven business models, unless they could demonstrate to investors the dynamic capabilities to realize synergies and minimize antagonisms. Then we surveyed where the boundaries of the future pharmaceutical business model might lie. We concluded that they would be narrowly defined but that firms would exist in a symbiotic network of suppliers and partners, something between the vertically integrated company of the past and the virtual company that some have predicted. Finally, we asked what structure the core of the organization might take in order to develop and employ the differentiating capabilities demanded by their chosen habitat. The answer would seem to be a tribe of 150, or perhaps a loosely connected alliance of tribes of that size, in order to meet the constraints implied by the human brain.

On reaching our conclusion, we survey a strange industry. A lichen of what, by today's standards, are small companies embedded in a complex web of suppliers and partners, not just of the kind we see today, like academic departments and clinical research organizations, but perhaps of retailers, healthcare providers and consumer goods companies. Only by tracing the legal ties between some of the hubs can we detect something that we might recognize as the pharmaceutical company of today.

Although very different from the structures with which we are familiar, this lichen is a viable, valuable entity. Parts of it produce good quality, basic drugs, so cheap that almost everyone can afford them. Other parts allow individuals to manage their own health either modestly or by spending lots of money to buy many years of extra life. The lichen allows states and other institutions to provide dramatically better 'bang for bucks' than today, by reducing the costs of curing illness and by preventing it in the first place. Finally, an important part of the lichen will deliver advanced medicines that we all, especially those looking towards the second half of our lives, desperately want.

But, to steal a title of a John Wyndham science fiction story, the trouble with lichen is that it is not what we have now. We have great beasts striding the landscape, smaller creatures weaving between them and myriad insects and little birds living off them. The question is: how will firms make that transition from today to tomorrow? How will they change their DNA of organizational routines and how will that express new organizational capabilities? How will they build and apply new distinctive competencies, and how will they change their shape to fit their new habitat? Those questions are the subject of Chapter 9.

References

(1)   Daly, J. 2000. Sage Advice: An Exclusive Interview with Peter Drucker. *Business 2.0*. August 2000.

(2)   McDonald, M.H.B. 1990. Some Methodological Comments on The Directional Policy Matrix. *Journal of Marketing Management*; 6(1):59–68.

(3)   Robinson, S.J.Q., Hichens, R.E. and Wade, D.P. 1978. The Directional Policy Matrix-Tool for Strategic Planning. *Long Range Planning*; 11(3):8–15.

(4)   Jensen, M.C. 1986. Agency Costs of Free Cash Flow, Corporate Finance, and Takeovers. *American Economic Review*; 76(2):323.

(5)   Jensen, M.C. and Murphy, K.J. 1990. Performance Pay and Top-Management Incentives. *Journal of Political Economy*; 98(2):225–64.

(6)   Berger, P.G. and Ofek, E. 1995. Diversification's Effect on Firm Value. *Journal of Financial Economics*; 37(1):39–65.

(7)   Lang, L.H.P. and Stulz, R.M. 1994. Tobin's Q, Corporate Diversification, and Firm Performance. *Journal of Political Economy*; 102(6):1248.

(8)   Chandler, A.D. 1977. *The Visible Hand*. Cambridge MA: Belknapp Press.

(9)   Matsusaka, J.G. 2001. Corporate Diversification, Valu Maximization, and Organizational Capabilities. *Journal of Business*; 74(3):409.

(10)   Villalonga, B. 2000. Privatization and Efficiency: Differentiating Ownership Effects From Political, Organizational. *Journal of Economic Behavior & Organization*; 42(1):43.

(11)   Jing, L., Dawar, N. and Lemmink, J. 2008. Negative Spillover in Brand Portfolios: Exploring the Antecedents of Asymmetric Effects. *Journal of Marketing*; 72(3):111–23.

(12)   Coase, R. 1937. The Nature of the Firm. *Economica*; 4(16):386–405.

(13)   Williamson, O.E. 2010. Transaction Cost Economics: The Origins. *Journal of Retailing*; 86(3):227–31.

(14)   Cavalla, D. 1997. *Modern Strategy for Preclinical Pharmaceutical R&D: Towards the Virtual Research Company*. Chichester: Wiley.

(15)   Williamson, O.E. 1975. *Markets and Hierarchies*. New York: Fre Press.

(16)   Pisano, G.P. 1990. The R&D Boundaries of the Firm: An Empirical Analysis. *Administrative Science Quarterly*; 35(1):153–76.

(17)   Reitzig, M. and Wagner, S. 2010. The Hidden Costs of Outsourcing: Evidence From Patent Data. *Strategic Management Journal*; 31(11):1183–201.

(18)   Armour, H.O. and Teece, D.J. 1980. Vertical Integration and Technological Innovation. *Review of Economics & Statistics*; 62(3):470.

(19)   McGahan, A.M. 1994. Industry Structure and Competitive Advantage. *Harvard Business Review*; 72(6):115–24.

(20)   Li, D., Eden, L.O.R.R., Hitt, M.A. and Ireland, D.R. 2008. Friends, Acquaintences or Strangers? Partner Selection in R&D Alliances. *Academy of Management Journal*; 51(2):315–34.

(21)   Rothaermel, F.T., Hitt, M.A. and Jobe, L.A. 2006. Balancing Vertical Integration and Strategic Outsourcing: Effects on Product Portfolio, Product Success, and Firm Performance. *Strategic Management Journal*; 27(11):1033–56.

(22)   Festel, G., Schicker, A. and Boutellier, R. 2010. Performance Improvement in Pharmaceutical R&D through New Outsourcing Models. *Journal of Business Chemistry*; 7(2):89–96.

(23)   Pisano, G.P. and Verganti, R. 2008. Which Kind of Collaboration is Right for You? *Harvard Business Review*; 86(12):78–86.

(24)   Smith, B.D. and Raspin, P.J. *Creating Market Insight*. 1st ed. London: Wiley.

(25)   Smith, B.D., Wilson, H.N. and Clark, M. 2006. Creating and Using Customer Insight: 12 Rules of Best Practice. *Journal of Medical Marketing*; 6(2):135–9.

(26)   Smith, B.D. 2005. *Making Marketing Happen*. Oxford: Elsevier.

(27)   Mintzberg, H., Ahlstrand, B. and Lampel, J. *Strategy Safari*. 1st ed. New York: The Free Press.

(28)   Meyer, J.P., Becker, T.E. and Vandenberghe, C. 2004. Employee Commitment and Motivation: A Conceptual Analysis and Integrative Model. *Journal of Applied Psychology*; 89(6):991–1007.

(29)   Smith, B.D. 2009. Maybe I Will, Maybe I Won't: What the Connected Perspectives of Motivation Theory and Organizational Commitment May Contribute to our Understanding of Strategy Implementation. *Journal of Strategic Marketing*; 17(6):469–81.

(30)   Smith, B.D. 2011. Turf Wars: What the Intraorganizational Conflict Literature May Contribute to Our Understanding of Marketing Strategy Literature Implementation. *Journal of Strategic Marketing*; 19(1):25–42.

(31)   Hodgkinson, G.P. and Sparrow, P.R. 2002. *The Competent Organization*. 1st ed. Open University Press;.

(32)   Nonaka, I. 1991. The Knowledge-Creating Company. *Harvard Business Review*; 69(6):96–105.

(33)   Argyris, C. and Schon, D.A. 1978. *Organizational Learning: A Theory in Action Perspective*. Reading MA: Addison-Wesley.

(34)   Aiello, L. and Dunbar, R.I.M. 1991. Neocortex Size, Group Size and the Evolution of Language. *Current Anthropology*; 34:184–93.

(35)   Gladwell, M. 2001. *The Tipping Point*. Abacus.

(36)   Serenko, A., Bontis, N. and Hardie, T. 2007. Organizational Size and Knowledge Flow: A Theoretical Link. *Journal of Intellectual Capital*; 8(4):610–27.

(37)   Garnier, J-P. 2008. Rebuilding the R&D Engine in Big Pharma. *Harvard Business Review*; 69–76.

CHAPTER

9 *Gales of Creative Destruction: The Turmoil Ahead of the Pharmaceutical Industry*

'Economic progress, in capitalist society, means turmoil'

Joseph Schumpeter

In the last three chapters, we've painted a picture of the future of the pharmaceutical industry that is very different from its past and present. Its customers, value propositions, organizational structures and distinctive competencies will be qualitatively different from those we see today. That difference implies a a great change of course, but how quickly will that change happen? Will it be incremental or will it be revolutionary?

Again, we can look to the theory of evolution for guidance. Since change in complex adaptive systems is an evolutionary process, its speed will be dictated by the rate of change of the social and technological environments with which the industry is co-evolving. We see those environments changing rapidly around us every day. Some of those changes are gradual, such as the increasing pro-activism of the public; others appear to be happening rapidly, such as the spread of personal information technology. Some, such as the shift in the global economic centre of gravity and the maturing of the value concept, may have been accelerated by the economic crisis that began in 2007. The pace of change of these environments suggests that the industry may change very quickly, in the sort of spurt of evolution predicted by the punctuated equilibrium hypothesis, as discussed in Chapter 6. Economists talk about the same phenomenon in a different way. Joseph Schumpeter popularized the phrase 'gales of creative destruction', although the idea has its origins in Karl Marx (1). By it he meant relatively sudden shifts in the economic conditions that swept away the economic structures, such as industries, that we are used to.

So, having derived from management science and evolutionary theory a view of the future of pharma that is very different from the present, we should expect change. And, without being able to predict a precise timetable for that change, we would be complacent to expect it to happen gradually and at a pace we can manage easily. Rather, both evolutionary and economic theory suggest that we should expect change to hit the industry like an economic storm, sweeping away the pharmaceutical industry we are all familiar with and replacing it with a new one, all in a relatively short period of time. If so, we should anticipate the change and prepare for it.

Most of us accept the proposition, expressed by Abraham Lincoln in the quote at the head of Chapter 1, that by understanding the future we can in some way prepare for it. So, for those who work in or with the industry and, indeed, for those of us who expect to need its products in the future, this prediction of rapid change prompts two questions. The first: what can we predict about how that change will come about? The second: how might we use that prediction to prepare for and, if possible, control our journey into the future?

This chapter will try to answer those two questions, albeit still bearing in mind Neils Bohr's admonition, at the head of Chapter 5, about the difficulty of predicting the future. Following our definition of a business model (Chapter 5, page 93), we will discuss how change in the strategies, capabilities and organizational structures of the pharmaceutical industry might come about and what that implies for executive action. Then we will discuss some of the barriers to change that might hinder our preparation for the coming storm. Before we do either of those things, however, let us discuss something we've deliberately omitted so far: organizational culture.

Changing the Water: Cultural Change in the Pharmaceutical Industry

Our decision not to discuss organizational culture up until now was made so as to avoid burdening the reader with yet another new concept. But the omission of organizational culture does not imply that this area of research is irrelevant, quite the opposite. Organizational culture is a domain of management science that contributes powerfully to the understanding of almost every management question. And it is perhaps especially germane to the topic of organizational change, which is why we've kept it in reserve until now. What we know about organizational culture has important implications for how we might manage the storm that is approaching the industry. So we will start with a brief overview of what management researchers have found out about organizational culture, then we will draw out the practical implications for the pharmaceutical industry, how it might change and what executives should consider.

The most important thing we know about organizational culture is how important it is. Peter Drucker, describing how it affects everything a firm tries to do, called it 'persistent and pervasive'(2). Some researchers have gone as far as to say that an organization does not have a culture; it is its culture (3). Others have said that executives are as aware of the culture in which they work, as fish are of the water in which they swim (4). There is, in the management literature, a strong consensus that organizational culture underpins everything (see for example (5)), so it will undoubtedly play a part in the future of pharma. Organizational culture has been described as 'the way we do things around here' and 'the habits of the organization'. But to understand and manage it, we need a more refined understanding of what organizational culture is and how it works. The most practical tool we have for that is found in the work of Edgar Schein (6;7)(see Figure 9.1).

Schein, who is regarded as one of the leading thinkers in the organizational culture field, asserted that culture has its origins in the fundamental assumptions made by the founders of the company. These assumptions, about what will and what won't make the company succeed, are numerous but are usually implicit, unspoken and lost in the mists of corporate history. If they are good assumptions, the company thrives and they become embedded into the company culture. If they are poor assumptions, the company fails and there is no company culture to consider. Subtly, imperceptibly, these assumptions create the values of the company, the beliefs that are taken for granted, and which govern how everybody in the company behaves.

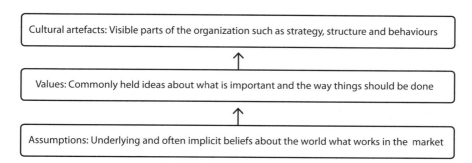

Cultural artefacts: Visible parts of the organization such as strategy, structure and behaviours

↑

Values: Commonly held ideas about what is important and the way things should be done

↑

Assumptions: Underlying and often implicit beliefs about the world what works in the market

Figure 9.1 Schein's model of organizational culture

Although some values are explicitly stated, most value systems are invisible, but they are observable through their effects. Everything we see in the company, from its strategies and structure to little things like dress code and punctuality, is an expression of its values. In Schein's scheme, these things are called artefacts of the culture. The assumptions, values and artefacts that add up to a company culture are, at a detailed level, unique to each firm. However, in an industry like pharmaceuticals, there is so much sharing of people that there is a lot of commonality of culture between companies in the same industry. So, just as regions in a country share a common culture, there is, to some extent, an industry culture that underpins individual company cultures.

The valuable thing about Schein's three-layer explanation of organizational culture is that it allows us to understand a number of important things that seem to apply to the culture of all companies and which are relevant to how the industry will change. The first is the pervasive nature of organizational culture. Nothing seems to happen in an organization that is not shaped by its culture and any organizational change that goes against the grain of the culture rarely takes hold.

The second is its immutability. Executives often fiddle with the artefacts of a culture. They reorganize, make minor process changes and rename things, then call it culture change. However, if the underlying assumptions and values are left unchanged, the culture restores itself and nothing, in practice, is really different. Thirdly, we know that when cultural change is achieved it begins with a firm's leadership. Cultural change is rarely driven by middle managers; in fact they are quite often the source of most resistance to cultural change. We also know that the transmission of new cultural assumptions and values through an organization happens via a class of employee known as culture carriers. Such people may not be particularly senior but they are often long-standing employees and respected by their peers. Without culture carriers, change tends to stay in the boardroom and outside the boardroom it is only feigned. One set of management researchers coined a beautiful phrase to describe this phenomenon of going along with, but not really committing to, cultural change. They called it 'resigned behavioural compliance' (8). Finally, we know that effective leaders change the underlying assumptions and then use a technique of 'dynamic symbolism'(9). This simply means doing things that visibly demonstrate changes in the firm's basic assumptions. A perfect example of this was Zhang Ruimin, CEO of the Chinese household appliances firm Haier. To demonstrate changes in culture with respect to product quality, he staged events at which, in front of his employees, he took a sledgehammer to poor quality products.

Taken as a whole, our understanding of organizational culture tells us something about how change will occur in the pharmaceutical industry and how we might manage it. Firstly, we can now see that change in any organization will be preceded and supported by real change in its cultural assumptions, not just fiddling with its artefacts. The assumptions at the root of current pharmaceutical company business models are correct for the industry as it is, or was until recently. Its corresponding values and artefacts are therefore similarly correct for the market conditions in which they developed. The industry's business models, its organizational routines, capabilities, strategies and structures are all artefacts of its culture. But as the market environment – the social and technological environments and the fitness landscape – changes, the old assumptions will become less valid and, if the firm is to survive, it will need to change. One possible prediction is that a change in the industry will involve its leaders changing their minds, to some extent, about what it takes to succeed in the industry. Then, that those new assumptions will lead to sustainable change in the organization's values and that, finally, those changes will support the transformation of its artefacts, including its strategies, structures and capabilities. Conversely, we could predict that change will fail when leaders fiddle with strategy, structure and capabilities without paying attention to cultural change.

The research for this book informed prediction of how organizational culture will influence change and it also allows us to provide some guidance to the executives who must manage that change. They are advised against starting with a strategy review and reorganization, however tempting that is. Instead, they are recommended to start by explicating the firm's underlying assumptions, challenging them and, where they see those assumptions to be outdated, changing them.

For some firms, this might be painful. Many pharmaceutical companies have, deeply embedded in their culture, the belief that success comes almost exclusively from scientific innovation, with perhaps a little selling competency on top. As the fitness criteria of the market change, especially in the Core State Provision habitat, this assumption will need to be revised. Similarly, firms adopting a Trust Manager model may need to revise their assumptions about the value of marketing strategy capabilities such as segmentation and branding. Our knowledge of how cultures change also allows us to predict the executive behaviour that will be successful in enabling cultural change. Dynamic symbolism and judicious use of culture carriers will succeed; grandiloquent statements alone will not. In summary, any pharmaceutical executive planning to change his or her firm to meet the demands of the future will need to address the organization's culture.

Careful, informed cultural change will be the first necessary step in riding out the storm that will hit the pharmaceutical industry. But it will not be sufficient. Surviving and thriving in the future of pharma will also require firms to adapt strategies, as we discuss in the next section.

Weaving New Patterns: Changing the Strategies of the Pharmaceutical Industry

Our prediction for the future of pharma implies that many strategies that have served the industry well in the past will not work in the future. The business models of big pharma, speciality pharma and generics will not meet the fitness criteria of the new landscape. They simply will not create enough comparative value, or they will target the wrong customers, or both. Every firm currently operating in the industry, and those seeking to enter it, will need to adapt their strategy to meet the specific demands of the habitats in which they choose to compete. This is unlikely to be a trivial, incremental adaptation to current strategies, involving only small tweaks to the customers addressed and the value propositions made. It will involve, for all firms, a significant shift in which customers they target and what they offer them. As discussed in Chapter 7, these new strategies will involve the development and employment of new capabilities, both core and differentiating. By definition, it will require the development and employment of the dynamic capabilities that lead to these new core and differentiating capabilities. We will discuss, later in the chapter, how firms will develop new capabilities, but for now we can use what we learned in Chapter 7 to agree that there will be at least four dynamic capabilities that will be essential to developing and implementing new strategies. These will be the capabilities to create market insight, to make new strategies, to execute them effectively and then to learn from what was done. We know quite a lot about how firms do these four things, about what works and what doesn't. So we will start with a brief overview of what management researchers have found out about these topics, then we will draw out the practical implications for the pharmaceutical industry, how it might change and what executives should consider.

Starting with the creation of market insight, we know quite a lot about both what insight is and how it is created. We know from research into knowledge management that effectiveness in this area involves an iterative loop that transforms data to information, information to knowledge and knowledge to insight (10). In particular, we know that the large majority of the knowledge a firm creates is operational knowledge, essential to its operation, but which doesn't create competitive advantage. Only a tiny subset of an organization's knowledge, which we call insight, meets the specific criteria to do that. We know that, to be insight, knowledge has to be valuable, rare, hard to copy and usable by the firm. We also know that the creating of insight is more complex and less rational than one might expect. In particular, we know that market insight rarely comes from positivistic, quantitative, data-crunching alone (11). Instead, it usually requires more synthesis than analysis, using a combination of methodologies guided by a pragmatic epistemology. In short, it's not just about the numbers.

A similar picture emerges when we review what we know about how firms make strategy. Despite what some business schools teach, the rational, planning approach to making strategy is 'a poor description of reality' (12;13). Instead, we know that firms use a mixture of processes, implicit and explicit, to make their strategic decisions (14) (15). Further, we know that none of these hybrid strategy-making processes works better than the others. Instead, all we can say is that 'what works is what fits' and that, for any given context of organization and market, there is a blend of strategy-making processes that works better than other blends (16). Of particular relevance to our discussion, we know that formal planning processes do not cope well with market turbulence and, to be effective, they need to be augmented by visionary leadership and incremental experimentation. We also know that, whatever process firms use to create strategies, effective strategies have a number of characteristic features. These features, all of which increase the probability of the strategy being successful, add up to a process of marketing due diligence (17). In summary, we know that effective companies are not slaves to bureaucratic, formalized strategic planning processes, especially in turbulent markets. They use hybrid, context-specific strategy processes to create tailored strategies that have a known and managed level of business risk.

Consistent with our knowledge of insight and strategy creation processes, we know that strategy execution is more complex and less systematic than we might have expected. In particular, we know that much strategy implementation depends on discretionary activity that cannot easily be measured and controlled (18). Such activity, typically the creative activity of knowledge workers rather than the routine activity of manual workers, is crucial to the implementation of complex, value adding strategies. It follows that good strategy execution is not just about command and control, but about the motivation and commitment of individuals and the effective cross-functional working of different expertise groups. The Dunbar-sized tribes described in Chapter 8 will reduce some of these discretionary implementation problems, but we can be sure that managing individual motivation and intra-organizational conflict will be important to strategy execution. We also know that many current management practices, such as the internal customer concept and geographically-dispersed working, hinder strategy implementation (19;20). In summary, effective strategy execution is at least as much an issue of organizational psychology as it is one of metrics and incentives.

Finally, our knowledge of organizational learning tells us that, to sustain competitiveness, firms will continue to build their knowledge base by drawing lessons from the success or failure of their strategy implementation (21). We know that this is a difficult process to formalize and that, inasmuch as it can be turned into a process, there seem to be two complementary processes: the inductive and the deductive(22;23). In the former, knowledge emerges from the data as patterns of information form. In the latter, firms create and test hypotheses. Both ways of organizational learning seem to be very sensitive to organizational cultural norms. In particular, organizational learning seems to be more effective when firms try to minimize blame and allow experimentation. It also seems to rely on the 'displacement of concepts' idea that we discussed earlier in the book. It is probably fair to say that organizational learning is not a topic that is as well codified and understood as some other areas of management science, but what we do know tells us that it benefits from some degree of deliberate design and that importing ideas from other contexts is an important part of it.

We can use this knowledge about insight, strategizing, execution and learning, reviewed very briefly here, to predict how the industry will change its strategies. We can predict that effective new strategies will be based strongly on insight, not just knowledge, and that insight will have been created by intelligent, pragmatic synthesis rather than formal, positivistic analysis. Those strategies will be formed not by textbook planning alone, but by a hybrid strategy-making approach that fits the context of the company and market. In particular, visionary leadership will play a bigger part in strategy making. The resultant strategy will have a well-understood risk profile. The successful implementation of this strategy will rely on the motivation and commitment of individuals and on effective cross-functional working within business units. And effective strategies will maintain and renew themselves by deliberate learning and 'displacement' of ideas.

That prediction allows us to give some guidance to executives tasked with changing their firm's strategies. Effective executives will learn to differentiate between insight and other forms of knowledge. They will also learn to create insight by blending together multiple sources of information and not relying too heavily on data analysis. They will learn to create hybrid strategy-making processes that fit their situation, rather than follow the text book slavishly. And they will test the outputs of those strategy-making processes using a process of marketing due diligence. Importantly, they will not 'fire and forget' their strategy. Instead, they will carefully manage its implementation by predicting and pre-empting the individual and organizational barriers to discretionary activity. Then they will reiterate the whole strategy process by learning from what they did and feeding it back into the insight creation process.

Adopting an organizational culture perspective, how the pharmaceutical makes strategy is an artefact of its culture. At present, the artefacts we observe most frequently – data-driven, formalized processes, command and control systems – all suggest a set of assumptions derived from the industry's heritage in the natural sciences. It is as if the industry thought that markets and people were like atoms and molecules, susceptible to measurement and manipulation. In the future of pharma, we anticipate (and indeed recommend) that these assumptions will shift to something more like those found in the social sciences; markets and people are imperfectly measurable and can only be managed in a contingent, context dependent manner. This shift in assumptions, and the change in approach to strategy making that it will lead to, will be part of the way in which pharmaceutical companies will adapt to their future.

Old Dogs and Upstarts: Changing the Routines and Capabilities of the Pharmaceutical Industry

Whatever choices a pharmaceutical company or, indeed, a new industry entrant makes regarding how to adapt to the future pharmaceutical fitness landscape, it will need to adapt not only its culture and strategy but also its organizational capabilities. Even those firms with an excellent set of capabilities for today's market will need to adapt as the social and technological environments change. In particular, each of the eleven habitats will demand different distinctive competencies. As discussed in Chapter 7, distinctive competencies are an aggregate of a firm's capabilities, and capabilities are, in turn, the net result of clusters of organizational routines. So, at the basis of competitiveness in changing markets lies a firm's ability to adapt its organizational routines and capabilities. This idea is reinforced if we remind ourselves that organizational routines and capabilities are the analogues of genes and proteins in biological systems.

As with culture and strategy, management researchers have uncovered a lot of useful knowledge about organizational routines and capabilities. Reviewing that knowledge allows us to predict how pharmaceutical companies will change what they are able to do, and that prediction may guide executives who are responsible for developing their firm's capabilities.

The best place to start is with what we know about the nature of organization routines, much of which I've drawn from Markus Becker (24) and the references that work guided me to. We know that these recurrent patterns of interaction are dispersed around the organization, typically involving several people or groups. We know that they are valuable for storing knowledge, especially tacit knowledge, and that they act as coordination mechanisms. They are especially efficient because, to an extent, they become automatic and, in doing so, they economize on management time and effort. They do indeed resemble genes, in that they are triggered either by internal or external cues, and they act together to form a cumulative outcome. In short, they are complex, embedded entities that are much more than a simple, explicit, business process.

However, we also know something about how new organizational routines are created. They are heavily path dependent, in other words, they are shaped and, to some extent, constrained by the history of the organization. Organizational routines, whilst they are repetitive, are not absolutely fixed and they constantly vary to some degree. This allows the first way in which adaptation of organizational routines can take place. Like genes, variation occurs and, if that variant works well, it is selected for.

The second way an organization is able to change its routines is by importing or transplanting from another organization. The capacity for doing this is, however, limited because organizational routines are very context specific and they do not usually transplant directly from one context to another without some kind of adaptation. So, in the development of new routines, firms face a trade-off between the in-house adaptation of existing routines that is relatively slow, but likely to succeed, and the absorption of routines from outside that is relatively slow, but which risks rejection.

The other very interesting thing we know about change in organizational routines is that a delicate balance of conditions is needed for new ones to grow. On the one hand, development of new routines is hindered rather than helped by pressure on time or other resources. When placed under stressful conditions, organizations tend not to adopt new routines, but to fall back on old ones that they trust, even if they are sub-optimal. On the other hand, organizations tend to fall into competency traps. That is, if a routine is working well enough they will stick with it and are reluctant to adopt a new routine, even if it is superior. So, new organizational routines seem to develop best in a kind of Goldilocks zone, where there is enough pressure to remove complacency but not so much as to trigger a retreat into comfort zones.

What we know about changing organizational capabilities complements what we know about organizational routines. We know that core and differentiating capabilities, themselves the result of clusters of organizational routines, tend not to change much unless acted upon by a dynamic capability. For example, the core capability to get a drug through regulatory approval will not be upgraded to getting through regulatory and economic approval unless the firm has the dynamic capability to change and adapt its drug development processes. But dynamic capabilities are themselves the result of organizational routines and, if those routines can develop either by gradual variation or more discrete importation of new ideas, we might expect to see similar differences in the development mechanism for dynamic capabilities as we do for organizational routine. And indeed we do. There seem to be three levels of dynamic capabilities (25): incremental, renewing and regenerative. The first two of these would seem to be the result of gradual variation and selection of existing routines, the third the result of importing new ones. Dynamic capabilities of the incremental and renewing variety tend to involve tweaking and fine-tuning the organization; the regenerative kind seems to involve restructuring the firm's structure and processes.

What we know about how organizational routines and capabilities change allows us to predict what might happen when companies successfully adapt to the changing market. Firstly, we can predict that firms will actively seek to change their routines and capabilities, both core and differentiating. We can predict that this will be by a combination of gradual development of existing activity and the importation of ideas from elsewhere. We can also predict that the ability to develop capabilities will be a major factor in separating those firms who successfully adapt to the market from those that don't.

In terms of guiding what executives do, the research into capabilities suggests three things. Firstly, because routines are so context specific, simplistically importing new routines, via consultants for example, might be naive. It is more likely that imported routines will need careful adaptation and contextualization. Secondly, executives seeking to improve their routines and capabilities will have to ensure that pressure does not inhibit development by leading to reversion to old routines. On the other hand, they will need to avoid the opposite problems of a competency trap. Finally, firms will need to develop regenerative capabilities that involve reconfiguring the organization to improve its dynamic capabilities, not just its core and differentiating capabilities.

Metamorphosis: Changing the Shape of the Pharmaceutical Company

In Chapter 8, we suggested that the structure of the pharmaceutical industry would evolve into a network structure, analogous to lichen. The components of this network will be chaebol-like clusters of symbiotic firms, each made up of one or more Dunbar-sized tribes of around 150 people. This is perhaps one of the more radical suggestions to emerge from the research, indicating that the large, hierarchical and integrated organizational structures of the late-20th and early-21st Centuries have run their course as the optimal structural form. But the early indications of structural change in the pharmaceutical industry that we do have, of downsizing, outsourcing and partnering, seem to indicate that this trajectory, which is created by the demands of the new fitness landscape, has already started. The lichen-like picture may, like most predictions, be wrong at a detailed level, but a major change in the structure of pharmaceutical companies does seem likely, and at least some of the characteristics of the lichen model will be part of the picture. Whatever the details of the end result, it would be useful to know how that structural change process will play out and how, if at all, industry executives can manage it. That is the purpose of this section. As with the preceding sections, we'll quickly review what we know about organizational change before drawing implications for the future of pharma.

The anecdotal view of change in organizations is that it is difficult, slow and messy. This is borne out by many decades of research. As early as 1957, researchers recorded that, whilst bureaucracies were important to allow organizations to function, they hindered change by adhering too strictly to procedures and rejecting innovation(26). Others have noted that organizations get locked into a vicious circle of rigidity (27). In the body of research known as organizational ecology, researchers talk about the concept of structural inertia and observe that firms seem to be much less able to change their structure than is demanded by the environment (28;29). Structural inertia seems to increase with the age, size and complexity of the organization and has a number of internal and external components. Internally, these include the need for investment, limited information flows and vested interests. Externally, pressures by investors and regulators also hinder change. This reluctance of organizations to change is not necessarily a bad thing, however. In the short term at least, organizational change is often associated with a reduction in effectiveness. For example, the succession of a new leader sometimes reduces team cohesion and increases conflict (30) (31). Researchers who have studied situations where structural change has occurred note three things about it. Firstly, it is often triggered by changes in the technological environment (32). Secondly, it seems to work best when change reflects existing capabilities (33) and, thirdly, it seems to be most likely to happen when the organization's survival is threatened by market changes (34).

The conditions described above, from bureaucratic rigidity to change triggered by new technology and market changes, are all recognizable features of the pharmaceutical industry as much as any other. This gives us general guidance about how structural change in companies might play out. This general knowledge is supported by a small body of research that looks specifically at organizational changes in the pharmaceutical industry. This work presents a narrow, uneven picture but still carries some useful lessons. It is narrow because it largely considers only the structuring of organizational relationships in the research and development part of the industry's value chain and pays relatively little attention to the structuring of the customer management or operations parts of the value chain. Paulina Ramirez, for example, has studied the globalization of pharmaceutical research and development and found it to be very uneven, varying greatly between US- and EU-based companies and, in the period she studied, heavily biased towards investment in the US (35). Other work has also shown that changes in the pharmaceutical industry have been uneven, reflecting firm-specific differences in their research and development pipelines and their attitudes towards outsourcing drug discovery (36). This work also shows that change via merger, acquisition or other partnering arrangement seems to be the industry's preferred mechanism of adapting its structures. Other, complementary, work in this area shows that how pharmaceutical firms form alliances is strongly idiosyncratic and context-specific (37). In short, there is no model to follow; relationships form on a case by case, pragmatic basis.

Compared to the areas of strategy, capabilities and culture, what we know about how firms restructure themselves is relatively limited and it is just as useful for what it does not say as it is for what it does. For example, we cannot point to an obvious single migration pathway from the large integrated firm to the networked symbiote structure we are suggesting for the future of pharma.

We can, however, say that significant structural change creating completely new structures is rare in comparison to gradual change. We can point to the internal and external reasons for that – things like internal politics and organizational complexity – and we can say that, in most cases, we would expect pharmaceutical companies to change only in an incremental manner, rarely in big, dramatic steps. We can expect those small steps to be in response to directly observable changes in the environment, such as new technologies or changes in the market. And we can expect much of the significant structural change in the industry to arise from mergers, acquisitions and partnership, rather than endogenous change. Of equal importance, we can say that each pathway from the present structure to the future will be idiosyncratic, reflecting the context of each firm and its market habitats. In short, there is no 'planned' model of how pharmaceutical companies will change their organizational structures, but early evidence is that it will happen as a process of slow, internal incrementalism combined with bigger leaps of merger or alliance activity.

Even this limited picture of how the industry will change its structure allows us to give some guidance to executives. Firstly, we can advise against looking for an industry standard, best practice migration path from the present structure to the future. The best guide we can offer is a picture of the destination, a lichen with the distinctive competencies to address the chosen habitat, and to take deliberate but pragmatic steps towards that end. Secondly, we can suggest that the organizational development path will be a series of incremental steps responding to particular pressures faced by the firm. Historically, these have often been responses to the needs of the research and development pipeline but, if firms are heading towards business models based on customer management or operational efficiency, they are as likely to be steps to acquire capabilities in those areas. This implies that executives should be sensitive to the environmental changes and alliance opportunities that allow them to take a positive incremental step. Finally, it looks as if the weight of structural inertia means that it will always be easier to change new parts of the organization than to change the old, embedded structures. For this reason, we can suggest that each new merger, acquisition, joint venture or partnership allows an opportunity to take a leap towards the new structure, whilst old structures may best be changed only gradually or allowed to wither until change is essential. For executives, this implies that they should seize the opportunity provided by merger, acquisition or alliance to start the process of building a lichen-like network and they should challenge the inertia of keeping old, existing structures.

CHANGING THE BUSINESS MODEL: CHANCE FAVOURS THE PREPARED MIND

In this chapter, we have tried again to combine two areas of knowledge to get a practical result. We have taken the picture of the future of the pharmaceutical industry, developed in Chapters 5, 6, 7 and 8, and combined that picture with what we know about how organizations change their culture, strategy, capabilities and structure. In other words, we tried to understand how we might manage the transition from present day pharma to the future of pharma.

What comes out of that combination is complex in detail, but simple in its fundamentals. Change will be difficult, but it will be impossible for those firms that do not start with their cultural assumptions. Most firms will need to change their strategy quite radically and for many of them this will mean a more sophisticated, less rigid approach to strategic planning. Whatever strategy is adopted, new capabilities will almost certainly need to be developed. This won't happen by enthusiastically chasing the latest industry 'best practice' fad; it will happen through careful understanding of and searching for new organizational routines. And all of this will need to be delivered by a new organizational structure that will not come from a single restructuring exercise. The new shape of the pharmaceutical company will emerge from gradual internal changes combined with larger leaps as new relationships are made. All of this will be difficult and, to some extent, haphazard. But with good leadership it will be a kind of guided haphazardness. There will be a large element of chance in how any individual firm evolves its structure but, as Louis Pasteur famously said, 'Chance favours the prepared mind'.

The Keys to the Iron Cage

We've now, almost, reached the end of this book. It's been a long journey, reflecting the complexity of the industry and the problems facing it.

In the first section of this book, we described the importance of the pharmaceutical industry and the danger that its contribution to our society and economy may stall. We then introduced the idea of evolutionary theory as a way to explain, predict and perhaps manage that situation.

In the second section of this book, we drew on the primary research to understand what social and technological forces were shaping the industry's fitness landscape. That allowed us to predict how the landscape will fragment into eleven habitats and how seven new pharma business models will evolve to meet the fitness criteria of those habitats. In doing so, we identified the targeted habitats of each model, the offer each model would make to its customers and the distinctive competencies each model will need to do that.

In this final section of the book, we've described the capabilities required by each of the new business models and the organizational structures that will evolve to deliver those capabilities. In this chapter, we explored how changes in the cultures, strategies, capabilities and organizational structures of the industry may play out and we provided some guidance for executives who need to manage those changes.

Throughout this book, we've used evolutionary theory to guide us and occasionally used biological analogies and metaphors to help explain what is going on in the industry. But there is one important difference between the evolution of industries and that of biological systems that we ought to consider before we end this book. In biology, evolution is unguided, driven by random variations in DNA that are selected and amplified. It is the capacity of unguided evolutionary processes to 'build' wonderfully complex and ordered organisms, what Dawkins called 'The Blind Watchmaker' (38), that makes evolutionary theory such a brilliant intellectual achievement and, for some, so hard to understand.

By contrast, in economic evolution, the process is neither blind nor random. Variation of organizational routines, the analogue of genes, is driven by deliberate human action. One might expect that to allow us to drive the evolution of industries faster and towards a more desirable outcome although, as we discussed in Chapter 6, our track record for that is not great. By and large, the evolution of industries is no more efficient than that of biological systems. It implies that, even if a new industry structure does emerge in the long run, the wastefulness of the evolutionary process might mean that we don't get the societal and economic benefits we desire as quickly as we want them. This is worrying for those of us hoping the industry will make our lives richer and better.

So the final words of this book are addressed to those who work in and with the pharmaceutical industry and they lie somewhere between a plea and a challenge. Our predecessors in the industry have done great things, saving and improving lives on a scale that is, literally, awesome. For the most part, this admirable achievement rests on the practical application of the natural sciences. But the challenges that lie ahead are even greater than those conquered by our predecessors. The diseases we have yet to defeat are much more challenging and we must do it for billions instead of millions of people. That challenge will not be overcome by the natural sciences alone. We will need to harness all the knowledge we have in management science too, managing strategy, culture and capabilities as well as we manage chemistry, biology and pharmacology. This book, I hope, makes a small contribution to that challenge.

References

(1)   Schumpter, J.A. 1943. *Capitalism, Socialism and Democracy*. London: Routledge.

(2)   Drucker, P.F. 1993. Corporate Culture: Use It, Don't Lose It, in *Managing for the Future*, edited by P.F. Drucker. 1st ed. Oxford: Butterworth Heinemann. pp. 150–4.

(3)   Smircich, L. 1983. Concepts of Culture and Organizational Analysis. *Administrative Science Quarterly*; 28(3):339–58.

(4)   Cameron, K.S. and Quinn, R.E. 1999. *Diagnosing and Changing Organizational Culture*. 1st ed. Reading, MA: Addison-Wesley Publishing Company.

(5)   Deal, T.E. and Kennedy, A.A. 1982. *Corporate Cultures: The Rites and Rituals of Corporate Life*. 1st ed. Reading:MA: Addison-Wesley;.

(6)   Schein, E.H. 1984. Coming to a New Awareness of Organizational Culture. *Sloan Management Review*; 25(2):3–16.

(7)   Schein, E.H. 1991. What is Culture? in *Reframing Organizational Culture*, edited by P.J. Frost, L.F. Moore, M.R. Louis and C.C. Lundberg. 1st ed. Newbury Park, California: Sage. pp. 243–53.

(8)   Ogbonna, E. 1993. Managing Organizational Culture: Fantasy or Reality? *Human Resource Management Journal*; 3(2):42–54.

(9)   Hatch, M.J. 1999. The Cultural Dynamics of Organizational Change, in *The Handbook of Organizational Culture and Climate*, edited by N.M. Ashkanasy, C. Wilderom. and M.F. Peterson, Thousand Oaks CA: Sage.

(10)   Smith, B.D., Wilson, H.N. and Clark, M. 2006. Creating and Using Customer Insight: 12 Rules of Best Practice. *Journal of Medical Marketing*; 6(2):135–9.

(11)   Smith, B.D. and Raspin, P.J. 2008. *Creating Market Insight*. 1st ed. London: Wiley.

(12)   Eisenhardt, K.M. and Zbaracki, M.J. 1992. Strategic Decision Making. *Strategic Management Journal*; 13(Special Issue):17–37.

(13)   Rajagopalan, N., Rasheed, A.M.A. and Datta, D.K. 1993. Strategic Decision Processes: Critical Review and Future Directions. *Journal of Management*; 19(2):349–84.

(14)   Mintzberg, H., Ahlstrand, B. and Lampel, J. 1998. *Strategy Safari*. 1st ed. New York: The Free Press.

(15)   McDonald, M.H.B. 1996. Strategic Marketing Planning: Theory, Practice, & Research Agendas. *Journal of Marketing Management*; 12:5–27.

(16)   Smith, B.D. 2003. Making Marketing Happen: How Great Medical Companies Make Strategic Marketing Planning Work For Them. *International Journal of Medical Marketing*; 4(2):129–42.

(17)   McDonald, M.H.B., Smith, B.D. and Ward, K.R. 2005. *Marketing Due Diligence: Reconnecting Strategy to Share Price*. Oxford: Elsevier.

(18)   Meyer, J.P., Becker, T.E. and Vandenberghe, C. 2004. Employee Commitment and Motivation: A Conceptual Analysis and Integrative Model. *Journal of Applied Psychology*; 89(6):991–1007.

(19)   Smith, B.D. 2009. Maybe I Will, Maybe I Won't: What the Connected Perspectives of Motivation Theory and Organizational Commitment May Contribute to our Understanding of Strategy Implementation. *Journal of Strategic Marketing*; 17(6):469–81.

(20)   Smith, B.D. 2011. Turf Wars: What the Intraorganizational Conflict Literature May Contribute to Our Understanding of Marketing Strategy Literature Implementation. *Journal of Strategic Marketing*; 19(1):25–42.

(21)   Hodgkinson, G.P. and Sparrow, P.R. 2002. *The Competent Organization*. 1st ed. Milton Keynes, UK: Open University Press.

(22)   Argyris, C. and Schon, D.A. *Organizational Learning: A Theory in Action Perspective*. Reading MA: Addison–Wesley;.

(23)   Bell, S.J., Whitwell, G.J. and Lukas, B.A. Schools of Thought in Organizational Learning. *Journal of the Academy of Marketing Science*; 30(1):70–86.

(24)   Becker, M.C. 2004. Organizational Routines: A Review of the Literature. *Industrial & Corporate Change*; 13(4):643–77.

(25)   Ambrosini, V., Bowman, C. and Collier, N. 2009. Dynamic Capabilities: An Exploration of How Firms Renew their Resource Base. *British Journal of Management*; 20:S9–S24.

(26)   Merton, R.K.1957. *Social Structure and Social Theory*. Glencoe IL: Free Press.

(27)   Crozier, M. *The Bureaucratic Phenomenon*. Chicago University Press.

(28)   Hannan, M.T. and Freeman, J.H. 1977. The Population Ecology of Organizations. *American Journal of Sociology*; 82(5):929–64.

(29)   Hannan, M.T. and Freeman, J.H. 1984. Structural Inertia and Organizational Change. *American Sociology Review*; 49(2):149–64.

(30)   Gouldner, A.W. 1960. *Patterns of Industrial Bureaucracy*. Glencoe IL: Free Press.

(31)   Grusky, O. 1960. Administrative Succession in Formal Organizations. *Social Forces*; 39:105–15.

(32)   Colombo, M.G. and Delmastro, M. 2002. The Determinants of Organizational Change and Structural Inertia: Technological and Organizational Factors. *Journal of Economics & Management Strategy*; 11(4):595–635.

(33)   Hakonsson, D.D., Klaas, P. and Carroll, T.N. 2009. Organizational Adaptation, Continuous Change and the Positive Role of Inertia. Academy of Management Annual Meeting Proceedings; 1–6.

(34)   Haveman, H.A. 1992. Between a Rock and a Hard Place: Organizational Change and Performance under Conditions of Fundamental Environmental Transformation. *Administrative Science Quarterly*; 37(1):48–75.

(35)   Ramirez, P. 2006. The Globalization of Research in the Pharmaceutical Industry: A Case of Uneven Development. *Technology Analysis & Strategic Management*; 18(2):143–67.

(36)   Mittra, J. 2007. Life Science Innovation and the Restructuring of the Pharmaceutical Industry: Merger, Acquisition and Strategic Alliance Behaviour of Large Firms. *Technology Analysis & Strategic Management*; 19(3):279–301.

(37)   Zhang, J. and Baden-Fuller, C. 2010. The Influence of Technological Knowledge Base and Organizational Structure on Technology Collaboration. *Journal of Management Studies*; 47(4):679–704.

(38)   Dawkins, R. 1988. *The Blind Watchmaker*. London: Penguin.

Epilogue:
Unanswered Questions and Speculative Answers

'If the world were good for nothing else, it is a fine subject for speculation.'
William Hazlitt

The Future of Pharma is built on a substantial piece of research but, as all professional researchers will tell you, good research always produces the same result: more questions. As the research progressed, three questions emerged that were important, relevant but, frustratingly, out of the scope of this particular research project. To answer these questions authoritatively, to design the research, scour the literature, gather the data and analyse it with rigour would have been another book, or perhaps two or three. Naturally, I formed some opinions about what the answers to those questions might be but, without the detailed research, they can only be speculative. I don't have the data to support these particular opinions and they don't deserve to sit next to my substantiated conclusions about the industry landscape and business models that I've recorded in the main chapters of this book. But I anticipate that some readers will get to the end of the *The Future of Pharma* and will want to know more; so this short epilogue presents those questions and their speculative answers.

The three questions that this work can only speculate upon are:

- If the industry is to evolve in this way, how fast will it happen?
- What will happen to the current major players in the industry?
- What might come out of the blue to change this picture?

With respect to the speed at which the industry will evolve, it is almost impossible to design a piece of research that could predict that with any validity. We can look at other industries but the particular conditions of the pharmaceutical industry always make it difficult to draw lessons. We can look at the history of our own industry, which shows steady progression interspersed with leaps forward but, again, the particular conditions of any period make it hard to draw comparisons. So, in the absence of a reliable research approach, we're left with speculation, albeit well-informed speculation. In the main part of the book, we've covered lots of things that seem to point to the acceleration of the industry's evolution, such as the financial pressure on governments as a result of the financial crisis and the breathtaking advance of many technologies, especially in information and communications. We've also discussed things that seem to hold the industry back, such as risk-averse regulation and its own structural inertia. The picture in my mind is one of a fast moving river of social and technological developments, on which the industry rides like a lot of logs beings carried downstream. But right now the logs are perhaps caught in a logjam and, despite the rush of water and furious jostling, not much is moving. We've discussed in the main chapters how the new knowledge of Biology 2.0 seems to throw up as many questions as answers and is proving slower than expected at delivering fundamentally new treatments. We can also see that our politicians are struggling to reconcile the dilemma of unlimited demand and limited supply. But when logjams clear, they tend to clear suddenly. Something happens, there's a sudden rush of water and one log moves, which creates a knock-on effect. This frees things up and everything hurtles downstream again. I see the logjam as a metaphor for the pharmaceutical industry. And it would fit, of course, with the ideas of punctuated equilibrium and Schumpeter's gales of creative destruction. So my answer to this question is that I don't know, but I think the industry will evolve in spurts, perhaps triggered by a big event. By their nature, those big events are unpredictable, but the financial crisis may be just such a tipping point, as might some new technological breakthrough or some innovative competitive move by one of the major pharma companies.

As to the future of the major players, the picture is clouded by complexity and media-relations spin. I can see a general picture, but the more specific one tries to be, the more margin of error there is. I was genuinely very impressed by the executives who granted my interviews. To a man and woman, they were very bright people addressing difficult questions in a serious way. And all of them were honest enough to admit that their view of the future was full of uncertainty. From what I've gathered in this research, I think I can see three broad things happening to the major firms in the industry.

Firstly, the speciality pharmaceutical firms have, in some ways, the easiest transition to make. They are part-way to the lichen model and have less restructuring to do. Also, since many of them are privately owned, I think that gives them some adaptive capacity that the huge multinationals do not have. Some of the smaller speciality pharma companies will go under, but some will fit nicely into the symbiotic network, as many are now beginning to do. The differentiator will be in their leadership vision. Specialized companies who still yearn to be 'big pharma' are probably wrong. Those that see the opportunity to find and dominate their place in the industry's ecosystem are more likely to adapt to the future.

Secondly, the larger firms will bifurcate into those that focus and become Genii and those who try to operate several models. There are signs of this already, of course, and we can see the direction of some leading firms. As I wrote this paragraph, news came in of Merck expanding research and development at the same time as Pfizer cut it back and of Pfizer acquiring a consumer health company. These, and many other news stories emerging every day, suggest to me that the likes of Merck, Roche and AstraZeneca will try to be focussed Genii whilst Pfizer, GSK, Novartis/Sandoz and others will try to run several models.

I envisage a future in which both focussed and diversified models exist, but both strategies are difficult to implement and some large companies will fail to achieve either of them. My intuition is that the diversified approach is harder to pull off. The focussed model is a better cultural fit for research-based companies and doesn't require the multiple business management capabilities that a diversified approach does. But the focussed model is necessarily limited and, if a company still wants to be huge, diversification may be necessary.

Which companies will succeed where is an altogether more difficult question. I am impressed, for example, by Roche's focus and Johnson & Johnson's strong history of diversification, to name just two examples. There are other companies that appear to be drowning strategically, grabbing at acquisitions and licensing opportunities like a drowning man clutching at straws.

The third factor affecting major firms will be the entrance of non-pharma companies. Nestlé and the other nutraceutical companies are hints of this. Insurance companies, retailers, IT companies and others will all, I'm sure, enter the industry as parts of the symbiotic lichen. It may sound crazy to think of a China-Mobile or Wal-mart or ING as pharmaceutical companies, but those sorts of companies will be part of the industry because they bring necessary capabilities. In a world where the molecule is only part of the value, they have a role to play. With less structural inertia and fewer cultural hindrances, a pharma/insurance/telecoms chaebol may be just the right organisation to dominate some habitats.

The most intriguing question is that about gamechangers, the low probability, high impact things that will happen to change the evolutionary path of the industry. I could speculate endlessly on this, but there are perhaps three that I can see that are possible and would change the game. The first is that the regulatory environment will go against social trends and start to balance risk and benefit more rationally. This might be manifested by incremental licensing or even allowing much more off-licence use. This would make development easier and cheaper, allowing Genii to take much more of the market. The second is the entry of a politically supported giant from the emerging markets. This might involve a western big pharma company failing because of a series of misfortunes and then being acquired by a Chinese, Indian or Brazilian company acting as a national champion. Armed with the capabilities of a top-ten company but freed of cultural constraints and able to restructure quickly, an emerging market big pharma might change the cost structure of the research based part of the industry and so start a cascade of events that might change the world quite radically. The third is sudden collapse of state healthcare systems, perhaps triggered by an economic collapse. If state provision was cut back to a safety net covering only the barest essentials, and personal insurance and self-insurance had to expand to fill its place, that too would change the pharmaceutical world drastically. It might involve governments doing what right-wing think tanks have urged them to do, forcing individuals to take responsibility for their lifestyle. Insurance companies and charities might rush to fill some gaps created in this scenario, but the world where the costs of healthcare are disconnected from the user would be gone forever, with huge consequences for the industry and indeed society as a whole.

These three unanswered questions are only the most obvious and my speculations are just the tip of the iceberg of possible answers. There are, of course, many other unanswered questions that might be asked and much more research would be needed to answer them fully. If you have read this far, I admire your patience and I hope it will enable you to wait for the next edition of this book.

Appendix 1:
A Pragmatic Research Approach

In writing this book, I wanted to avoid the sort of extended opinion piece that many business books become. The research programme that led to this book was therefore designed as a serious piece of research. It began with my PhD, on the effectiveness of strategy in medical markets, and then transmogrified into a second phase of work looking specifically at the future of the pharmaceutical industry.

Like most management research, this second phase began with a real-world problem, the apparent stalling of the industry. My research cannot, of course, claim to have discovered this stalling; it is quite obvious to anyone familiar with the sector. Instead, it began by investigating the details of the stalling, as described in Chapter 1. Having characterized this phenomenon, my research then looked around for a viable theory that might explain it. As discussed, evolutionary theory, especially the economic, social science variant of it developed by Nelson and Winter and others, was the obvious choice. Having a phenomenon and a working theory allows management researchers to hone the research questions to be answered. In this case, I settled on a set of six complementary research questions:

1. What are the changes in the social environment that are driving the evolution of the pharmaceutical industry's business models?
2. What are the changes in the technological environment that are driving the evolution of the pharmaceutical industry's business models?
3. What changes in the fitness landscape of the pharmaceutical industry are suggested by those changes in the social and technological environments?
4. How might we expect pharmaceutical industry business models to evolve in response to the changed fitness landscape?
5. What new organizational routines and capabilities might pharmaceutical companies need to develop in order to change their business models?
6. What are the practical implications for pharmaceutical companies attempting to deliberately evolve their business models?

Broadly speaking, Question 1 is addressed in Chapter 3; Question 2 in Chapter 4; Question 3 in Chapter 5; Question 4 in Chapter 6; Question 5 in Chapter 7; and Question 6 in Chapters 8 and 9.

The selection of these research questions provided most, but not all, of the basis for designing a research methodology. The missing component was an epistemological position. Those readers who are unfamiliar with the ways of academic management research need not worry too much about this, but I'll attempt a simple explanation for those who are interested in this important but arcane area. Of those readers familiar with epistemology, I beg your forbearance of the following gross simplification.

In simple terms, epistemology is about the way that one considers the phenomena that one observes in research. Some management researchers regard all phenomena as real, objective and measurable. This group (who I will loosely label 'positivists') are closest in outlook to physical scientists like chemists and physicists. Other management researchers regard all phenomena as essentially subjective and 'socially constructed' in the minds of the researcher. Many management scientists take this view, especially those working outside the United States. In between these two extremes lies an epistemological position known as pragmatism, which sees all phenomena as real but not everything as measurable. In essence, pragmatists believe that whatever makes a difference is real and can be measured, even if not quantified, and they do not worry too much about the rest. Having started my career as a research chemist, I was naturally inclined to be a positivist. However, my years as a management researcher have turned me into a pragmatist and I took that approach with me into the research programme. This, in essence, means that I think that things can be assessed objectively but that I am sceptical of those that think that you can reduce everything to hard data.

In practice, being a pragmatic management researcher had two implications for how to examine the pharmaceutical industry and answer the research questions. Firstly, it meant I could gather data and try to interpret it, much like a positivist physics experiment. Secondly, it meant that I decided against quantitative survey-type methods. Long experience of strategy research has taught me that, in a situation like this, surveys do not work very well because respondents interpret heavily the wording of questionnaires and try to guess the 'right' answer. In addition, surveys may tell you about what you ask about, but if you don't ask the right questions you don't get the right answers. Qualitative approaches allow the answer to emerge from the data, even if you don't fully understand what you're trying to find out. For these reasons, I opted for a qualitative approach, albeit laced with some formal analysis in order to preserve objectivity as much as possible.

The data-gathering itself was in three main parts. Firstly, I carried out an extensive literature search for prior research relevant to the evolution of industries. Mostly, the published work is not industry specific but a small part of it looks at specific aspects of pharmaceutical industry evolution. Readers interested in this very specific and academically oriented work are recommended to the work of Mazzucato and Dosi (1). It is excellent work and contributed significantly to the thinking in this book, but it is written for academics, not executives, and that is reflected in its style. Secondly, I gathered and read all the published material available concerning the development of the pharmaceutical industry. Almost none of this work took a truly evolutionary perspective, although the word evolution was used a lot in its commonplace sense of gradual change. Some of this was peer-reviewed academic material from journals; some of it was equally rigorous work published in books. Some of it was 'practitioner' literature such as trade press articles and reports published by consultancies. This last category of material is often frowned upon by academics because of its obvious biases, incompleteness and lack of rigour. I took the more catholic view that what such work lacked in rigour it made up for in relevance and so I included it in the analysis, albeit with a critical eye.

The final, and most arduous, part of the data-gathering was the primary research phase. I approached some 60–70 organizations, mostly pharmaceutical companies but also some related organizations such as investors, think tanks and companies to whom pharma companies outsource. Of these, 34 agreed to be interviewed. In all cases, I interviewed someone senior enough to answer the questions well. Since the questions were of a broad, strategic nature, this was typically a Chief Executive Officer, Chief Strategy Officer or similar. A full list of interviewees is provided in Appendix 2. Each interview was about an hour long and was transcribed with minimum editing. These interview transcripts, a total of about 300,000 words, then underwent a process of content analysis in which recurring themes were identified and structured.

Hence the findings and conclusions described in the following pages are a balanced synthesis of rigorous academic research and informed industry opinion together with new qualitative data from the primary interviews. Like every other management researcher, I cannot claim this methodology is perfect. I can, however, claim that it was carried out without preconceptions and in the spirit of genuine scientific enquiry. Above all, it was guided by the advice given to me by my PhD supervisor, Professor Malcolm McDonald, who many years ago told me the secret to good management research: don't worry too much about proving something, concentrate instead on understanding. Armed with those wise words, my research revealed the fundamental forces that are shaping the industry and a prediction of the future of pharma.

Appendix 2:
List of Research Interviewees

The following people kindly granted interviews during the research phase of this book. Their deep and extensive knowledge of the industry was invaluable but the conclusions drawn from the research are the author's and do not necessarily represent the views of any individual interviewee.

Rolf Badenhoop	Associate Principal, ZS Associates
G Steven Burrill	Chief Executive Officer, Burrill & Company
George Chressanthis	Professor, The Fox School of Business, Temple University
Luciano Conde	Director, Almirall
Jonathan De Pass	Chief Executive Officer, EvaluatePharma
Brik Eyre	General Manager, Baxter Healthcare Biopharma
Andreas Fibig	Chief Executive Officer, Bayer Schering Pharma
Jeff George	Head of Sandoz
Osagie Imasogie	Senior Managing Partner, Phoenix IP Ventures
Joe Jimenez	Chief Executive Officer, Novartis
Ken Jones	Chief Operating Officer, Astellas Pharma Europe Ltd
Jeff Keisling	Chief Information Officer, Pfizer
Andrew MacGarvey	Commercial Director, Quanticate
Julia Manning	Chief Executive Officer, 2020 Health
Peter Martin	Chief Operating Officer, Norgine
Sean McCrae	Senior Vice President, PharmaForce International
Doug McCutcheon	Head of Healthcare for Europe, Middle East and Africa and Asia-Pacific, UBS
Brian McNamee	Managing Director, CSL Biotherapies
David Norton	Company Group Chairman, Johnson & Johnson
Mike Rawlins	Chairman, National Institute for Health and Clinical Excellence
David Redfern	Chief Strategy Officer, GSK
Amit Roy	Head of Pharmaceuticals Research, Nomura
Angus Russell	Chief Executive Officer, Shire Pharmaceuticals
Aharon Schwartz	Vice President, Teva
Warwick Smith	Director, British Generic Manufacturers' Association
Peter Stein	Chief Executive Officer, Norgine
Harald Stock	Chief Executive Officer, Grünenthal Group

Richard Sykes	Chairman, The Royal Institution of Great Britain
Mike Thomas	Principal, A.T. Kearney
Sophia Tickell	Director, PharmaFutures
Moish Tov	Chief Executive Officer, Skila Inc
Merv Turner	Chief Strategy Officer, Merck & Co. Inc
Blane Walter	Chief Executive Officer, Inventiv Health
Bert Tjeenk Willink	Member of the Board of Managing Directors Boehringer Ingelheim, responsible for the Corporate Board Division Marketing and Sales Human Pharma
Chris Wright	Managing Principal, ZS Associates

Index

**If you have found this book useful you may
be interested in other titles from Gower**

Brand Planning for the Pharmaceutical Industry
Janice MacLennan
Hardback: 978-0-566-08520-8

**Business Development for the Biotechnology
and Pharmaceutical Industry**
Martin Austin
Hardback: 978-0-566-08781-3
e-book: 9978-0-7546-8138-0

**ePro:
Electronic Solutions for Patient-Reported Data**
Edited by
Bill Byrom and Brian Tiplady
Hardback: 978-0-566-08771-4
e-book: 978-1-4094-1242-7

**Forecasting for the Pharmaceutical Industry:
Models for New Product and In-Market
Forecasting and How to Use Them**
Arthur G. Cook
Hardback: 978-0-566-08675-5
e-book: 978-0-7546-8557-9

GOWER

The Price of Global Health:
Drug Pricing Strategies to Balance Patient
Access and the Funding of Innovation
Ed Schoonveld
Hardback: 978-1-4094-2052-1
e-book: 978-1-4094-2053-8

Outsourcing Clinical Development:
Strategies for Working with CROs and Other Partners
Edited by
Jane E. Winter and Jane Baguley
Hardback: 978-0-566-08686-1
e-book: 978-0-7546-8556-2

Patient Compliance:
Sweetening the Pill
Edited by
Madhu Davies and Faiz Kermani
Hardback: 978-0-566-08658-8
e-book: 978-0-7546-8304-9

Pharmaceutical Metrics:
Measuring and Improving R & D Performance
David S. Zuckerman
Hardback: 978-0-566-08676-2

Visit **www.gowerpublishing.com** and

- search the entire catalogue of Gower books in print
- order titles online at 10% discount
- take advantage of special offers
- sign up for our monthly e-mail update service
- download free sample chapters from all recent titles
- download or order our catalogue